UNDER NAZI NOSES

How Walraven van Hall Raised $1 Billion
for the Resistance—Mostly Heisted
from the Nazi-Run State Bank

John Tepper Marlin

Translated, Edited, and Annotated from
Erik Schaap's Astonishing Dutch Story

BOISSEVAIN BOOKS LLC
New York, New York | East Hampton, New York

BOISSEVAIN
BOOKS LLC

New York, New York | East Hampton, New York
2024

CONTENTS

Preface   v

1 | The Van Hall Family (1768–1906)   1

2 | Young Walraven (1906–1940)   11

3 | Zaandam Union Leader (1940–1941)   35

4 | The Seamen's Fund (1941–1943)   53

5 | Resistance Banker (1943–1944)   95

6 | The Railway Strike and Bank Heist (1944–1945)   153

7 | Betrayal and Execution (1945)   197

Endnotes   239

Walraven and Tilly van Hall on holiday in France, shortly after their wedding in 1932. Hitler has not yet come to power. The Second World War seems far away. (Van Hall Foundation)

Preface to the First Edition with Photos

THIS TRANSLATION is the culmination of a life-long process of discovering how deeply involved my Dutch relatives were in the Resistance to the Nazi Occupation. World War II and its aftermath loomed like a menacing cloud over my childhood. Born in 1942, I was a "war baby" in a family darkened by wartime loss. My father was in Europe with the O.S.S. Our much-adored Uncle Willem van Stockum, pilot on an RAF Halifax bomber, executed six missions during the two weeks around D-Day, June 6, 1944. Willem's plane was shot down over France on June 10, with no survivors. He is buried in France.

You should read this story because it shows how dearly bought is our freedom. It reminds us how inhumane human beings can be. It shows how political poisons can contribute to horrific outcomes. It shows how good intentions can go awry. It is inspiring because it shows that persistent, honorable, reasonable behavior can accomplish astonishingly good things. It underscores the sacrifices made over two years by the people of Ukraine.

My education about the Dutch Resistance began with my grandmother and mother, who read letters from Europe about the war's deadly toll on their relatives. They spoke Dutch at home when they talked about it, worried I was too young to deal with the stress. But I could see and hear— bad things were happening to people they loved. My not understanding much Dutch made these impressions more vivid. When my granny spat out the words *Vreselijk!* ("Horrible!") or *Verschrikkelijk* ("Evil"), you knew it was something bad. So the effort I put into translating and annotating this book is motivated by questions that originated more than seventy years ago.

My mother wrote a popular book for children about the Dutch Resistance, *The Winged Watchman* (Farrar Straus, 1962 and Bethlehem Books, 1995). It features "Kees Kip" as leader of the Resistance to the Nazi Occupation. In the second-last chapter he successfully rescues hostages but is himself caught and executed. In the year my mother died, 2006, I discovered a Dutch book about the real leader of the Resistance, Walraven van Hall. He was my mother's cousin and clearly the model for her book's Kees Kip.

This is an English translation of this fascinating book. I greatly appreciate the cooperation and assistance of Erik Schaap of Zaandam, the author of the Dutch biography. He did exhaustive research for his Dutch book, *Walraven van Hall*, whom he calls Prime Minister of the Resistance.

Thanks to my wife Alice for her important continuing feedback on issues raised by the book, her edits, and her forbearance with my night-owl writing habits. I also thank other readers, especially Constantine Valhouli, Iaira Boissevain, Marie-Louise Boissevain, my brother Randal Marlin, the Indian River County Library Writing Group in Vero Beach, Florida, especially Kathryn den Houter, and the Poets and Writers Group at the Harvard Club of New York City, being led by Teresa Brady.

This edition is being released with some photos to obtain feedback prior to indexing the book for a hard-cover edition. For every quote, I have sought to provide a source, but often my reference lacks detail. Part of the value I can add to the Dutch version is to generate additional notes for English-speaking readers. Your corrections or suggestions would be gratefully received.

John Tepper Marlin
New York, N.Y. and East Hampton, N.Y.
April 2024

1 | Money, Justice, Truth: The Van Halls (1768–1906)

"You cannot compromise with the truth"
—ANNE VAN HALL, 1836

WALRAVEN VAN HALL is the descendant of a distinguished family,[1] whose legends helped shape his outlook. The family was proud of its privileged economic status and, it seems, secretly proud of the rebels who flourished among them.

The Van Hall family tree includes many professional-class ancestors who married their peers, such as the Boissevains,[2] the Den Texes, and Van Lenneps. Their familiarity with poverty is mostly second-hand, through hearsay or charity work for the Civil Poor Board.

This family wealth originated during the Dutch Renaissance, in the 16th century.[3] Originally farmers and market gardeners,[4] by the 18th century, the Van Halls had chosen city life. The Van Halls started appearing as patricians in the family tree in 1750, around the time the Dutch became independent of Spain.[5]

Maurits Cornelis van Hall

The story of Walraven van Hall (known by many, affectionately and gratefully, as Wally)[6] starts with the progenitor of the Amsterdam Van Halls, Maurits Cornelis van Hall (1768-1858).

He was the son of Floris Adriaan (1736-1808) and Anna van Noorle, and grandson of Adriaan van Hall (1698-1783) and his wife Sara de Keyzer. She

1

was said to be descended from Admiral Piet Hein, except that Hein had no legal offspring.[7] Maurits followed his parents' advice, studying law.

(Maurits's brother Adriaan Teyler van Hall was ahead of his time in adding his wife E. R. Teyler's surname Teyler to his own.[8] He also started the first half of his life sedately, as an Amsterdam city council member and bank officer,[9] but in 1803, he and a shipowning partner sailed off as privateers[10] and also, it seems, as actual pirates.[11])

Maurits Cornelis van Hall first settled in near Utrecht, but fled[12] the area in 1787 after it was attacked by the Prussians, who plundered Maurits's first home. He and his family took refuge with his privateer brother Adriaan in Amsterdam. Maurits had assisted the Van Tuyl regiment in their losing battle with the King of Prussia, who invaded the Low Countries with 20,000 troops. (As we shall see, the name Van Tuyl resurfaces later as Walraven's most-used Resistance name in the fight against the Nazi occupiers.) But Maurits van Hall's regiment failed to stop the northward advance of the Prussians. Retired safely in Amsterdam, Maurits returned to his law studies and was duly registered as a lawyer. He was appointed city attorney, a position between public prosecutor and chief of police.

In his city attorney role, Maurits had a strong sense of justice. While walking on Dam Square in September 1795, he discovered that an elderly Jewish street vendor being beaten up by a fellow townsman.[13] The victim lay on the ground, covered in blood. Maurits confronted the man who did the beating, who justified his action on the basis that: "It's just a damn Jew." Though Jews were then held in low esteem, Maurits arrested the townsman, who was sentenced by the summary court to time in the stocks,[14] then a public flogging, followed by six years in a workhouse (*rasphuis*).[15]

In 1798, the eloquent Maurits and his brother Adriaan Teyler (the later pirate) were appointed members of the Senate of the Representative Body of the Batavian People,[16] a forerunner of the today's Dutch House of Representatives. The brothers were the first in a long line of Van Hall politicians. Maurits's eldest son Floris Adriaan became Minister of Justice and then Minister of Finance. His grandson Jacob became alderman and deputy mayor in The Hague. For four years, Maurits van Hall defended bills submitted by his son in the Senate, to which he was nominated by King Willem II. Maurits remained an intermittent member of parliament until 1848, when he joined a committee with his son to revise the Constitution, probably because of the criminal prosecution and the premature death of another son, whose name was (confusingly for an English-speaking reader) Anne.[17] Anne was Walraven van Hall's great-grandfather.

Justice: Anne Maurits Cornelis van Hall

Anne (pronounced AHN-ah) Maurits Cornelis (1808-1838)[18] is an important ancestor because he exemplifies the strain of rebellion in his support of a growing movement of dissident Protestants. He lived a carefree boyhood in Amsterdam and successfully studied literature and law in Leiden.[19] In the autumn of 1830, Belgium threatened to revolt against the Netherlands and young Anne van Hall joined his fellow youths and volunteered to join the army to defend his country. With some other young men, he traveled by steamer to Den Bosch,[20] close to the front. However, instead of engaging with the Belgians, they boarded at the fancy Bishop's Palace and had profound religious conversations. Although previous generations of Van Halls grew up loyal Protestant churchgoers (and a few became pastors),[21] Anne Maurits was so shaken by the Belgian conflict, and the consequent massive cholera epidemic, that he became a strictly orthodox pastor, caring for cholera victims in Amsterdam. He explained to his brother in 1832:

> Insurrection and violence have spread throughout Europe and the most terrible civil wars in France and England, and part of Germany, are about to break out. This proves to me that men, notwithstanding our much-praised civilization, enlightenment, etc., are sinners by nature. These conflicts are the fruits of a prevailing loss of faith. (*Source:* Letter from Anne Maurits Cornelis van Hall to his brother Floris Adriaan, November 21, 1832.)

3

Anne and some friends launched a counter-offensive, a magazine with the wide-ranging title *Dutch Voices for Religion, State, History, and Literature*.[22] He also contributed related articles to the *Journal of Law*.

On October 14, 1834, lightning struck. A large majority of the congregation of the Dutch Reformed Church in Ulrum, Groningen, signed the "Act of Secession and Return" and broke away from the Dutch State Protestant Church. The following year, Anne became a major defender of some of these dissidents,[23] whose popularity was growing.

The government was fearful of dissenters and now panicked. Although the Netherlands had famously enshrined freedom of conscience and religion in its 1529 Constitution drawn up in Utrecht when the first Dutch Republic was established,[24] in practice the dissenters were harassed.[25] "True believers" molested, dismissed, and boycotted the troublemakers, mostly farmers, fishermen, and agricultural workers with few resources to defend themselves. Instead of protecting the dissidents, the government joined in hunting for them. It banned meetings of more than twenty dissidents.

On July 12, 1835, a large group of dissidents, far more than twenty, gathered for worship in the Vuren[26] in Gelderland. The participants were fined. They appealed. Anne van Hall prepared a 57-page-long fiery plea for them. He filed it at the court and published it as *The Freedom of Divine Service*. It was a model for other appeals, but the fines were upheld.

Overwhelmed at the injustice, Anne and his wife Suze in 1836 converted to the religion of the persecuted dissenters, now called Separatists. They lost some friends. The Van Hall law firm lost clients. Some people openly abused Suze and Anne. His father Maurits and his brother Floris tried in vain to get Anne back on what they believed to be the right path. But Anne replied firmly: "You cannot compromise with religion, with the truth."[27]

The couple moved with their family to The Hague, where Anne took appeals for convicted secessionists. That did not go well. During a plea in one of the many cases, Van Hall asked: "Does the People consider it appropriate to punish my client in the name of public tranquility?" The exasperated Advocate General Van Appeltere saw his opportunity. He said: "The honorable defender acts as a public accuser against His Majesty the King!"

Van Appeltere argued that by "people" Van Hall meant King Willem I himself. He charged Anne with the crime of *lèse majesté*, treasonous disrespect for the king.[28] The President of the Court piled on. Shocked and disillusioned by the unfair attacks, Anne was silenced.

A broken man, Anne quit the legal profession and lived only two more years. He worked as a deacon and an elder until 1838, when he died of tuberculosis at thirty years of age. His family made clear that, while they did not adhere to Anne's religious dissension, they respected their brother and his beliefs. In a remarkable display of family solidarity, the funeral procession of fourteen coaches[29] passed through The Hague, with a brother or sister of the deceased in each carriage.

Suze was also infected with tuberculosis and five years later, in 1844, she too succumbed to it. Anne and Suze left behind three young children. A month before her death, she wrote a religious will, a "beautiful legacy,"[30] addressed to them.

"My Maurits, spitting image of your Father, may you also share his faith and mind," she prayed. For Johanna she pleaded: "Oh my daughter, give your heart to the Lord. Oh! God save you from the false lips and the flattering tongue!" She asked the younger son Floris to become "a servant of the Lord." Her penciled farewell said: "Goodbye! Farewell! I cannot stay any longer. Almighty God, Thou knowest the battle."[31]

Orphans: Maurits, Johanna, and Floris van Hall

The three orphaned children of the felled Anne and Suze – Maurits Cornelis (seven years old), Johanna Justina (six) and Floris Adriaan (five) – were raised in Utrecht by their Mennonite Van Schermbeek aunt.[32] The family had enough money to provide them with a carefree childhood and a good education. However, their guardians, Grandpa Maurits Cornelis van Hall and Uncle Floris, anxiously kept them from the ever-expanding community of dissenting Protestants.[33] So her children did not hear or heed their mother's desperate deathbed cries from the heart. Instead, their daughter Johanna at a young age married Johan Gleichman, who became the Dutch Finance Minister and State

Minister, and their two sons went to law school on the recommendation of their grandfather and uncle.

The younger son, Floris Adriaan (1839-1929), became a banker, a left-liberal municipal councilor in Utrecht and chairman of the supervisory board of the Amsterdam Palace of Industry.[34] In that gigantic glass and steel building, he regularly extended hospitality to the fast-growing labor movement, which met and demonstrated there. Childless, he retired to the Palace in his old age, a somewhat eccentric multi-millionaire. Popular Dutch author Geert Mak has quoted a 1929 drama critic describing in the *Algemeen Handelsblad* the impact of Floris's appearance at an opera performance at the Palace Hall:

> All eyes of the audience suddenly turned to the board box. There stood, as if appearing out of nowhere, a very old, skinny, stooped man, with a faded, sharp bird's face. The figure leaned out of the box, the trembling hand leaned on the velvet rim, and the mouth mumbled. This strange, almost ghostly figure, dressed in a woolen dressing gown, his head covered by a cloth skullcap, looked for a while into the dark room and fascinated hundreds of visitors, who stared back at the peculiar apparition." (Mak, *Een kleine geschiedenis van Amsterdam*, "A Little History of Amsterdam," Amsterdam, 1961, translated into English as *Amsterdam: A Brief Biography*, 1999.)[35]

"Uncle Floris was a genius, but crazy," Walraven's father used to tell his children in the early twentieth century.[36] On February 24, 1929, Floris Adriaan van Hall, aged 90, died alone in his palace apartment. Less than two months later, the majestic Palace burned to the ground.

His older brother Maurits Cornelis van Hall (1836-1900), after studying law, entered the Amsterdam banking industry, where he rose quickly. He became co-director of the Nederlandsche Crediet- en Depositobank, co-founder and director of the Amsterdam branch of the Banque de Paris et des Pays-Bas[37] and, together with Floris, supervisory board member of the Peat and Industrial Company, NV,[38] in Nieuweroord (in the farming province of Drenthe, deep in the less-populated interior of the Netherlands bordering on Germany). He also won a seat in the Provincial Council of North Holland and the Senate.[39] His parents' faith appears to have failed to take root in him, as Maurits developed into a liberal in the tradition of Thorbecke.[40]

In 1883 Maurits and his wife, Debora Cremer Eindhoven, moved into *Herengracht* (Men's Canal) 475. Over the years he had built up a considerable fortune and paid 82,000 guilders cash—for this grand house,[41] located on the Golden Bend of the canal belt. It provided enough space for the nine children he and Debora brought into the world.[42] The rest of the family benefited from its luxurious location in the canal belt.

> "In our early youth we stayed a few times with Grandma Van Hall, at 475 Herengracht," a grandson[43] said. "We all still vividly remember how we had to be disinfected every time we came in from the canal. Large white sheets were spread in the children's room, to the left of the entrance under the steps. Our mittens, coats, shawls,[44] and shoes were treated with sulfur. All because someone once brought tuberculosis into the home, killing our Van Hall great-grandparents. (*Source:* Maurits Cornelis van Hall, translated by Michael C. van Hall, *Three Centuries*, 93.)

Debora van Hall took no risks with germs. The laundry went to the Veluwe[45] twice a year, because the stream water there was much purer than in the capital. After countless baskets of clean linen came back, the house staff first sprinkled it all with sulfur.[46] She closely monitored food hygiene. Milk can contain dangerous bacteria, so she brought jennies[47] to the *Herengracht* (Men's Canal) and milked them on the spot, under the supervision of a maid or Grandmother Debora herself. The fish from Zandvoort had to pass her critical eye before the cook was allowed to work with it in the "*palazzo* Van Hall." To limit further any urban dangers, Father Van Hall had a house built in Baarn as a summer camp, where he brought his family, the nanny, and several maids—far from the unsanitary[48] canal belt.

Maurits Cornelis van Hall died at the turn of the century. Debora followed him on April 6, 1906, having just gotten to know her grandson Walraven, born two months earlier.

Adriaan (Aat) van Hall and Nel Boissevain

Maurits and Debora van Hall left behind in 1906 eight surviving children (the ninth had died in 1895). Each of the children inherited many tens of thousands of guilders and were assured of a financially worry-free future. Most of the heirs followed in the footsteps of their ancestors. The youngest daughter, for example, married the mayor's son, Sjoerd Vening Meinesz.

Two other children, Adriaan (Aat) and Jan, married the daughters of two Boissevain brothers. It was no accident. When Jan van Hall married Hester Boissevain, the Boissevains put on a lavish party and that is where Jan's brother Aat took a fancy to Hester's first cousin Nel Boissevain. These two unions were the heart of a powerful family nexus that would play an important role in making the Resistance leadership effective in World War II.

The wedding of Jan and Hester in 1895 was a collective display of wealth and family connections. Hester was a favorite daughter of the *Algemeen Handelsblad* editor-publisher Charles Boissevain.[49] The lavish festivities, summarized well by Maurits van Hall in his book *Drie Eeuwen* (translated by his grandson Michael C. van Hall, *Three Centuries),*[50] began on February 20, 1895, with a twelve-course dinner for 52 people, ranging from pasties and venison to pheasants, lobster and *pâté de foie gras.*[51] On February 22 an intimate family supper included fourteen people, followed two days later by a reception at the bride's home. On February 25, the Riche banquet hall on the Rokin in Amsterdam hosted a *soirée dansante.* On February 27, a dinner for 24 people was followed by theater and ballet. On March 2, a grand ball with stage performances was accompanied by a six-course *supper.* On March 3, *afternoon tea.* On March 4, another ball, this time at the groom's house. Finally, on March 7, the main event of the marriage concluded, as we might expect, with a large dinner.

Jan's brother Adriaan ("Aat"), Walraven's father, grew up in the security of a well-off family in a confidently growing Amsterdam. The Oranjesluizen locks, completed in 1872, connected the port of Amsterdam with the North and South Seas.[52] Shipping to the city increased four-fold during the next quarter-century. In the new Amsterdam, banking and shipping families like the Van Eeghens, Boissevains, Van Lenneps, and Van Halls prospered greatly. Within two or

The Van Hall family around 1920 posing in the garden of their home on the Keizersgracht. Standing, from left to right: Suzelène, Gijs, Nelleke and her husband René, Walraven. Seated: Maria, Floris, Johan Bernard, mother Petronella Johanna (Nel), father Adriaan Floris (Aat), Hester, Debora, and Vera. (Amsterdam City Archives)

three decades the city changed from a collection of poor, sleepy neighborhoods to a bustling mini-metropolis. Money was not a problem among the well-off Amsterdammers.

On his 26th birthday, Aat took the plunge and married Hester Boissevain's cousin, Petronella Johanna, known as Nel. Like his father, by the time Aat was married, he had already completed a law degree. In the year of his marriage, he obtained his advanced doctorate in jurisprudence.[53] Also like his father, Aat ended up in the financial world. He accepted an appointment as a supervisory director[54] at the banking and insurance firm H. Oyens & Sons. For decades he served as a board member of the Dutch Securities Trading Association and he was on the boards of the political associations Progress and the Liberal Union. He accepted a directorship at Koninklijke Hollandsche Lloyd. At the end of his life, Aat had dozens of jobs, board memberships, and directorships, judiciously selected from many options. These organizations and spheres of interest were reflected in the lives of his sons Walraven and Gijsbert.

In 1905, their parents bought the luxurious residential-and-office building, *Keizersgracht* (King's Canal) 327. It was another palace, decorated with high, ornamented ceilings and chandeliers. Paintings by Dutch masters hung on the walls. In 1906 Adriaan also purchased *Herengracht* (Men's Canal) 330 and 334, followed four years later by number 332. With this, the growing family owned a significant compound of connected stately homes in the most expensive part of Amsterdam. Their marriage further resulted in Adriaan and Nel owning the *Zonnehof* villa and the *De Ebbinge* estate in Bentveld, although these properties, unlike the other real estate, remained in Nel's name—a fact that would later be of importance.

Their family ties were close. Some Van Halls lived in the canal belt, but Adriaan also had two brothers in Hattem,[55] a town on the Eastern end of the Veluwe, often voted by the Dutch as the most scenic part of the Netherlands and the home of the Veluwezoom National Park.[56] Family, friends and business associates came and went, both in Amsterdam and in Hattem, where Adriaan and Nel were having a second home built. Their cousin Maurits wrote about the Van Hall summer house in Hattem, the "Rabbit Mountain:"[57]

> Uncle Aat and Aunt Nel had the most hospitable houses one can imagine. They spent their summer holidays with their ten children in their country house in Hattem. Each child had a double bedroom and was allowed to invite a boyfriend or girlfriend. Our family consisted of eight children. During World War I, when it was impossible to travel abroad, we were together in the summer with fifty young people. We were allowed to go out with sailing boats and canoes, camp, swim in the IJssel and the Kolk,[58] and go on hiking and cycling trips. (*Source:* Maurits Cornelis van Hall, translated by Michael van Hall, *Three Centuries*, 94.)

This is the environment into which Walraven was born on February 10, 1906, surrounded by bankers and administrators, liberal and reformed. The baby boy was born with a silver spoon in his mouth, or as they say in the Netherlands, he was tucked into a comfortable crib.[59]

2 | Young Walraven (1906-1940)

"Wally could not live with tension."
—TONNY EGGINK

WALRAVEN WAS BORN in Amsterdam on February 10, 1906, the sixth Van Hall child in a family that expanded to ten children over two decades. He was nine years younger than his eldest sibling, a sister, and ten years older than his youngest sibling, a brother. When his father took him to the birth registry office, the plan was that the baby would be named after his mother Nel Boissevain's brother, Walrave.[60] But the clerk on duty miswrote the baby's name as the more common Dutch name, Walraven. The family was easy and decided not to fix the error.

The family's lackadaisical reaction to the mistake fit with those mellow days in Amsterdam. Three years earlier, the city's giant stock exchange, the *Beurs van Berlage*,[61] opened amidst praise for its Dutch architect, Hendrik Petrus Berlage.[62] The startup of a new electric tramway was hailed as a sign of progress. The year before, the fast-growing Free University, founded by descendants of secessionists from the State Church, celebrated its 25th anniversary.

Walraven's banker grandfather, Maurits Cornelis van Hall,[63] was one of the big winners from the city's success. His active participation in the global-trading economy enriched him. When he passed away in 1900, his legacies to his children made money plentiful. For example, in the ancient town of Hattem in 1915, fewer than twenty residents owned a telephone, and three of them bore the name Van Hall. Walraven's parents had both a phone in their Hattem country house and one in their history-laden Amsterdam canal house. Few of the six million Dutch people of the day could afford such a luxury, two home phones.

11

Poverty in Amsterdam

Wealth shone on the canals and in the country houses, but the Amsterdam slums harbored many social problems. Amsterdam had grown faster than its social services. The city's population doubled to more than half a million residents. Many people lived in damp basement dwellings. Infant mortality was high. The city was plagued with beggars. In 1901 the government stepped in, via its Housing Act, to build homes for workers. That year, a director of Haarlem's Bank for Small Loans estimated that sixty percent of its borrowers were indigent.[64] Dock workers lacked job security—they had to show up at a café to wait for casual work and then return afterwards to get paid. Alcohol abuse was the order of the day. Government posters showed a malnourished child begging a man entering a bar: "Oh father! No more!"[65]

In 1903, the same year the doors of Berlage's palace of a stock exchange swung open, Amsterdam's railway employees went on strike to protest social conditions. "All the wheels will stand still if your mighty arm wills," was the rallying cry of the rising socialist movement. Karl Marx's theories of industrial impoverishment appeared to explain what was happening in Amsterdam.[66] As the wealthy became richer, the slums also grew, along with extreme misery, desperate toil, slavery, ignorance, and rudeness. This was the underside of Dutch society, in which everyone had to earn their living, but work opportunities for the uneducated were limited and often degrading.

The leaders of a workers' revolt quoted Marx in their speeches. In July 1917, a potato riot broke out in Amsterdam's Jordaan neighborhood,[67] as workers who lived there campaigned for affordable and sufficient food. The police and army fired on the protesting-and-plundering crowd. The demonstration ended with nine deaths and 114 injuries. Four months later, after the Russian Revolution, another protest occurred. David Wijnkoop, Ferdinand Domela Nieuwenhuis, and Henriette Roland Holst[68] enthusiastically addressed their massed supporters at the diamond exchange. The evening ended with another demonstration along the barracks on Sarphatistraat. Soldiers again opened fire. Three people were killed and eighteen injured. Guns crushed another protest of the *have-nots*.

Employees of the Civil Poor Board, making the rounds to relieve distress, encountered appalling situations, such as that of an unemployed skipper's assistant, Evert Agema. At the end of the nineteenth century, he moved with his wife from the landlocked Eastern Netherlands to Amsterdam, hoping to benefit from the explosive growth of the city's port. He had little success. A visitor found a desperate, crying man who had failed to find work for the umpteenth consecutive day:

> The children yearned to know whether father had earned something, because they were so hungry. Household goods, clothes, blankets, and even the children's bed had all been left as collateral with the Bank for Small Loans,[69] to buy food. His wife Aaltje, who had been seriously ill after giving birth to a stillborn child, languished for lack of food. Because her footwear was pawned, she went barefoot. (*Source: The Green Amsterdammer.*[70])

Although young Walraven mainly spent his days in the well-off parts of the canal belt, the immense gap between rich and poor did not completely escape him. Mother Nel wrote approvingly of her son, who came home on an ice-cold day in the winter and with excitement said to his father:

> "Father, you have to help me. We walked in the Vondelpark [the largest park in Amsterdam, named after a poet] and seven children were crying. The police took them all away." According to the nanny, Wally did not rest until she went to the police station and told them that the children had been left behind in the Vondelpark by their father, because their mother was in the hospital and he did not know what to do with them. (*Source:* Letter from Nel Boissevain van Hall.)

Father van Hall, chairman of the Civil Poor Board, in this case provided assistance.

The family felt responsible for social distress. Adriaan ("Aat") and Petronella ("Nel") raised their children to respect the idea of *noblesse oblige*, that affluence brings responsibility. They rarely sought publicity for their assistance, but several examples of their concern for the less fortunate can be told. For example, at his wife's request, Adriaan tried to have a playground built for workers' children in the Jordaan. He purchased the necessary land, but the plan failed because of the cost of safety investments required by the city council. The family provided a hospitable welcome to Belgian refugees in their Amsterdam canal home during World War II. Mother Nel offered job opportunities to unemployed young people, personally combating the immense unemployment during the 1930s. The Van Halls even sponsored a talented girl who could not afford to go to university. Dozens of orphaned children and girls in the workshops of the fashion houses in Amsterdam[71] were allowed to stay in the country house.

Van Hall Homes and Schools

In 1911 the Van Hall couple sold their house at Herengracht 334, bought when Walraven was born, five years earlier. They sold the two adjacent buildings as well, the following year. Adriaan's sister Helena Suzanna (Suzie) van Hall[72] purchased them. Young Walraven moved with his parents, brothers, sisters, and dog "Fikkie," to *Keizersgracht* (Emperor's Canal) 327. Like their previous homes, it was a house with a history,[73] built in the seventeenth century for Nicolaas Witsen, then mayor of Amsterdam.[74] Aunt Suzie's garden was on the other side of the back wall of the new home. Uncle Walrave Boissevain,[75] later a liberal alderman and parliamentarian, lived three houses away.

In the winter, the family lived in Amsterdam and in the summer they all traveled by train to their "Rabbit Mountain" *(Konijnenberg)* home in Hattem, where as many as twenty family members and guests were in residence. Over the years, Aat and Nel van Hall welcomed not only their ten children, seven sons- and daughters-in-law, and eighteen grandchildren, but also ten nephews and nieces over whom they had temporary custody. There was room for everyone at the huge house and the twelve acres of land around it. Father Van Hall even had a bell tower built in front of the entrance and required that the bell be rung before the start of each meal, to make sure everyone was at the table on time.

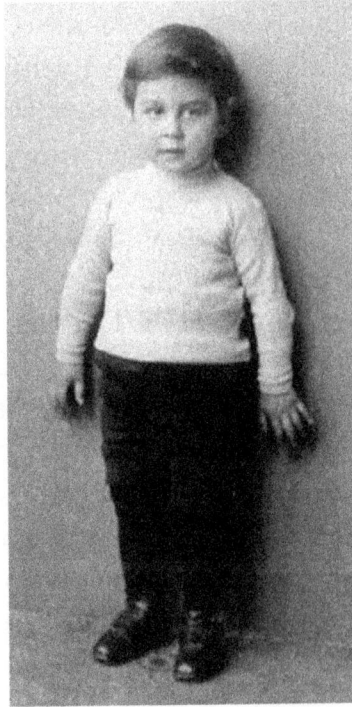

Walraven as a toddler.
(Van Hall Foundation)

Walraven had a sunny childhood. His mother Nel said that he was "an active child, very physically strong, full of a sense of humor. Even when he was mischievous, he always managed to disarm people with his witty and humorous answers and cheerful laugh."[76] Only a few forms of distress troubled his joyful days. One was that his mother almost constantly felt ill, had "nervous fits," or suffered from melancholy. She regularly underwent health therapies in foreign spas.[77] Her children often traveled with her.

Nel's son-in-law, neurologist Dr. René de Monchy,[78] prescribed for her a regimen of permanent rest:

> Mother's nervous system can bear little at home, is not able to withstand the emotional pressures and stimuli that her numerous children necessarily bring. She should live in her house as in a hotel, with no care, responsibility, or questions. (*Source:* Dr. René de Monchy, prescription.)

15

Despite this adverse diagnosis, Nel Boissevain van Hall[79] lived until she was ninety-six years old, surviving all but four of her ten children.[80]

Walraven's first years of private school education were another dark period in his generally joyful life, because of a teacher whom his mother, Nel, described as "incompetent." He was also, for a while, sick at home like his mother. He fell behind in his learning at his primary school on the *Keizersgracht* (Emperor's Canal). Over the years, he managed to catch up sufficiently to obtain his first school diploma. In 1919 he followed his older brother Gijsbert ("Gijs") to the Amsterdam Lyceum.

The Van Halls were among the first students at this novel Lyceum. Its curriculum combined a traditional high school with the Dutch gymnasium, which prepared students for university entrance exams.[81] The secondary school, founded in 1917, was the second-oldest lyceum in the Netherlands. The school's Latin motto was apocalyptic: *Potius deficere quam desperare* ("Rather perish than despair.") The young founder Dr. Christiaan Pieter Gunning[82] tried to impart to his students his special humanistic vision, unique for the times.

> An alumnus of the school, publisher/author Johan Polak, said everything in the school reflected the outlook of the founder—the construction of the classrooms, the layout of the auditorium, the protracted speeches of the rector that resembled sermons in a reformed church (Dr. Gunning liked to hear himself speak). So also did the school board elected by students, the class book, the high school tie (sky blue, white, bright yellow) have the unmistakable taste, flair and style of Gunning. He was a noble, cordial, warm, brave, and somewhat solemn man. I myself learned a lot from Dr. Gunning and I never wanted to hear a bad word about him. I don't believe there was any evil in him beyond a normal allotment of vanity. (*Source:* Johan Polak.)

Gijs van Hall was also positive about the school's extracurricular activities and School Council, which encouraged communication among teachers and pupils, offering all kinds of clubs:

Walraven as a twelve year old, drawn by his cousin Maurits Cornelis van Hall. (Van Hall Foundation)

For older students the Brugman debating society[83] provided a place for fervent argument about all kinds of subjects. All students had to play hockey under the guidance of the gymnastics teacher once a week. In short, this was not a school where the students were only prepared for the final exams! (*Source:* Gijs van Hall.)

In 1939, Headmaster Gunning addressed the people of Amsterdam in a full-page article featured in an anti-fascist door-to-door paper, "The Bellows" (*De Blaasbalg*),[84] warning that Nazism[85] threatens Dutch people with the ruin of its highest and most sacred possessions:

Through the ages these have been the inalienable property of our people. What we are already observing here in this country: the empty phraseology, the deliberate ignorance of the true value and meaning of democracy and parliamentary government, the suppression of free, personal expression, the organized power apparatus, the putting of violence before discussion, the appalling and degrading anti-Semitism— all that tells us enough. (*Source:* Gunning, in *De Blaasbalg*, 1939.)

17

*Walraven, on the far left, in a bench of the nautical
college on Terschelling. (Johan van der Wal)*

Gunning's lashing out at the Nazis was an outgrowth of his sense of responsibility. The views of this radical-democratic school founder must have made a deep impression on generations of pupils besides Gijs and Walraven van Hall.

Walraven spent two years at the Amsterdam Lyceum. In 1920 he transferred from the Amsterdam school on Valeriusplein to the Kennemer Lyceum in rural Overveen. His father Adriaan van Hall and his family were forced to give up their Amsterdam house because Adriaan had invested in Russian railway bonds, which all became worthless after the 1917 Russian Revolution.[86] He lost much of his wealth, but not he family's summer house, which as previously mentioned was in the name of Adriaan's wife Nel. They moved from Amsterdam to this summer house in Bentveld, a hamlet between Haarlem and Zandvoort,[87] on the edge of the dunes.

From then on, Adriaan took the electric tram from Bentveld to work in Amsterdam. Walraven attended the Kenner Lyceum, which had fewer than 180 fellow students, yet with excellent teachers like Jacobus P. Thijsse for natural history and Anton Pieck for drawing. The students were given much freedom. The school motto was *Communis salus singulis constat* ("Common salvation rests with each individual"), which would fit Walraven like a glove.

Kennemer Lyceum was also within walking distance of the North Sea. That was a godsend for Walraven, who became a fanatical sailor, reveling in high waves and strong winds. He clearly wanted a future on the sea. Thanks to extra tutoring, he got through the third year of the HBS program[88] at the Kennemer Lyceum. In July 1922 he received his diploma. Later in the year he went on to study at the nautical school, Willem Barentsz on Terschelling, where he felt even more at home.

Walraven the Sailor

Walraven's long-cherished wish to go to sea became a reality. On vacations, he served as an apprentice on various ships that sailed to Germany, Portugal, the Cape Verde Islands, and other places. His father gave him the gift of a Staverse sailboat.[89] When the school holidays were over, he would pick up his boat from its mooring in a side canal of the Spaarne,[90] and would sail, rain or shine, via the Zuiderzee and the Wadden Sea to Terschelling.

Friends and family were invited on board his sailboat for long cruises. "It was a dubious pleasure," according to his younger brother Johan Bernard (nicknamed Beppo). "Wally objected quite a bit to my operation of the foresail. In a booming voice, he gave directions that were not crystal clear to me."[91] In a letter to his older brother Gijs, Walraven reminisced about a stay near the Frisian Heegermeer where they smeared themselves with margarine "to get a tan." According to his father, Walraven was "the moving spirit in most groups. He is cheerful, and at the same time he is a young dog and a thoughtful lad."

Walraven had barely started his seaman's training when his parents received a message that a police action had been drawn up against him at Terschelling. During confrontations between the local police and some students at the nautical school, Walraven was accused of entering a restricted area. During the court case in Harlingen, Adriaan van Hall represented his son. He dryly explained to the judge that according to the section of the law stated in the summons, Walraven kept chickens without a municipal permit, an accusation for which no evidence had been produced. There was some consternation among the court staff, until they realized that the clerk's office accidentally used the Harlingen regulation number instead of the one for Terschelling. The judge had no choice but to acquit.

Although Walraven was not first in his class, he passed his exam with flying colors after three years of nautical school. He was ready now to start his sailing career. He did not have to sign up for military service, because his brother Gijs's service exempted him. But since he was a minor, he was required to bring a letter of permission from his father, a month after he received his diploma. With this letter in hand, he was ready to sail with the Royal Holland Lloyd.[92]

He was examined and deemed fit to sail, and in August 1925 he joined the crew of the 360-foot steamship *Amstelland* as a mate's apprentice. Six months later, he joined the somewhat larger 1,160-passenger *Flandria*, sailing to South America. After two years, Walraven obtained his third-mate certificate and in 1928 his radiotelegraphy certificate.

Now an officer in the merchant marine, Walraven was eagerly anticipating his third ship, the *Eemland*. He had settled into a happy life as a seafarer. His love of travel and adventure was conveyed by the obvious relish with which he described some nautical mishaps, like the following one, when his ship went through a field of three-foot-thick ice and lost one of its two anchors and chains:

> The force of the ice dragged the anchor and chain and we were carried away. We dropped the second anchor and the drag was so great that the brake pin on the anchor did not hold. Sparks[93] flew off, but no one could do a thing about it. The chain tightened. We let it out and finally had to cut it loose—we lost one anchor and chain. The fog was thick, so we kept blowing the ship's whistle as a warning to other ships. We barely cleared another boat and were then pushed against another ship that was anchored. Fortunately, this ship had a high galleon bow, so the only damage was to our superstructure and the sloop deck.[94] (*Source:* Walraven van Hall, Letter, March 14, 1929.)

Walraven at the
Zonnehof in Bentveld
with his ouistiti Apie.
(Van Hall Foundation)

His mother Nel wrote that when Walraven came back from a trip "something unexpected always happened." For example once he came home and took out of his pocket a dwarf monkey that he had brought from Brazil in a cigar box.

> He was very attached to this monkey. It made many journeys with him subsequently, until, on a rough lurch of the ship, it lost its balance, fell into the sea, and drowned. Later he brought several monkeys and even a very special tropical bird, which everyone said he couldn't possibly keep alive in winter. (*Source:* Letter from Nel Boissevain van Hall.)

His younger brother Beppo remembered when Walraven came home in wintertime having bought four marmosets during his travels and went to the Groote Club[95] on Dam Square to get a haircut. The monkeys were no bigger than squirrels and he put them in the inside pocket of his jacket:

> The marmosets were warm and settled in his pockets. Walraven handed his jacket over to the porter and went down to the barber of the Groote Club. It was nice and warm in the wardrobe. The monkeys

went to investigate and a little later the doorman came by the barber: "Mr Van Hall, your monkeys have broken loose!" With his hair half-cropped, Wally went on a monkey hunt and with some difficulty—a few coats fell off their hooks—he got hold of them, after which they were locked up in a cake box." (*Source:* Beppo van Hall, letter.)

In 1927, between two trips, Walraven and Gijs bought a Remington[96] "light car," a sports car with a sliding roof, for the hefty sum of 100 guilders.[97] Wally's brother Beppo wrote that the engine was not strong and to get it started with three people in, they had a routine:

> Passengers had to jerk forward on an order from Wally, whereupon the car would sputter and belch a thick cloud of smoke. I can still see Mrs. Van Dedem's stunned face as we three, on Wally's command ("full speed ahead!") all jerked forward, after which mother said goodbye with a royal gesture." (*Source:* Beppo van Hall.)

When the car broke down a short time later, Walraven was allowed to use one of two cars that his father purchased in 1928. With dancer sister Suzy, always dressed in *haute couture*, he regularly attended *concours d'élégances*, shows of luxury automobiles. The duo won many prizes for their presentations.

Van Hall loved cars and especially loved to drive them fast. Once he was driving above the limit on the Zandvoortselaan near his parental home. He was pulled over by a police officer, who approached him with a pen and a printed form in his hand.

> Police Officer: "What is your occupation?"
> Walraven: "Sailor."
> Police Officer: "Your address?"
> Walraven: "On board the Eemland."
> The officer paused . . . and then tore up the speeding ticket.
> Police Officer (laughing): "You won't get to the sea that way. Don't drive so fast!" (*Source:* Beppo van Hall.)

The Emland. (Collection of Erik Schaap)

However, Walraven's sailor's luck didn't last much longer. After he obtained yet another diploma, his career was all over. At previous physical examinations he had been approved, despite his requiring glasses. This time his eyesight was no longer deemed good enough to be a crew member on a large ship. As he summarized the situation in a letter two years later:

> In 1929 I made my last trip as 4th mate radio operator on the Eemland of the Royal Holland Lloyd. After the trip was over, when the ship arrived in June, I wanted to study for my officer rank as 2nd mate. But my eyes wouldn't let me. (*Source:* Walraven van Hall, Letter, 1931.)

With an honorable discharge and an extremely positive recommendation in his pocket ("His conduct as well as his diligence and ability have been very good throughout his employment."),[98] he turned his back on the sea. The forced farewell was an immense disappointment for him. His younger brother Beppo wrote: "It was of course a great sadness for Wally that he was rejected because of his eyes. He had always been expecting that in the end he would be approved."[99]

New York City, 1929-1930

He could not immediately leave behind the shipping world. In August 1929 he sailed on the *Statendam* to the United States, expecting to find a suitable job there in shipping. Walraven shared a room in a five-story walk-up near New York University in Greenwich Village at 83 Washington Place[100] with his compatriot Jimmy Huizinga—a son of the Leiden historian Johan Huizinga—where his older brother Gijs and his wife Emma, both still in New York City, formerly lived. His younger brother Beppo commented:

> Cleaning, for them—Walraven and Gijs—was not something they liked to do regularly. They would wait until there was a strong wind. Then they opened all the windows and swept the room so that the dust flew out the windows. (*Source:* Beppo van Hall.)

Walraven came to New York City hoping to join a shipping company. (That is, after all, what three cousins of his did—Robert, Jan, and Eugen Boissevain.) But the global economic crisis[101] threw a spanner in the works. The company could not take him on.[102] His brother Gijs was also in New York. He had a job at a bank[103] and so was in a position to help Walraven. The sailor followed in the footsteps of his father and grandfather and became a banker, albeit initially at a level far below his ability. To support himself, he also translated German and French letters into English. He had lovely months in Manhattan and the surrounding area, according to his friend Nico van Heek:

> What a wonderful time we had. Wally was then tireless. We often partied late into the night, but I remember he was always on time for work the next day and did not leave until the last of his colleagues had finished their day's work. He had countless acquaintances in New York, which made me wonder sometimes how he managed to get to know all those people so quickly. (*Source:* Nico van Heek.)

*Walraven and his brothers Floor, Beppo and Gijs
at the parental home in Bentveld. (Van Hall Foundation)*

The shocks of the Great Depression were becoming increasingly intrusive, but that wasn't reason enough for the Van Hall boys to cut back on their fun. Gijs wrote home:

> Yesterday, Tuesday, we celebrated Wally's [24th] birthday with a big party. With five boys and five girls we went for cocktails, then ate in a Russian restaurant on 52nd street and finally danced until two in the morning at the Plaza Hotel. We were still tired from this exertion on Sunday. But next Saturday we will do it all again and will have a big party here for our acquaintances. For this we will decorate the whole house. (*Source:* Gijs van Hall, letter from New York City to his parents, February 12, 1930.)

Walraven enjoyed the city, the parties, his old and new friends, and the countryside around New York. But the job-search part was a different matter. He was continually faced with the challenge of finding work during a period of prolonged and catastrophic financial panic and economic destruction. The former sailor was unfamiliar with this world of work and longed to be back in the shipping world. He wrote to his father in March 1930 somewhat desperately, asking:

> How is the Holland Lloyd doing? I heard nothing more about that and wanted to know about it with a view to future plans. The chances of me getting anything here in New York are very slim unless there is a huge change in the coming months, which I don't expect. The pickup of business is of course constantly being predicted, but I have learned not to believe any of it. You, of course, are a better judge then I of the chances of me getting into the banking business in Holland. I got the impression when you were here last time that you weren't very optimistic about it. (*Source:* Walraven van Hall to his father, March 1930.)

Walraven tried the Dutch network in New York,[104] hoping to find a better job. He considered becoming a naturalized American citizen,[105] but decided against it because of the economic downturn. Signing on for the Holland-America Line was another option. He thought hard about it, even considering a move to the Dutch East Indies, where he might work for shipping company De Nederland.[106] He wrote:

> Yesterday I spoke to Mr. Van Hengel, who would see what he could do for me in New York. But he said that De Nederland never hired anyone in the Indies without a commitment for a stay in the East Indies of at least two years. I heard back from him and he was friendly, but not encouraging. (*Source:* Walraven, letter to his father Adriaan Floris van Hall)

His mother sympathized. Nel responded to his letter in October 1930: "I so hope that you will be successful at the Lloyd and that you will return to your own element."[107]

At one point in his searches in the liquidity-parched Wall Street offices, he was persuaded to invest in a corporation that was promoting a medicinal radium cushion. Walraven asked his father if he could borrow $2,000 ($34,000 in 2024 dollars) to participate. He told the home front:

> We have already drawn up a draft contract. It is a matter of urgency, since these days everyone has rheumatic pains and stomach pains, so it's a good time to start something like that. (*Source:* Walraven van Hall, letter to his father Adriaan Floris van Hall.)

Father Van Hall did, indulgently, transfer the requested amount to his son.[108] He said: "If it fails, you don't have to repay anything. If it succeeds, and you can repay it from the what you earn back from the investment, then yes. In the latter case I will charge you seven percent interest." But the investment faded away quietly, its death shrouded in silence.[109] A year later, Walraven was back in the Netherlands. Looking back on his time in New York, he wrote:

> Life in New York naturally had attractions for a young person like me, but the life was ultimately unsatisfying for a European used to engaging with individuals, not joining with a disorganized and thoughtless herd[110] in New York. It was really amazing to see how little the young people I met there made of their lives with the many possibilities they had. Office life, on the other hand, was very interesting."[111] (*Source:* Walraven van Hall letter, Stadsarchief Amsterdam.)

Walraven left Wall Street after a year and a half. He was required to return home by his visa. According to U.S. visa rules, he had to go back to the Netherlands at the end of his two-year visa in order to extend it.[112]

Zutphen Banker, 1931

Back in the Netherlands, something came up. His father was director of the Amsterdam-based bank H. Oyens & Sons and was able to obtain for Walraven the opportunity to become co-director of the bank's Zutphen branch. He seized it, and—after first taking a long vacation trip through Scandinavia—began a new phase in his working life on February 10, 1931, his 25th birthday.

A month into his new job, in March 1931, he wrote to his former headmaster, C. P. Gunning: "Here I am, sitting here in Zutphen, but I must add that if someone had predicted this to me two years ago, I would never have thought it possible." The ambiance of the old Hanseatic city suited him well.

> After more than four years of sailing and almost a year and a half of a hurried and busy life in New York, I suddenly find myself in quiet Zutphen, which makes me happy, because I think a Dutchman always finds Holland is the best country on this globe. (*Source:* Walraven van Hall, letter to C. P. Gunning,. March 1931.)

The bank was at a distinguished location, a white corner building on the long IJsselkade in Zutphen. But he was not so keen on the type of work he was assigned to. His aunt Dea reported:

> He didn't really like the banking profession, but he never complained about it and did a more than decent job. He took advantage of the IJssel, where he engaged in joyous sailing with the dinghy he renovated himself." (*Source:* Dea van Hall, letter.)

Gradually he held various administrative positions in local association life. Over the years he became a member of a tourist board that wrote a hotel plan for the Salland region[113] and started as treasurer at the local Red Cross branch. Another Zutphen organization, the local Borgstellingsfonds (the Agricultural Guarantee Fund Foundation) also used his services. His mother Nel wrote:

Walraven in his sailing boat Hollebolletje. (Van Hall Foundation)

The social side of Walraven's banking work had special appeal for him. He had a borrower from his bank, an instrument maker, who had become completely apathetic. His business was neglected, his house was filthy. Wally got him some work at a farm, where he had to be present every morning at six o'clock, to shake him out of his apathy. The man was able to pay off his debts with the money he earned. Wally visited him regularly and checked that he maintained everything properly. The man returned to a normal life." (*Source:* Nel Boissevain van Hall,[114] letter.)

The financial crises of 1929 and the early thirties[115] hit hard—not only this instrument maker but also the Van Hall family. Father Aat had invested heavily in Küchenmeister's International Company for Acoustics. This company sought to profit from opportunities to add sound to films, which was something new.[116] In the summer of 1931, the company's share price collapsed, and Aat and Nel van Hall lost tens of thousands of guilders.[117] Worse, their investment company, Oyens & Sons—Walraven's and Adriaan's employer—almost collapsed because of its investments in Küchenmeister's. This debacle got Aat pushed off the board, although his son remained at the firm. Walraven wrote later: "It was a bad time for father. Everyone asked him why he left the firm, because he had not yet reached retirement age. It was an especially bitter pill for him that he no longer had an office in Amsterdam."[118]

Because of his progressive social attitudes during the 1930s, in Zutphen Walraven was nicknamed "the Red Banker." This nickname did not refer to any particular political activism—he was not then a member of a political party and, with the exception of the short time he was later active in the Dutch Union, never would be. But, as Louis de Jong wrote in his official World War II history, Walraven did think in a progressive way:

> Walraven believed that a "new beginning" was possible for the Netherlands, especially regarding economic-social relations, if those of goodwill would just find one another. Promoting that greatly suited him—he had a remarkable ability to strip sharp disagreements from their emotional context and to present the two sides of a business negotiation. This approach made agreement easier, if it was possible. (*Source:* Louis de Jong, History of the Second World War, in Dutch.)

That quality came in handy a decade later when he presided over meetings of the Dutch Resistance.

In 1936, Walraven recruited as an apprentice[119] a recently graduated lawyer, Wim Schukking, six years his junior. Walraven taught him the tricks of the banking trade in a comradely way and regularly invited Schukking and his wife to dinner. This friendship continued during the war. Wim Schukking writes in his memoirs: "In 1944, we spent a holiday in their house. Only afterward did we learn how dangerous that had been. Not only were concealed firearms in the toilet cistern, but Wally himself was already being hunted by the SS."[120]

However, Walraven's longing for the sea continued to gnaw at him. He regularly drove his car out towards the coast. Tonny Eggink, who spent a lot of time with him then, said:

*Walraven in front of
'his' bank in Zutphen.
(Van Hall Foundation)*

Because we would otherwise run out of things to say to each other, we always sang while driving. We sang songs from the nautical school, both seamen's and student songs, in tenor and bass. The sea was his great love, and we often drove there together. I would eventually leave him alone, and he would climb a dune, or just stare far out into the distance. At these times, he appreciated being left alone. (*Source:* Tonny Eggink.)

Walraven later described this period of his life in a letter to his fiancée as "hopelessly empty."[121] His brother Beppo wrote that they were together one evening in Beppo's car after Walraven had returned to the Netherlands. They were driving along the boulevard by the shore in Zandvoort.

Suddenly Wally said: "There goes the Eemland." He asked to take over the wheel, and raced to see the ship coming into IJmuiden.[122] But the road was narrow and winding. By the time we got there, the

Eemland had already been through the lock and was sailing through the North Sea Canal to Amsterdam. But we saw it, and that was enough for Wally. How he could recognize the distant silhouette above the bilge line was a mystery to me. (*Source:* Beppo van Hall, letter.)

Surviving film footage shows Walraven in his Staverse sailboat, given to him by his parents.[123] He called it the *Hollebolletje*.[124] He had rigged it for two sails before the mast. During his time in Zutphen, he purchased a new Finnish sailboat, which he outfitted again, with extra rigging. Nico van Heek said that he sailed for the first time in life in Walraven's *Hollebolletje*. In his case, the memories were cherished as wonderful and sunny. However:

> Those first sailing lessons did not go smoothly at all. I was often punished when I didn't react quickly enough or when I didn't immediately catch his sailor's commands and the names for the rigging. He always had the gift of saying things straight to the point without mincing words. But the sincerity of his intentions made everyone willing to accept it from him. That will certainly have been one of the reasons that he later exerted such a great influence and managed to get so much done through his friends and associates. (*Source:* Nico van Heek.)

Van Heek also noticed that the "lively, cheerful, and cordial" Walraven also had a serious side. "Afterwards, I decided that he just pretended to be less serious than he really was."[125] Eggink said: "Wally was only quiet when something bothered him. With a single word, he then indicated what it was. For example, he was very shocked when the monkey he had brought from South America for his mother died."[126]

Eggink and Van Hall saw each other in the Zutphen Men's Society, the meeting place for the local *upper middle class*.[127] Eggink described his friend as a pacesetter who would come up with one anecdote after another.

He would rip through the stuffy atmosphere. People shook with laughter. He would laugh along heartily while carefully directing the conversation. He would then whisper to me: "Continue, carry on. They all must go home late." People went home late, so their housemates were asleep, resulting in their housemates wanting to hear the stories first-hand from us newcomers. We received one invitation after another to many dinners and told many stories. (*Source:* Eggink.)

Eggink gave another example, when he and Walraven were both invited to an engagement party where the only thing being offered to drink was lemonade, and no smoking was permitted. Walraven saved the day:

In the middle of the party, Wally whispered to me: "If you want wine, come along." He brought me to the service elevator and called out in a fake lady's voice: "Jan, two wines." Jan replied: "Yes, ma'am," and two glasses came up. This was repeated several times. Wally had discovered that the lady served wine to some of the older guests and took it from the service elevator herself. We continued the game until Jan replied: "The bottle is finished, ma'am." (*Source:* Eggink. The story is also told in Michael C. Van Hall, *Three Centuries*, 107.)[128]

In their petit-bourgeois provincial town, Wally and his friends sometimes crossed what were considered proper boundaries.

We made great blunders, infringed on etiquette, and didn't always pay attention to the Zutphen customs. This caused tensions, and then Wally would mediate with his wonderful gift. Without exception, he would bring the parties back together through a conversation. He could not live with the tension. (*Source:* Eggink.)

Tilly den Tex

The move from New York City to sleepy Zutphen was a step away from excitement in the life of the 25-year-old banker. But his excitement returned as he fell in love with a young woman named Anna Mathilde—Tilly—den Tex. In early 1931, the two must have bumped into each other at a family party.[129] It was the first time since they were nine or ten that they had seen each other. "Wally fell in love instantly," a childhood friend of Tilly wrote in 1989.[130] "Wally couldn't hide from us that he was madly in love." Eggink wrote:

> One day, he told me about a girl called Tilly den Tex. He kept talking about her and disappeared to Amsterdam more often. I also got engaged. At the same time, we left behind our wild years. (*Source:* Eggink.)

During the summer of 1931, the Van Hall family and friends spent their holidays in Hattem,[131] where Walraven's Uncle Jan and Aunt Hessie had a house, called the "Kolkhuis" because it has a small lake (a Kolk) in the back. Walraven's brother Johan Bernard wrote:

> When Tilly joined the group and ventured into the Kolk to swim,[132] Wally only had eyes for her. She couldn't swim very well, so Wally (he said) always kept close to her just to be on the safe side and when Tilly wanted to rest for a while, he chased away the children, who found nothing more exciting than rocking back and forth on the raft. (*Source:* Johan Bernard van Hall, letter.)

Tilly also came from a patrician[133] Amsterdam family. One branch of Tilly's Den Tex family belonged to the nobility.[134] Tilly's father and grandfather were directors for a time of the Royal Netherlands Steamship Company, one of the five largest Dutch steamship companies.[135] Other Den Texes were employed in the financial world. One of Tilly's grandmothers was a Boissevain,[136] which was how she met Walraven in her childhood.

Walraven and Tilly were deeply in love, but during the first months of their relationship, they could visit each other only on weekends because of the long distance between them. In between, they spoke by telephone almost daily. Every week, passionate letters went from Zutphen to Amsterdam and vice versa. Soon they were engaged to be married. In September 1931, Walraven asked his fiancée to find out how her family felt about an early wedding:

> Father and mother are very conservative and probably expect us to be engaged for a year or at least three-quarters of a year. I suspect not the slightest opposition from them, but I would like to hear your thoughts. (*Source:* Walraven to Tilly, September 9, 1931.)

Tilly had set her sights on a quick marriage, but Walraven asked for more time. He had seen the American stock market crash up close and now daily saw it again in the crises at his employer, the stockbroker H. Oyens & Sons. He wrote to her the following month:

> You know I would like nothing more than to get married tomorrow. However, alas, the national and international situation is in such turmoil that we must wait for things to calm down. Read the newspaper tonight and see how bad things are, everywhere. We have to first try to get through all this mess and address the setbacks, which are inevitable. (*Source:* Walraven to Tilly, October 6, 1931.)

So the engagement continued.

This time the delay was short. Walraven wrote to Tilly on December 7 with big news: "When you read this letter, you will have a house in a week." He eagerly awaited his wife-to-be's arrival but also felt the weight of change, sharing his life with someone else

> Since the age of sixteen, I have hardly ever been home, and I was almost always living alone. So living with you means I suddenly get a companion with whom I can share joys and sorrows. I feel a

35

The wedding in Amsterdam and honeymoon in France, 1932. (Van Hall Foundation)

tremendous responsibility, taking you out of your cozy and pleasant home and asking you to share life's challenges with me. . . . I am sure that together we will succeed. If we both have the will, we shall be able to endure much. (*Source:* Walraven to Tilly, December 7, 1931.)

In mid-February 1932, the couple moved into an idyllic, well-situated house at IJsselkade 3a, right near Walraven's Zutphen workplace. On March 1, 1932, the eagerly desired marriage occurred in Amsterdam. On April 5, 1933, the young couple's first child, Adrienne (nicknamed Attie), was born in Zutphen. Her Aunt Dea wrote in a 1966 letter: "As a small baby, you were carried in a baby carrier[137] in Zutphen when your parents went out for dinner. That is more common now, but it was revolutionary then."[138] On July 28, 1936, Attie got a little brother, who was given the name Adriaan Floris, continuing the family's tradition of reusing their most illustrious names.

In 1933, the year of Attie's birth, Adolf Hitler came to power in Germany.[139] Nazi politics there and in Austria cast a shadow over the Netherlands. Debate reverberated in the dining rooms of the Van Hall family. Sixty years later, granddaughter Attie still remembered the discussions between Walraven's parents. "They always quarreled when there were elections because his father Aat (Adriaan) was conservative and voted liberal. His mother Nel was very progressive and voted social-democratic."[140]

When the couple together attended a Nazi meeting before the war, it quickly became too much for grandmother Van Hall. Her granddaughter Attie said they were near the front of the hall, in the middle of the row. Mussert was speaking and Nel Boissevain van Hall couldn't take it anymore.

> She shouted in a stentorian voice: "Bah![141] Come on Aat, let's go!" So half the row had to stand up in the middle of the lecture to let them pass. That some people did not appreciate this was revealed by an event near Zandvoort, on the Pentislaan,[142] where a few Dutch Nazi Party[143] members lived at the time. When Nel and an aunt walked by, the men said in a loud voice to each other: "Let's hang another old Jewess from our lamppost." (*Source:* Attie van Hall, letter dated November 3, 2005.)[144]

While driving through Germany in his car, Walraven saw the Nazi influence. He carried a movie camera and filmed scenes with swastikaed flags waving behind him. After the *Anschluss* with Austria and then Hitler's invasion of Poland, the threat of war was rising in the Netherlands. Like many others, Walraven believed he should volunteer his time to defending his country. Shortly before the start of World War II, he taught radio telegraphy in his spare time and helped create the Zutphen Air Defense Service.

Zaandam, 1940-1945

On March 1, 1940, Walraven joined the august banking and securities office Wed. J. te Veltrup & Son in Zaandam, partnering with the Zaandam securities broker Pieter Huijbert van der Goot. Two months before, they registered their partnership with a notary, contributing 25,000 guilders each,[145] plus their "knowledge, work and industry," and their "relationships."

West side 42, Zaandam. (Collection of Erik Schaap.)

The Van Hall family moved into a century-old mansion at Westside 42 in Zaandam. They rented it from Anna Maria Honig, who vacated it because her husband had died two years earlier. It was "a large house with a beautiful garden and a maid," reported daughter Attie van Hall, who was just six years old when the family moved into the home. "We had a beautiful garden there on the Zaan river."[146]

A playmate of Aad, Hans van de Stadt, lived a few houses away and had fond memories of the house. Though Hans rarely saw Walraven, he said the mother of the house was always there:

> She was very cordial when I came back with her son Aad. The garden was full of old trees that begged you to climb up and make a beautiful tree house. But such a house would have been superfluous, because the garden included a fully equipped children's playhouse. (*Source:* Hans van de Stadt, *Dakhaas bij gaslicht*, "Roof Hare by Gaslight," 2012.)

Walraven's bank office was less than a thousand feet from his home, at Westside 47. His new position meant that he became a member of the Association

Walraven and Tilly van Hall with their daughter Attie and son Aad,
shortly before the German invasion of the Netherlands. (Van Hall Foundation)

for Securities Trading and thus was admitted to the Amsterdam stock exchange. Every work day, Walraven made the five-minute walk from his home or the bank to the railway station and took the train to Amsterdam's Beursplein.[147]

Walraven also continued to volunteer with the Air Defense Service[148] in Zaandam. The Dutch Government created the Service in 1939 to address new dangers from the air, calling upon the army and the public: "Self-protection is the pillar of air protection." The message was heard and soon 140,000 Dutch people were members of the Service. After the German Occupation, as the impact of the air war on civilians was increasingly visible, membership increased to 230,000.[149]

Two weeks before Hitler invaded the Netherlands,[150] Walraven and Tilly's third child was born, a girl. She was named after two of Tilly's American friends—Mary Dawson Strawbridge and her mother Anna Hacker Strawbridge, Quakers from Philadelphia. With Mary-Ann, the Van Hall family was complete.[151]

The invasion of the Netherlands, May 1940. Rotterdam after the bombing, above, and German troops entering Amsterdam, below. (Public domain.)

3 | Zaandam Union Leader (1940–1941)

"The Dutch Union is just a way to resist the new order."
—WALRAVEN VAN HALL

ON MAY 10, 1940, without warning or provocation, at 4 am, the German Army invaded the Netherlands. An hour later, Zaandam's Air Defense Service[152] head, Cornelis (Cees) de Cock, nervously called Zaandam Mayor Joris in 't Veld[153] with the news. The mayor was incredulous. As he said later:

> At about 5 o'clock in the morning I woke up feeling something unusual was happening. I was hearing the roar of airplane engines and heavy anti-aircraft fire. Then the phone rang. The head of the Air Defense Service, very agitated, told me: "It's no mistake,[154] Mayor, the radio is full of reports of planes dropping paratroopers.[155] It's happening." I still didn't want to believe it. I clung to the hope that there might still be a misunderstanding. (*Source:* Joris in 't Veld.)

The quick-thinking chairman of the board of the State Artillery Devices Company[156] decided that Dutch capitulation was inevitable and proposed blowing up the Zaandam munitions factory. But General Henri Winkelman,[157] the nation's leader after the Queen left the Netherlands on May 13, said no. Frans den Hollander, president-director of the Dutch Railways and chairman of the Artillery Devices company, remembered:

When I asked the Dutch High Command whether we should proceed with blowing up the State Artillery Devices Company[158] factory, I was told everything should remain intact. So the enemy got a functioning arms factory that was of great value to them. At least we immediately closed it down and resisted early orders from the incoming Occupation to start it back up again. (*Source:* Frans den Hollander.)

The Early Months

The invasion was a shock. Few people tried to resist the Occupation government. The ones who did were looked upon with pity back in the early days of May 1940. Bernard IJzerdraat, a Haarlem tapestry restorer, did urge resistance to the Nazis, but people like him were rare as black swans.[159] On May 15, General Winkelman signed the Dutch surrender, in Rijsoord, near Rotterdam. The same day, IJzerdraat issued his *Geuzen*[160] *Message,* headlined: "The Battle Continues!"

Despite IJzerdraat's public appeal, most Dutch people were at first resigned to the Occupation. Unlike Germany, Belgium, or France, the Netherlands had not been occupied since 1813, when the Napoleonic occupation ended. The Dutch did not have the same frame of reference as the other three countries. Also, the Germans for a few months kept up a constant charade of wanting only the best for their Dutch cousins.[161]

The first Prime Minister in exile, Squire[162] Dirk Jan de Geer, who went with the Queen to Great Britain, even advised the Dutch via the BBC to help their occupiers. He said the duty of the Dutch was now to cooperate with the German authorities and serve the interests of the population as well as they could. The public, for their part, believed it was their duty to stay calm and orderly, to maintain normal services and refrain from anything that could complicate the country's new administration.

There was little criticism of the Occupation, and it was veiled. When Mayor In 't Veld of Zaandam gave a speech to open a residence for the German military on May 21, he started by putting in a good word for the royal family that had left for England, saying that the Queen had not fled Holland, merely relocated her government. "The House of Orange and the Netherlands belong together," he said to his audience, evincing sympathy for the royal family, although he was a dyed-in-the-wool anti-monarchy Republican.[163] Then he criticized the Occupation in the guise of going along with their new rules. Before the Occupation, municipalities had been able to negotiate with one another about where a military garrison should be located. But the German Occupation decided without any discussion:

> Perhaps these garrisons will be very temporary. I hope so. Not that we have anything personal against our new military friends. We Dutch are hospitable and make our guests comfortable. No, we want to help them return as soon as possible, as they themselves must want, to their own homes and workplaces. (*Source:* Joris in 't Veld.)

The mayor's message got national attention and was widely understood for what it was, an oblique call to resist.

However, this mayor was an exception. The political parties, which were still permitted in this early phase of the Occupation, kept quiet about resistance. Even the Communist Party of the Netherlands (CPN) was at first acquiescent. A year earlier, Nazi Germany had signed a non-aggression pact[164] with Stalin's Soviet Union, the great model of socialist government in the CPN's eyes. The Russian Foreign Minister was the first minister to congratulate Adolf Hitler on his conquest of the Low Countries. No wonder the CPN's secretary-general reassured his supporters of the good intentions of the Nazis and dismissed the idea of patriotic resistance as royal Orange propaganda. He advocated instead a "true neutrality" toward the Third Reich and a "correct attitude" toward Hitler.[165] Of course, none of this CPN kow-towing to the Occupation ingratiated the party to the Nazis. On July 20, 1940, the Germans banned the CPN, which pushed it right into the Resistance.[166]

In one area, the Occupation made some quick decisions. The Air Defense Service members were issued a special identification card (in German, the *Ausweis*) and were ordered to patrol the streets like night watchmen. Anyone without this identification was required to stay indoors during the curfew, between midnight and 4 am. But Air Defense workers were allowed out during air raids and at night. Thanks to his Air Defense work, Walraven van Hall could move freely at night.

Before the invasion, members of the Dutch Nazi Party (the NSB) were barred from becoming members of the Air Defense Services because their pro-German ideology was viewed as unpatriotic. Because of this history, Anton Mussert and his fellow Dutch Nazis held a grudge against the Air Defense. The Occupation acted swiftly in two ways. First, it welcomed Dutch Nazis as members of the Air Defense. Second, it required Jews to resign as of July 1, 1940.[167] So Air Defense was the first Dutch organization to enforcing an anti-Semitic measure. Zaandam's branch was still managed by Cornelis de Cock, a staunch opponent of pro-German politics before the war. Nonetheless, he enforced the new anti-Jewish decree. No protests followed in the Zaan region or anywhere else.

The next Occupation move was worse. The day after the Zaandam Air Defense order, a short newspaper article advised:

> All non-Aryan aliens who left Germany between January 1, 1933 and March 1, 1938 and now reside in Zaandam must register at the police station in Vinkenstraat within eight days. Failure to do so is punishable by a prison sentence of up to two months or a 1,000-guilder fine. (*Source:* "Non-Aryan Aliens Must Report," *The Zaanlander.*)

Again, no protests were heard.

The Dutch Nazis and the Dutch Union

During the first months of the Occupation, political activity was largely absent except for the Dutch Nazis[168] and their two allied parties—the National Socialist Dutch Workers' Party (NSNAP),[169] and the National Front. They lined up behind the Nazi Occupation. In early summer 1940, the NSNAP in

44

Walraven with Mary-Ann,
his youngest daughter (1940).
(Van Hall Foundation)

particular was active near Walraven's Amsterdam office. On June 7, supporters of this extremist party smashed eight large store windows at the Jewish-owned De Bijenkorf department store, next to the stock exchange.[170] Five days later, the party broke windows of the Plotske porcelain store in the main shopping street, Kalverstraat.[171] They were following the playbook of the German Nazi gangs.

The only sign of resistance was on Prince Bernhard's birthday, June 29, when Orange loyalists laid flowers at the palace on Dam Square. Some people wore the Prince's favorite flower, white carnations. Nazi collaborators soon organized street fights. NSNAP members provoked fights in the Kalverstraat. Near Central Station, inebriated German sailors beat up pedestrians. In the late afternoon, fights erupted on streets between Dam Square and Rembrandtplein. Especially in the area around the stock exchange (Dam, Spui, Rembrandtplein, and Kalverstraat), frequent fighting occurred between German- and Dutch-friendly groups.

The wait-and-see attitude of moderate democratic parties contrasted with the enthusiasm of the Nazi and Communist standard-bearers, creating a hole in the political center. The Dutch Union, created on July 24, 1940, filled this hole. The Dutch Union was founded by three people—the Groningen Queen's Commissioner Hans Linthorst Homan, Tilburg professor Jan de Quay, and Rotterdam police commissioner Louis Einthoven. They believed that political reform could continue even after the Occupation and that a new national movement could end the pre-war religious and ideological silo thinking (what they called "pillarization").[172] By promoting "national unity," they set out to use the Occupation as a time to address widespread Dutch dissatisfaction with the country's polarized parliamentary democracy in the 1930s.[173]

In this way, the Dutch Union became the first place where moderates could meet comfortably. Walraven van Hall's brother Gijs described his joy and relief at having this new political home as an emotional escape valve.[174]

The Dutch Union started a suburban[175] unit first and then started to recruit as many members as possible—but no Nazis! The campaign found sympathetic ears. Hundreds of people joined. According to Gijs van Hall, this great new influence in his daily life, this Union, was "one big demonstration against the NSB," against the Dutch Nazis. He commented: "I will not waste time debating the purpose of the Dutch Union, because it cannot openly declare itself a resistance organization."[176] Like Gijs van Hall, many others who joined the Dutch Union thereby became more confident in taking a position against Adolf Hitler and his Nazi partisans.

The Dutch Union started up immediately in the Zaan region. Two days after the national Union was established, the daily newspaper announced: "The Zaan Region is participating!" The text made the point that the time for talking was over. Its slogan, "Unity is Strength," was widely understood on the banks of the Zaan river.

> Nowhere else in the country can you find a region whose people act so boldly and smoothly and think so logically. Those who sympathize with the aim of the Dutch Union, please provide your name and address to the Zaan regional branch. Send your business card, with the words "Dutch Union." *Source: De Zaandlander,* July 26, 1940.

The appeal was signed: "J. J. Dinkelberg, Koog aan de Zaan."

De Zaanlander promoted the new Dutch Union more than any other regional newspaper. It supported their advertisements with promotional articles. Why? Because Dinkelberg was the newspaper's editor-in-chief.

With the help of people like Dinkelberg, enthusiasm for the new party grew, translating into a massive nationwide influx of members. A Haarlem newspaper reported:

> Three confidence-inspiring people have called for Dutch unity, and within two twenty-four-hour cycles they have received more than one hundred thousand expressions of support from all parts of the country and all layers of our society. (*Source: Haarlems Dagblad*, July 28, 1940.)

A day later, *De Zaanlander* mentioned broad interest in the Dutch Union. The Zaan regional branch was being joined by "shopkeepers and workers, yes, but also mayors and pastors of different religions." The newspaper urged its readers to join the new movement.

> The Zaan warhorses[177] also feel that we cannot just keep forever asking questions, hiding behind our fears. The Dutch Union is now available to offer guidance and open up possibilities for uniting Dutch people. The first hundred patriots in the Zaan region signed up in just two days. (*Source: De Zaanlander*, July 27, 1940.)

Walraven van Hall was one of the first Zaan residents to join.

Some voices were negative. The Social Democratic Party called the Union's declaration of principles a "program of meaningless noise." The editor of the Party news wrote:

> We believe in helping to build a better future for our country, in cooperation with everyone else with good will, provided that this good will is manifested in a clear program of action. But we have found neither good will nor clarity in the program of the Dutch Union. (*Source: Zaans Volksblad*, July 30, 1940.)

But this critique had no impact. On July 31, 1940, the local newspaper reported that registrations of new Dutch Union members in the region have been arriving every day. "Now more than five hundred statements of support have been received."[178]

Zaandam's Mayor supported the Union, but didn't care for *Zaandammer* editor-in-chief Dinkelberg. He sent a confidential letter to the Dutch Union complaining that Dinkelberg was miscast as their agent. " The man is unfit for that role. He is pushy. People will be put off by him. I promised some other mayors to tell you they want someone else."[179] His attempt failed, and Dinkelberg continued as the local contact person, for a little longer. But by 1942, Dinkelberg's *Zaandammer* paper was toeing the Nazi line, carrying Nazi news and describing the Soviets as the enemy.[180]

Arnold Meijer's National Front, a Dutch Nazi group, tried to suppress the Dutch Union, but only seven supporters showed up in early August in the Café Vigilance[181] in Koog aan de Zaan, north of Zaandam. Nonetheless, in the Gouw area, south of Zaandam, Nazi leader K. H. Tusenius announced that the Union would have "no chance" against the Nazis. "Every day the Union has to change its program, clarify it, and try to reach agreement through compromises. They cannot prevail over the power of our new program."[182] Sadly, Tusenius's prediction would be accurate.

The Largest Political Party in Dutch History

However, the Dutch Union meanwhile grew rapidly into the largest political party the Netherlands had ever seen, estimated at 600,000 to 900,000 members,[183] far more than the peak membership of the Dutch Nazi Party (NSB) at only 100,000 supporters. (The two smaller Nazi-friendly parties had only 25,000 members between them.)[184]

The Union's astonishing growth created its own administrative barriers to success. The Zaandam branch sent out a note apologizing for embarrassing delays:

> To the hundreds of ladies and gentlemen from the Zaan region who responded spontaneously a month ago to our call from the Dutch Union triumvirate and sent me their declarations of support: I hereby advise you that the Central Bureau in The Hague is still processing the flood of new memberships." (*Source:* Dinkelberg, *De Zaanlander.*)

The Union's head office, on Alexander Street in The Hague, was chaotic, as a full-time staff of forty people tried to cope with thousands of letters daily of advice, questions, and complaints. By mid-September, many members had still not received a membership card or magazine.

The greatest problem was that the unity cited in the name was based on one thing. People joined because they disliked the Nazis. They were not in fact unified. They were not even informed—few read the weekly magazine, *The Union*, faithfully, and those who did read it had to puzzle over its pro-German statements. Most assumed these statements were there to mislead the German Occupation. But the reality was that the Union's leadership was more pro-German than its members. The leaders were seeking compromise, if not consensus. Linthorst Homan wrote: "Anyone who joins us out of aversion to another [Nazi] political party has come to the wrong place."[185]

The Dutch Union leadership had good reason to worry about overt hostility toward the Germans, because the Occupation could ban them at any time. The Dutch Nazis (NSB) were not happy with the Union and in July 1940, NSB leader Meinoud Rost van Tonningen said so. Reichskommissar Seyss-Inquart had appointed Van Tonningen Commissioner of the Netherlands Social Democratic Workers Party, the SDAP,[186] a week earlier. In this new role, Van Tonningen controlled the socialist party's publications and activities, and ended its relevance. In a speech in Zaandam, Van Tonningen lashed out at the Union:

> Linthorst Homan and others were pillars of the old regime. They now rally with politicized Catholics under a new flag, because they finally appreciate that Dutch socialism is at last unleashed—a socialism that cannot be learned from books, but is the people's voice,

coming from their blood.[187] (*Source:* Van Tonningen, speaking at the Castle[188] in Zaandam, July 27, 1940.)

Van Tonningen's thinly veiled Nazi propaganda found few sympathetic ears in the far-left Zaan region. At the end of August, his regional NSB still had only 142 members.

The Dilemma for the Union's Leadership

However, the Union's popularity did not help the Union leadership figure out its path ahead. As historian Jacques Presser noted in his book *Demise:*[189] "The basic question is always whether one can sacrifice something *less important* to secure something *more important*."[190] The challenge for the Dutch Union's triumvirate was to propose compromises giving something small to the Germans while getting something big for the Dutch.

That never happened. The prospects were never very good. Look at the October 1940 issue of the member magazine, *The Union.* The Occupation banned promoting or hiring Jews or half-Jews[191] in the civil service. The Union leadership tried to find a middle way. It proposed a compromise. For recent Jewish immigrants, they proposed that "a restriction may be needed." But for "native" Jews, "who have been living and working in the Netherlands for generations," the ban on employment was unnecessary, "because in the Netherlands Jews do not take the positions and do not adopt the attitudes that have made the Jewish question acute in other countries."[192]

The anti-immigrant nature of this statement was an inevitable consequence of the Union leaders' search for unity. It meant accepting Germany as victor, and therefore meant opposing the Resistance. So the Union warned its members:

> The leadership of the Dutch Union has observed that many members of the Union are joining Resistance organizations. The leadership has, through its own channels and publicly, told its members

often not to oppose the party in power. Members must comply with this. (*Source:* Editorial, The Union, October 12, 1940.)

The leadership said again in a letter to branch[193] secretaries in mid-December 1940, that the Union is not rocking the boat:

> The Union is loyal to the Occupation. The Union will keep its word on this matter. It can, therefore, never allow Union members to join so-called secret (Resistance) organizations. Some elements in the Union are still engaging in such illegal activity. There is no place in the Union for Resistance members. All Union officials are instructed to strictly enforce this directive. (*Source:* "No place for Resistance members," Founders, Letter to Branch Secretaries, Dutch Union, December 15, 1940.)

In the Zaandam branch of the Union, a "provisional local committee"[194] was founded in Koog-Zaandijk. A Union storefront followed in Koog aan de Zaan. Members and non-members went there for party pins, magazines, and bicycle flags. But Dinkelberg's glory days in Union leader were swiftly ended on October 4, 1940, when Regional Secretary A. A. Aberson informed Dinkelberg that branch committees were needed in some Zaan municipalities "with the utmost urgency." He said Dinkelberg's role at the newspaper was a conflict of interest, so Dinkelberg would have to step down and make room for new representatives from local branches such as Zaandam and Wormerveer.[195]

The Zaandam branch of the Union (VPC-Zaandam) was formally created in November 1940.[196] The Union leadership asked Walraven van Hall to become its chairman. He said yes. Jaap Buijs, lumber trader in Zaandam and enthusiastic SDAP[197] member, became secretary-treasurer. The branch leadership was expanded to include a publicity officer and three general board members.

Little information about this Zaandam branch in 1940-41 has survived the war. Some lists of members and accounts remain, but most records were destroyed, probably deliberately, in December 1941, when the Occupation banned the Union. Only a few surviving documents show how the Zaandam branch functioned under Van Hall's leadership.

What we know is that hundreds of Zaandammers became members of the Union, including many Social Democrats. In March 1941, the membership count was 740; six months later, it was down to 663; but by December the count was back up to 956. During the first year, in some weeks, thirty to fifty new members signed up. Prominent figures such as Mayor In 't Veld joined the Union. Members went door-to-door, selling pins, flags, and brochures.

Starting in February 1941, Zaans-Waterland Union employees met every first Friday of the month, usually in the Reitsma Hotel near Van Hall's Westside home. They had much work to do because of the steady influx of new members. The provincial Union periodical, the *Regional Chronicle of North Holland*, exuded optimism: "Every month, thousands of magazines have been sold and another new branch has been set up ('North Holland already has 784 Union circles'). The Union has grown into an immense popular movement."[198]

Mixed in with the service announcements in the *Regional Chronicle*, the editors occasionally looked back wistfully at the pre-war situation and the new state:

> *It's May Again! We think so deep*
> *A year of war and blood, we weep.*
> *But with so much pain, we all must share,*
> *And be faithful, always to care!*
> —Anonymous.[199]

Everyone familiar with the *Wilhelmus* knew to whom that faithfulness was pledged unto death—King William I of Orange and the royal family descended from him.[200]

In March 1941, Arnold Meijer, the leader of the pro-Nazi National Front, expressed annoyance about a debate in the *Café De Jonge Prins* ("Café of the Young Prince") in Wormerveer:[201]

De Nederlandsche Unie

Stadgenooten,

Dit propagandanummer wordt U aangeboden door het Plaatselijk Comité van de Nederlandsche Unie, dat kort geleden geïnstalleerd werd om de denkbeelden van de Unie in Zaandam te verbreiden.

De Nederlandsche Unie richt zich tot U, want ook van U wordt gevraagd U te bezinnen op onze taak als Nederlanders.

Ons Volk moet zijn eenheid hervinden; teveel liepen wij langs elkaar heen, teveel spraken wij over wat ons verdeeld hield en te weinig over wat ons samenbindt.

Die samenbinding van allen, die zich Nederlanders weten en ons Vaderland liefhebben, wil de Nederlandsche Unie tot stand brengen.

Daarom komt de Nederlandsche Unie ook in Zaandam en bij U. Sluit U aan en helpt ons de Nederlandsche Zaak te dienen.

Binnenkort hoopt de afdeeling Zaandam een „UNIE-HUIS" te openen, waar U alle inlichtingen kunt ontvangen. Plaats en tijd van openstelling worden nader bekend gemaakt. In afwachting van deze opening zal voorloopig zitting gehouden worden in Hotel Reitsma, Westzijde 22 in de tuinzaal, ingang door den tuin, waar 's Zaterdags en 's Woensdags, tusschen 3 en 6 uur, voor het eerst op Zaterdag a.s. inlichtingen ingewonnen kunnen worden, propagandamateriaal beschikbaar zal zijn, en U gaarne ontvangen zult worden.

Wie zich als lid wenscht op te geven, verzoeken wij het hieronder gedrukte aanmeldingsformulier ingevuld te willen bezorgen bij een der onderstaande Comitéleden, of op gemelde uren aan het inlichtingsbureau.

Het plaatselijk Comité der Nederlandsche Unie,

W. VAN HALL, Voorzitter, Westzijde 42.
J. BUIJS, Secretaris-Penn., Rembrandtstraat 12.
B. VAN EIJCK, Hemkade 19.
Mevr. J. M. J. GLAZENBURG—DECKER,
                                        Parkstraat 82.
A. J. RAMAKER, Heijermansstraat 37.
A. W. VOORS, Westzanerdijk 317.

Hierlangs afknippen

Gaarne verklaar ik hierbij, dat ik volledig instem met de doelstelling van „De Nederlandsche Unie"; dat ik geboren Nederlander (Nederlandsche) ben en den leeftijd van 18 jaar heb bereikt. Ik verzoek U, mij als deelnemer (deelneemster) aan „De Nederlandsche Unie" te willen inschrijven, en teeken, hoogachtend,

Handteekening ....

Naam en voornamen ....

Beroep ....

Adres ....

Woonplaats ....

per maand **)
Contributie *) .... per kwartaal **)
per jaar **)
waarover kan worden beschikt.

*) Contributie naar draagkracht, minimum ƒ 0.59 per jaar.
**) Doorhalen wat niet verlangd wordt.

Registration form of the Dutch Union in Zaandam, 1941. (Collection of Erik Schaap.)

Major differences persist with respect to the Dutch Union. These differences could all be bridged with more discussions, but the Jewish question remains a sticking point. We cannot regard the Jew as a Dutchman, yet the Union refused to exclude the 1,500 to 2,000 Jews from its membership. Regrettably, this prevented unity." (*Source:* Nazi Arnold Meijer, *The Zaandammer,* March 11, 1941.)

Meijer was indirectly responding to protests that occurred two weeks before, in Amsterdam, Hilversum, and Zaanstreek. Workers stayed home, to show their outrage at the anti-Jewish measures of the Occupation, in what became known as the February Strike.

In May 1941, the Zaandam branch of the Union opened the Union House, in the center of Zaandam, on the Muffled Canal (*Gedempte Gracht*). Chairman Van Hall gave a speech:

He expressed his gratitude to members, who made a special effort to furnish the Union House so comfortably. He urged that a major campaign to recruit members start from this house. The number of one thousand members currently reached for Zaandam is still, he said, far too small. (*Source:* Walraven van Hall, May 17 speech to the Union house, reported in *The Zaandammer,* May 18, 1941.)

According to the local newspaper, the storefront was open daily. Meetings could be held in a back room. A department for social affairs was launched. Van Hall welcomed to the Union House the Union founders Einthoven, in June, and De Quay, at the end of August. Both leaders addressed local members.

The area around Zaandam, the *Zaanstreek,* is a diverse[202] region that is more socialist-inclined than the rest of the country. It was therefore ready to oppose the Nazis more than the Union triumvirate liked. In May 1941, therefore, the provincial party magazine published a notice which contained a double message:

The Zaan is a district with stamina and energy, which means its members are active but hard to control. Loyalty to one's former associations is, of course, something of value. Our Union work is not easy, but is no less important. The watchword for the Zaan must be: Persevere! Your hard work will be rewarded." (*Source: Regional Chronicle of North Holland*, provincial magazine, May 1941.)

The leadership was sending two different messages. First, to the public, to support the Zaan Union board. Second, to the Zaan Union boards, to control their unruly supporters.

The board's work did not go smoothly in mid-1941. Secretary Buijs had to inform the regional secretariat that the Green Police[203] occasionally confiscated the print run of the latest *Uniekrants* (the Union newspaper) when its content was deemed too critical of the Occupation. In the weekly report at the beginning of August 1941, Buijs wrote to the leadership: "The police raided the store. They found nothing."[204] At the end of August, he wrote:

> During the night, from Saturday to Sunday, our store door was kicked open, one shop window was destroyed, another was heavily damaged, brochures and distance cards were taken, and the donation box was stolen. (*Source:* Letter from Jaap Buijs, Secretary of the Zaandam branch of the Dutch Union, August 31, 1941.)

There was one consolation, according to a statement in a corner of the letter: "Damage will be compensated by the municipality of Zaandam, according to a telephone communication from Mr. Van Hall."[205]

Seeds of the Resistance

The abuses of power by the Green Police and NSB had a counterproductive effect on Buijs and Van Hall. They did not heed the Union triumvirate's ban on joining the Resistance. The two Zaan friends were in no way accepting of the actions of the Occupation. An example from December 1940 makes this clear. That month, an unsigned chain letter was sent to officials in the Netherlands.

We will probably soon be presented with a statement of approximately the following content: Do you sympathize with the NSB or its principles, or are you neutral towards it, or are you hostile to it? If everyone who is hostile to the NSB openly says so, they will do nothing to us. In The Hague it has been agreed among the officials concerned that they will put their name in the third category (i.e., anti). (*Source:* Anonymous letter, December 1940.)

The letter continued with the request to act against the NSB and pass on the message to fifteen colleagues. On behalf of the Union leadership, Jaap Buijs wrote to the regional secretariat:

I heard today from a civil servant that many want to answer "neutral" when asked how they feel about the NSB. Would it not be good if our magazine commented on this? When these questions are asked, it would be a disaster if most people declared themselves "neutral" out of cowardice. (*Source:* Buijs, letter to the regional secretariat.).

To emphasize his aversion to Anton Mussert's blackshirts, Buijs underlined the last sentence. Secretary Aberson tried to reassure him: "There is no good reason to assume that the NSB will present such a statement to civil servants."[206]

Another example of resistance from Zaandam was Buijs's message to the secretariat that Zaandammers "prefer not to sell raffle tickets for WinterAid,"[207] the Occupation's charity. He explained: "Our buyers should expect no raffle winners." fWalraven also resisted on the personal front. When ordered by local officials to report for a digging project, he got a statement from his doctor that he had serious back problems, which succeeded in getting him an exemption.

Walraven was ostensibly working for the Union. But when his old friend Tonny Eggink, early in that first year of the Occupation, met Walraven, he found him to be "fired up against the Germans, looking for a way to make himself useful."[208] Walraven's Resistance work had started.

It was not hard for Walraven and others to find useful work to do of a resistance nature. The Union leadership regularly sent to Zaandam a tireless propagandist for North Holland, Hemmo Leeuw. At the home of the Van Halls, Leeuw, a former SDAP council member, advised on association activities and explained articles that appeared in the national party magazine, *De Unie*. In addition, however, Leeuw discussed other matters, such as forging identity cards for people wanted by the Nazis.[209] Like Walraven and his brother Gijs, Leeuw moved on from the Union and engaged more deeply in Resistance work through other organizations.

Did the Van Hall brothers consider leaving the Union, given that the Union leadership ordered their members to stay out of the Resistance? That was out of the question. In May 1941 Buijs even took a seat in the Union's regional administration.

In this way, the Union for a while served as a cover for Resistance activities. The Occupation allowed meetings to be held in the Union Houses, provided they did not exceed twenty participants. In the relative privacy of such small local meetings, serious discussions took place about problems created by the German Occupation. Naturally, some of the participants were prepared to oppose the Occupation.

The patriotic action of a Union house employee from Zaandam fit into this picture. Regional secretary Aberson reported to the local Union's three leaders: "In Zaandam the janitor of the store reported that '**1 year of Union is / 1 year of treason**' had been scrawled on the sidewalk in front of the store. The janitor cleaned off only the first half of the message."[210] Walraven van Hall undoubtedly smiled on hearing of this selective cleaning.

The Occupation cracked down in stages on political freedom. First, the German government[211] announced that almost all pre-war political parties were dissolved as of July 5, 1941. The only four exceptions were the three Nazi parties—the NSB, the NSNAP,[212] and the National Front, all instruments of the Occupation——*and* the Dutch Union. The Union was too popular to be abolished so soon. Almost every place in North Holland now had a Union branch, about one hundred branches in total.

The Occupation suppressed journalistic dissent first and then turned its attention to suppressing political dissent.[213] For a little longer, the Occupation

ABOVE AND OPPOSITE: *At the beginning of August 1941, opponents of the Dutch Union destroyed and robbed the party store in Zaandam. "A nice advertisement at the start of the home visit campaign," writes Union Secretary Jaap Buijs cynically to the regional secretariat. (Municipal Archives of Zaanstad/Netherlands Institute for War Documentation)*

accepted the Union's maneuvering at the margin and for a little longer, Union leaders searched for compromises. But the Occupation on July 28, 1941, ended the Union's right to put up posters, distribute newspapers, or display party pins in public.

On December 14, 1941, finally, all Union activities were banned, along with those of the smaller Nazi parties, NSNAP and the National Front. It was a tenth-birthday present to the NSB, Mussert's Dutch Nazi party, which was the only political party left standing.

But the Dutch Union had gotten the Resistance under way. It had created friendships. Buijs and Van Hall were strangers to each other before the founding of the Union. Their work in the Union engaged them more deeply in the fight against the Occupation, to the point of total commitment. Buijs noted after the war:

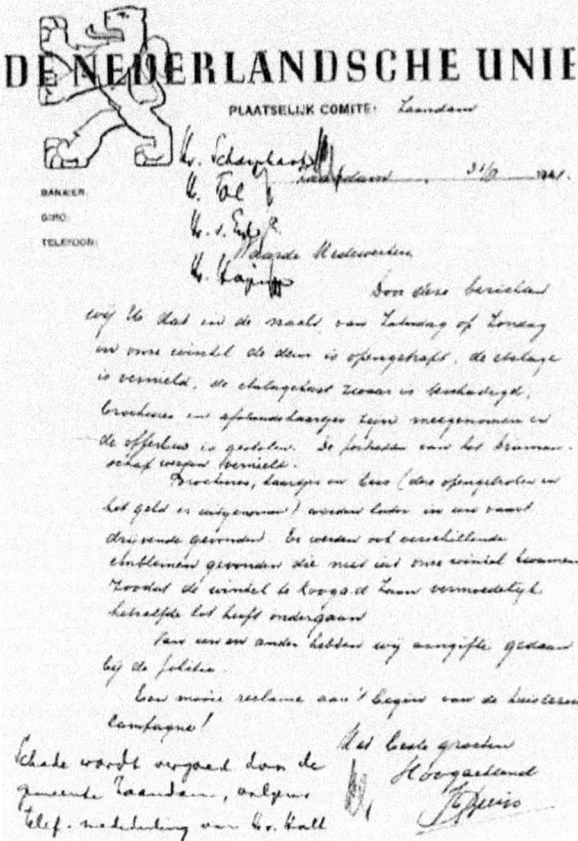

When the Union was banned in 1941, a great hatred arose in us against the Germans, because of their oppression of the Dutch and their cruel measures against our people, especially towards the Jews. When the Union was banned, we discussed what to do next. We decided to join the Resistance and intensify our battle against the enemy. (*Source:* Buijs, Diary.)

The Dutch Union was a precursor of, and catalyst for, a fortified Resistance.

4 | The Seamen's Fund (1941-1943)

"We will find a way"

—WALRAVEN VAN HALL

THIS CHAPTER SHOWS how Walraven got involved in funding the Dutch Resistance. It started with a modest cause that he could not resist—supporting the families of his former colleagues in the merchant marine. The Queen's government in exile asked all sailors to remain abroad and not return to the Netherlands. Walraven took on paying their wives and widows.

Walraven van Hall started his second full-time job as a broker on the Amsterdam stock exchange[214] in early March 1940, two months before the Germans invaded the Netherlands. On the day the invasion began, the exchange locked its doors, not to reopen for the next two months. The doors reopened on July 15 thanks to the hard work of two people—the exchange chairman, Franciscus Joseph Maria van Ogtrop, and Walraven's father, Adriaan Floris van Hall. They were both members of the exchange operating board. Both of them at first felt too old to head up the exchange in the face of the Nazi Occupation. But in August 1940, 69-year-old Van Hall agreed to step up and succeed Van Ogtrop as the exchange's chairman. He viewed his papacy as an interim position, keeping the exchange open and implementing an existing plan to reorganize.

During the two-month closure, Walraven organized meetings with fellow securities-firm employees. These meetings continued after the market reopened. After the war, in August 1945, his initiative led to the creation of the Association of Brokerage Houses.[215] A stock trader wrote of Walraven:

His bringing together like-minded stock brokers came from his desire for more unity among them once the Krauts, as he called the Occupation officials, disappeared. Had Wally's life been spared, he would doubtless have become the presiding judge for us, his friends. (*Source:* Stock trader.)[216]

One of Walraven's concerns was German bias against, and restrictions on, Jewish brokers. Father and son Van Hall saw these measures up close. The February Strike, initiated in particular by Communist workers, had repercussions on the stock exchange. On the morning of first day of the strike, February 25, 1941, the trading floor was noisy and distracted. Dutch Nazi[217] exchange members on their way to work were hissed at by staff and stock-exchange runners. Some employees wanted to shut down the stock market immediately in protest.

That morning, vice-chairman Carel [Charles] Overhoff called a meeting, since chairman Van Hall was absent that day. He told those present that he was appalled by recent measures taken against the Jews. The question they all faced was whether everyone should go to work as if nothing had happened.

My advice was not to do anything more than the existing demonstration. New countermeasures by the Occupation seemed certain. Furthermore, I did not consider additional action to be in the interest of the people[218] targeted by the Occupation. It would not help them. It was therefore unwise. (*Source:* Carel Overhoff.)

Overhoff's appeal won the day and the stock exchange resumed without further interruption.

Walraven Collects Donations for Seamen

Walraven's response to the strike was more empathetic. He collected money for its many victims, his first major activist step toward his eventual role as Banker for the Resistance. After the February Strike, the German Occupation imposed heavy fines on the strike centers, such as Amsterdam, Zaandam, and Hilver-sum.[219] They forced the municipality of Amsterdam to fire the large number of its employees who participated in the strike. By raising funds for them, Walraven sought to alleviate the suffering of those who had expressed solidarity with the Jewish victims—those who had been freed from their civil service jobs and many of whom went into hiding out of fear of what was to come.

Gijs van Hall said later that he was involved in this fundraising[220] early on through his cousin [Frits van Hall], a sculptor who later died in a concentration camp.[221] Frits came to him at the beginning of the war, after the February strike. Many strikers had been shot dead by the police in Amsterdam and others had been fired from their jobs, in either case creating financial problems for their families. Gijs said:

> A group of people, including Frits, raised money for these families. Frits asked me to help. I approached several friends and co-workers, who gave money every month. Initially, the donations were all small. Even so, many people were morbidly fearful of donating to the Resistance. In early 1941, soon after the February Strike, I approached a very important gentleman at the stock exchange and asked him to donate ten guilders. Just ten guilders! Horrified, he said no. He said that if I were to be caught and arrested, he would be as well, because they would find his ten-guilder note on me. I then assured him that I could walk the streets with an extra ten-guilder note in my wallet without arousing any suspicion! This was an extreme example of how terrified people were that a gift would be recorded and traced back to them. (*Source:* Gijs van Hall, Het Nationaal Steun Fonds, 1943-1945, Amsterdam, 1948.)

According to Gijs, the "very important gentleman" was Arnold Jan d'Ailly, director of the Cash Association (*Kas-Vereeniging*), a bank.[222] Later, d'Ailly did join in fundraising for the Resistance and after the war, in 1946, he became Mayor of Amsterdam for the next decade.[223]

Occupation Bars Jews from Stock Exchange

On March 10, Albert Bühler, a Commissioner[224] of the Netherlands Bank,[225] convened the board of the Association of Stockbrokers[226] to convey the message that Jewish members would no longer be permitted to enter the exchange. Carel Overhoff reported on the meeting:

> Bühler informed us that Jewish members could continue their business outside the exchange. Mr. Van Hall,[227] chairman, raised objections, which Bühler dismissed. Finally, we were asked for comments. Bühler said he would be happy to receive them and pass them on. However, he made clear that the Occupation couldn't have different rules from the ones in Germany. Bühler said he, as a human being, deplored these events, but... etc., etc. (*Source:* Carel F. Overhoff, *Oorlogsherinneringen,* "War Memories," Amsterdam, 1949, in Dutch.)

The board searched for a way to convey the new message without overly distressing exchange members, and asked for permission to prepare a memorandum. Bühler allowed this, but said it would be a waste of time and would not affect the order to implement the new rule. Overhoff cautiously argued in his March 17 memorandum that the number of Jewish members in the exchange was so small that excluding them would have little impact.

As Bühler predicted, the Nazis ignored the memorandum. The Occupation ordered the board to enforce the ban against visits by Jewish members starting May 1. That morning, Chairman Van Hall addressed the members of the exchange, none of whom was now Jewish. Although the audience included some Dutch Nazi Party members, he said the board would keep treating their Jewish colleagues as full members, even though they would in future be barred from entering the exchange. Van Hall warned against protesting the German measures. The secretary noted: "Members refrained from comment."

For a short time, Jewish brokers continued to participate in the securities trade via the Koopmans Exchange. However, this access was also ended at the instigation of Dutch Nazi Party members. The ban affected 80 people, 12

Walraven and his father. (Van Hall Foundation)

percent of the total membership. In addition, 58 Jewish staff members immediately lost their jobs.

Later that year, father Van Hall resigned as chairman, citing his age. In November, vice-chairman Overhoff succeeded him as chairman,[228] and the same month, the Germans ordered Jewish members to give up their Association of Stockbrokers (VvdE) memberships. When the stock exchange unveiled a war memorial in May 1949, it bore the names of 85 members and staff who were killed by the Nazis. Of these, at least 72 were Jewish.

Many Dutch ships were under the control of the Dutch government in exile. At the time of the German invasion, more than 90 percent of the merchant fleet was offshore. As early as the summer of 1940, the Occupation tried to force these Dutch ships to return home. But few of the 18,000 people on the ships returned to the Netherlands after the German invasion. The Dutch Shipowners' Association, despite German pressure, refused to appeal to its members to stay out of the war. To prevent sanctions against these shipping companies, the Secretary-General of the Department of Agriculture and Fisheries, Hans Hirschfeld, then sent a telegram, dictated by the Germans, to the Dutch merchant navy. He correctly assumed that every captain would understand the telegram was sent under Nazi duress, and would ignore the order.

Occupation Bars Payments to Seamen Overseas

The Germans therefore took stronger measures. On April 11, 1941, Radio Hilversum aired a message from the Occupation, claiming that the British government was prepared to prohibit Dutch shipping companies from sending money to sailors' relatives if they refused to sail under the British flag.[229] The story was invented by the Germans, but it served as a segue to a shocking follow-up announcement:

> Hitherto, shipping companies have paid the wages of all seamen to family members living here. In future, however, these payments to family members will be discontinued for any Dutch sailor found to be in the service of England or working for any ship found to be sailing in the interests of England. (*Source:* Radio Hilversum. Message from the *Kommissar für die See- und Binnenschiffahrt*, the Occupation's Commissioner for Maritime and Inland Waterways, April 11, 1941.)

The Dutch government in London responded a week later via Radio Orange. Through her minister Steenberghe,[230] Queen Wilhelmina guaranteed all payments that had been or would be made to close relatives of Dutch seamen:

> Insofar as the action by the Occupation may result in a payment less than the family is entitled to, I appeal to compatriots in the occupied territory to support or continue to support those concerned. You can be assured that the amounts you spend on this will be fully repaid in due time. (*Source:* Radio Orange—in Dutch, Radio Oranje—Statement of Minister Steenberghe, April 18, 1941.)[231]

During the summer, the Occupation took no further action. Almost all Dutch seafarers remained loyal to the Queen, but their salaries and pension payments continued. Only in September did the Occupation take action. The shipping companies were told that benefits to families of seafarers must be reduced starting in October.

From then on, a sailor's wife was scheduled to receive a maximum of 90 guilders per month plus 40 guilders for the first child, 25 guilders for the second, and 15 guilders for each subsequent child. This was a big cut for senior officers. In 1939 a second-class engineer earned 240 guilders a month, a sailor 89 guilders, and a boiler boy[232] 22 guilders. Initially, only the families of merchant-navy captains and ship's officers were victims of the new rule, but as of February 1, 1942, benefits were reduced further, for families of both merchant navy employees and naval personnel.

To make up for the loss of income for the affected families, committees formed to collect money in cities like Amsterdam and Dordrecht. In Rotterdam, the effort was led by Abraham Filippo, former captain of the *Statendam*, flagship of the Holland-America Line. The Amsterdam committee soon found Walraven van Hall because, as a former officer of the Royal Hollandsche Lloyd line, he felt it his duty to help the merchant navy members and their families. Together with Jaap Buijs, he raised money to pay the missing benefits for about fifty seamen's households in the Zaan region. In the first phase, they raised 1,500 guilders per month for fifty seamen's households—75,000 guilders per month.

These committees contacted one another in the winter of 1941-1942 and decided to ease the administration of these funds by bundling them under the name Seaman's Fund.[233] This was a major step toward creating in the Netherlands what would eventually become the best-funded resistance group in Europe. Money-collector and stockbroker Johann van Marle[234] explained how the fund became so formidable. At the beginning of 1942, an official of a Rotterdam shipping company with which he did business came to his office and told him:

A committee had been formed in Rotterdam to support seamen's families. A few Rotterdam residents had raised 150,000 guilders for them, and he asked whether people could do the same in Amsterdam. He mentioned a man named Van Meerveld as a local contact who could join them in the afternoon. When he came back, he brought Wally, who took great pleasure at my surprise that he was the Van Meerveld contact. [Walraven van Hall was his cousin by marriage.] The three of us then prepared a plan to coordinate the committees dealing with seamen, to divide up the work and be more effective. (*Source:* Johann van Marle, postwar letter to Walraven's parents, reprinted in Michael C. Van Hall, *Three Centuries,* cited, 2018, 101–102.)[235]

Abraham Filippo got in touch with Walraven van Hall. Filippo later explained to Walraven's brother Gijs: "I was looking for someone to shake up the Amsterdam gentlemen and get them to pay attention to the plight of Dutch sailors' wives and families. I had already tried several times, but I didn't get very far."[236]

The first contributions to the sailors naturally came from the port city of Rotterdam:

> The Rotterdam funds for families in Amsterdam went through Mr. Vos de Mooij. In January 1942, through a friend,[237] I contacted Mr. W. van Hall, bank manager in Zaandam, who immediately agreed to work in Amsterdam and the surrounding area.[238] (*Source:* Abraham Filippo, 1945 report.)

An early Seamen's Fund worker, Andries Teunissen, said: "During the winter of 1941-1942 I was told by Mr. Feenstra, board member of the Dutch Machinists Union,[239] that W. van Hall, Zaandam banker, would work with us, and could generate significant funds though his connections."[240] In his letter to Gijs van Hall, Filippo continued: "In February 1942 I left Dordrecht with Mr. Teunissen for Zaandam, where we introduced ourselves as representatives of the 'Hollandia factories.'"[241] The meeting of the captain and banker was delayed. Teunissen said: "Filippo had a problem with his leg and got stuck in Amsterdam. I was the one to go on to Zaandam and it came together. But it was difficult for me to arrange for Van Hall to join the Seaman's Fund board, given Rotterdam's attitudes."[242] Difficult or not, Van Hall was immediately included on the board of the Seamen's Fund after an introduction to Captain Filippo:

Mr. Van Hall accepted Filippo's invitation to manage payments in Amsterdam and the surrounding area. From then on, he was constantly approaching friends and acquaintances to beg for money for the charity. The Zaan region was administered for him by Buijs. Van Hall realized the dangers of his clandestine work and increasingly used his pseudonym—at first, Van Meerveld,[243] and, later, Van Tuyl. (*Source:* Andries Teunissen.)

Van Heek was at the time also working in the financial world and was annoyed that so few people were supporting the sailors' families. "Others, who may have more resources, may not want to risk supporting them. That is their decision. But I will not now abandon comrades with whom I have sailed."[244]

Van Heek was also impressed by Walraven's directness and ambitious goals. He said: "[Van Hall] knew exactly what he wanted. He instructed me to get for him quickly 50,000 guilders."[245] Van Heek agreed and succeeded.

Another person to be impressed was Amsterdam worker Dirk Vos de Mooij. Almost from the start, Walraven van Hall aimed high, making clear he was beyond looking for nickels and dimes. He needed big money. Amsterdam worker Dirk Vos de Mooij initially thought that Van Hall was grandiose in his thinking. Early in 1942 he traveled with Van Hall by train and tram to Hillegersberg, the home of Abraham Filippo. According to Vos de Mooij, Van Hall told the meeting: "Gentlemen, if we want to do this work well, we will have to see to it that we get a ton[246] (100,000 guilders) together as soon as possible." Vos de Mooij added:

> Shortly after this meeting, Captain Filippo asked me what I thought of Wally. I said I found him very sympathetic and enthusiastic, but had his sights set a bit too high. Filippo agreed. A few years later, we had changed our minds. We both admitted we didn't have any idea of Wally's great ability to raise money. (*Source:* Dirk Vos de Mooij.)[247]

Van Hall was one of the few to work with the Resistance early on, before the Allies had driven back the Germans in some places. Not until late

*Walraven in his time
as helmsman. "I think
about my comrades,
with whom I have sailed
together, now forsaken."
(Van Hall Foundation)*

summer 1942 did the organized Resistance start to grow significantly, eventually encompassing about 45,000 people, less than half of one percent of the population.[248] During the first two years of the Occupation, the Resistance was actively supported by only a few hundred people, including Van Hall, for whom participating in the Seamen's Fund was a given.

Another early entry into the Resistance was Iman Jacob ("Co") van den Bosch, a Philips employee in Eindhoven. In 1940 he led the Tromp-annex Birthday Fund.[249] Since few seafaring families lived in Eindhoven, from October 1941 the Birthday Fund distributed a large portion of its income in the Amsterdam region. Management of the Birthday Fund in this area rested with Jacobus Lootsma (after his pseudonym, the representatives there were called the Bakker Group). At the end of 1941 and in early 1942, the schoolmaster started with 27 townspeople, mainly teachers, providing money to Amsterdam seamen's families. Amsterdam therefore had two support funds for families of seafarers, although they did not know about each other. In the autumn of 1942, Van Hall and Lootsma connected:

In September 1942 my closest colleague told me: "Now we know who is behind that other group—Wally van Hall." A meeting at my house followed, and we divided up our work. From 1943 on, Amsterdam was left to Van Hall. My organization took care of the disbursements to smaller places in the area. Brandsma,[250] with whom Van Hall put me in touch, took on support of the officers. Van Hall provided all the money. We exchanged names and addresses of our clients, and divided them up flexibly. Money for new families, however, was distributed according to agreed guidelines. (*Source:* Jacobus Lootsma.)

The Seamen's Fund Is Founded

The new organization started on January 1, 1943. Soon afterward, the organizers decided to offer the sailors' wives food as well as money. "Van Hall was also behind this, assisted by Lieutenant Bottema (alias Van Buren), a naval officer from Den Helder," said Lootsma.[251]

Van Hall was working with both Filippo's and Van den Bosch's groups, when a new coalition was added. At the end of 1942, three young men figured out that their Resistance work should be coordinated with others—Deni Mesritz, who was *Praes* [President][252] of the Nijmegen Student Corps, and two representatives of the student resistance group Council of Nine, namely Jos van Hövell tot Westerflier and Han Gelder. Looking for more experienced organizers, they approached Arie van Velsen, whom they know had Resistance contacts. He arranged a few meetings of like-minded people. Van Velsen describes one such meeting:

On a sunny, cold winter morning, at the end of January 1943, a group of people[253] came together from different parts of the country and different parts of our Dutch society. We were brought together on the Leidsegracht with identification—such as a coin with a special cross or a word with a special meaning—and we represented people based on the principle that our minds should be focused on one thing, fighting the Germans. There, in the quiet, spacious back room of the home of Wally's mother-in-law,[254] we laid the solid foundation for a collaboration that continued and deepened and broadened over the years. (*Source:* Arie van Velsen, postwar letter to Tilly van Hall.)

In an earlier letter to Wally's wife Tilly, Van Velsen wrote: "We were there together in that room because Professor Heringa had heard through Nieuwenhuijsen and through the Medical Contact that we were working along the same lines as Van Hall."[255]

This was the beginning of the National Committee of Resistance (NC), an organization that initially had the ambitious goal of guiding the multitude of Resistance groups in the country, but eventually became another Resistance organization.[256] It was one with which Walraven and his colleagues worked well through the end of the war. NC inspiration Van Velsen said:

> With his fierce eyes and his barely controlled urge to get us to work as a team, Van Hall sat in the middle of that circle, listening. He called himself 'just a listener.' Wally always helped us past points of detail, to keep us focused on the big picture. He didn't make things easy. He was not satisfied with loose commitments and he always briefly explained the consequences of agreements and the need to translate one into this or that action. (Source: Arie van Velsen.)[257]

The thinker and the doer were united in the Zaan banker and these qualities emerged under the pressure of the extraordinary conditions of the Occupation.

Sometime in 1941, the political cartoonist and Social Democratic activist Jan Rot met Walraven under the auspices of the by-now-illegal Social Democratic Workers' Party, the SDAP.[258] Rot was born and raised in Zaandam, but had lived in Amsterdam since the 1920s. He regularly returned to the Zaan region[259] to attend meetings of his party. Rot said that his friend Jaap Buijs introduced him to Van Tuyl,[260] who, he said, had come along as an "interested person:"

Van Tuyl made a big contribution to the discussion. I did not entirely agree with him—Van Tuyl had definite political expectations, which were not in line with my own. And yet I did not argue with him. I have asked myself: "Why not?" I did not argue, because Van Tuyl had something special about him. He spoke with animation about how things would be immediately after the war, when the old political parties, particularly the Social-Democrat SDAP, would not be resurrected. Nothing of value would have come from debate then about the postwar path. But the ease with which he spoke about it—his manner, his words, his examples (he emphasized the work of the Quakers)—had for me the charm of a fresh perspective. (*Source:* Jan Rot.)[261]

Debate about the postwar path fascinated Van Hall. He often talked about the subject. Through Jaap Buijs he met Johannes Scheps, a former Social-Democrat SDAP council member who produced numerous illegal brochures, including one about the political future of the Netherlands after the war. Because the Germans were looking for him, Scheps kept moving around the Netherlands. He was a salesman. In Buijs's house he wrote a booklet advocating a fairer postwar judicial process, with anti-Nazi arguments. Van Hall gave him several opportunities to address Zaan manufacturers, bankers, and businessmen in his home, and thereby facilitated his winning recruits in the area. He also provided shelter to Scheps on September 9-10, 1943, when the Nazi SS's police, the *SiPo*,[262] were hot on the heels of this tireless anti-fascist propagandist. Two years after the war, in a warm commemorative article about Walraven, Scheps said:

Our thoughts drifted to Zaandam, to the house with the terribly squeaking gate.[263] It was in this house that we held several clandestine lectures, and in which, in the middle of the war, we gave an introduction to a subject of a religious nature. (Source: Johannes Hermanus Scheps, *Scheps Inventariseert,* "Scheps Inventories," Apeldoorn, 1973. Article on Walraven van Hall, in Dutch.)[264]

Van Hall was surrounded by countless Social Democrats—Scheps, Buijs, Rot, Leeuw, the future Labor Party[265] minister Neher, the postwar Labor Party alderman Prakken, and his brother Gijs. Many were members of the SDAP before the war and, like Gijs, were absorbed into the Labor Party after 1946. The Social Democrats, especially the moderates among them, were more to Walraven's taste than any other prewar party. Yet he never gave up the idea of a different kind of political organization—one that would unify the Netherlands after the war. His reasoning was that resurrecting the old parties was impossible because they made too many mistakes during the interwar period.

These Social Democrats brought in a large group of prominent politicians. A number of them—including the future prime minister Wim Schermerhorn, Marinus van der Goes van Naters and Jan de Quay—agreed on the formation of a broad postwar, progressive party, founded on principles of both Christianity and humanism. This "breakthrough" (Dutch: *Doorbraak*) idea resulted in the founding of the short-lived Dutch People's Movement (NVB) a week after the liberation.[266]

Walraven's ideas for a new political party became part of planning within the Resistance for after the war, according to Resistance leader Heinrich Douqué:

> We had been in touch with Van Tuyl and Knecht.[267] We were in a separate office in our former ration-card depot.[268] I had many conversations with Van Tuyl and at one point he told me about the start of the Dutch People's Movement. I got the original idea from him. He told me he was a member." (*Source:* Heinrich Douqué.)[269]

Walraven carried out his Resistance activities in addition to his regular work for the Zaandam investment banking firm Weduwe J. in Veltrup. He often combined both activities in the Amsterdam stock exchange, where he had to be almost daily. Walraven would briefly leave his workplace to perform a financial transaction that was outlawed by the Occupation. "I spoke to him several times on the Beursplein," recalled an employee of the Seaman's Fund. "He gave me money, usually 2,000 guilders."[270] The employee then distributed the banknotes to merchant and navy women outside Amsterdam.

After the war, it appeared that nearly 4,700 Dutch merchant-sailor families

*Walraven and
Gijs van Hall.
(Van Hall Foundation)*

had received money from the Seaman's Fund, plus 1,400 naval households and 300 army families. A few candidates got nothing. "We did not support NSB [Nazi Party] women, and those who had contact with the German overlords. Neither did we support those who led morally bad lives,"[271] said fund administrator Filippo. In 1941, the victims of the Nazi sanctions needed 10,000 guilders, paid out on a regular schedule.

Gijs remembered: "The first list of required funds totaled 18,000 guilders in aid, and Wally and I wondered how this needed amount—which was increasing very quickly—could be raised each month just from donations."[272] By 1944 that amount had grown to 2.9 million guilders. In total, the Seaman's Fund paid out more than 5.2 million guilders [about $50 million 2024 dollars][273] during more than three years of life.

It was a challenge to assemble such sums of money on a recurring and growing basis, under the eyes of the occupying forces, in extremely uncertain times. Van Hall, Filippo, Van den Bosch, and their employees at first depended primarily on donations from "good" Dutch people. The British government was reported to have made assurances that donations would be repaid after the war, which allowed the Seaman's Fund to negotiate large donations.[274] The amounts were often handed over in cash and in confidence—only the giver and receiver knew about the transaction. Walraven asked his brother Gijs to act as central cashier for Amsterdam and to keep lists of supported households with the corresponding IOUs for postwar repayment of the donations.

Fund Asks for Loans Against Queen's Guarantee

This "gifts" system functioned for months, but the funds raised could not keep up with demand for aid. Relying on small gifts meant that many people were approached, which increased the risks. Walraven realized that a formal loan approach was needed to attract larger amounts. He founded the Disconto Institute for Seamen[275] to separate the source of loans from payments to the families from the Seaman's Fund. To ensure that loans would be repaid after the war, lists were needed of lenders and amounts loaned. However, prospective lenders were properly worried about the risk of being on such a list, which might be discovered by the Germans.

Van Hall's brilliant solution to this problem was to give lenders, in exchange for their money, an arbitrarily selected worthless security from Tsarist Russia, or an old mark note, or a silver coupon, or a share of a long-defunct company—the main thing being that the document had some unique identifying number on it.[276] That number was put on a list, followed by the amount loaned, in a code. For example, a line might read: "Java Petroleum Society no. 492 100x," meaning that the owner of the certificate was entitled to 100,000 guilders after the war (the number before the x was to be multiplied by one thousand).

The loan list was kept by Gijs separate from records of the receipt or disbursement of the money. He wasn't prominently in the chain of collecting or distributing the money. Someone who found the list would have no idea who the lenders were. "However clever the German sniffer-dogs, they would have to be superhuman to find out who owned these certificates—a 4 ½ percent bond from Wladikawkas 1896 no. 91615 or a silver certificate of ƒ1 series

AX no. 65782," wrote Gijs van Hall.[277] At his office on the Vijgendam, Gijs administered the loans via the Disconto Institute, under the innocent name Wordeloze Securities:

> I kept the cash, registered the loans, received the receipts, and administered them. My only contact with the Seamen's Fund was Wally[278] and his loyal assistant, code-named Van den Brink (after the war, Lieutenant Weeda). (*Source:* Gijs van Hall, postwar report.)

Walraven set the minimum loan amount at 1,000 guilders to limit risks and administration.[279] Some money-collectors believed Walraven was over-optimistic and doubted enough people would want to lend as much as 1,000 guilders in such a risky way. Walraven's faith was soon justified. With their country a vassal state of Germany, wealthy Dutch people were prepared to take big gambles on loans to their fellow citizens. Many people made them.

The receipt system worked well for lenders. However, Resistance workers were concerned about the system, because they were trained not to write anything down, so as not to provide evidence to Nazi investigators in the event of arrests. Now, suddenly, the Seamen's Fund popped up, *requiring* them to write down illegal payments on paper. Iman van den Bosch was one person who balked. As Jacobus Lootsma reported:

> There was some friction. The Eindhoven group never asked for receipts, although they said to the wives: "Remember that it is an advance, to be settled later when your husband returns." But how did they plan to settle later if there was no record? Van Hall therefore insisted on receipts. (*Source:* Jacobus Lootsma.)

Arie Voorwinde from Eindhoven, who initially worked mainly with Van den Bosch, said:

> The only issue I remember on which Van Hall and Van den Bosch were sharply opposed was receipts. We strongly objected to receipts and

Iman J. van den Bosch.
(Van Hall Foundation)

told stories about some negative experiences. Where were we supposed to store those thousands of pieces of paper, anyway? Van Hall was not afraid of that question. 'We will find a way,' he said. Indeed, no receipts from the National Support Fund[280] were ever found in Nazi searches. That's amazing enough. There were hundreds of thousands of them on the sixth floor at Vijgendam. When I came to collect money there, things went amazingly smoothly. When the safe was opened, you saw a box with chocolate bars at the top. Beneath them lay rows of bundles of thousand-guilder notes! (*Source:* Arie Voorwinde from Eindhoven.)

It took some time for Van den Bosch and Voorwinde, and in their wake Filippo, to become familiar with the receipt system. They came to realize how important the system was, as other forms of contributions began to diminish, while demand for help was growing. As they were losing track of the money, they noticed the success that Van Hall was having. In 1942 they collected more than 500,000 guilders. After a few months, the leaders in Eindhoven and Rotterdam also switched to registering loans via expired shares and other numbered securities.

The Disconto Institute developed into an underground bank, the "Bank of the Resistance." The administrator, Gijs van Hall, in March 1943 even made a loan to himself, but Walraven consistently ensured a strict demarcation between what happened within the Disconto Institute and the activities outside it. Gijs van Hall said:

> Only Wally was fully aware of both the sources and uses of funds. Repeatedly people wanted to know from Wally what the Disconto Institute actually was. Captain Filippo easily resigned himself to Wally not wanting to share this for security reasons. But Van den Bosch and Gelderblom were determined to find out who and what this Disconto Institute was. Gelderblom in particular gave an ultimatum [presumably, threatening to quit] if they were not also informed, but Wally never told them." (*Source:* Gijs van Hall, postwar report.)

Resistance member Douwe Westra, who worked closely with Filippo in Rotterdam, also showed his curiosity, in vain. Gijs said: "Wally always kept it a secret. When Westra came to visit him, when Wally was staying with me in Blaricum, he said to Westra: 'Remember, my brother knows nothing.'"[281]

Walraven Helps Zaandam Jews

Walraven became more involved in nationwide Resistance activities through the Seaman's Fund, but he did not stop offering help to his neighbors. For example, a Jewish couple, Samuel and Margot Lewkowicz, lived near him in Zaandam. In the year Hitler assumed power in Germany, they had left the Ruhr area for the Netherlands[282] with their then three-year-old daughter Regina. They settled in Zaandam on September 25, 1933. They managed to earn a decent living through hard work, running a clothing workshop, the Arepa travel agency (at Westside 54a), and an import and export trade (at number 77). Soon after the invasion, the family had to deal with the rabid anti-Semitism of the Occupation. In November 1940 their travel agency was closed—little money was to be earned from the travel industry, in a Nazified Europe, and certainly not by Jews. Later, the other two companies were also closed.

On January 14, 1942, the Jewish Council ordered all Jews in Zaandam to move to Amsterdam within three days, the third being the Sabbath. However, it required refugees from Germany, Czechoslovakia, and Austria to report to the "Westerbork Foreigners Camp." Jews in Zaandam were the first in the Netherlands forced to move by a Jewish Exclusion (*Judenrein)* declaration.[283] The announcement said:

> You must lock your house and hand over the keys to the police. You can bring everything you or your family members can carry on Saturday. It is essential that you bring some linen and bedding. The costs of your provisional accommodation are for your own account. You must fire any Aryan personnel you employ. (*Source:* Circular.)

The Lewkowicz family knew the Van Halls, a few houses away. Decades later, Regina Lewkowicz remembered the events of those three days of panic, before leaving for Westerbork:

> We were unable to accommodate any furniture. My father had an acquaintance with whom he worked, who came to take some things from us, and I brought some toys to the Van Hall family. I visited with them and played with the children. They had a very big house with huge rooms, children's rooms, nannies, a special canning kitchen, a gazebo in the back of the garden, a tea house, a children's house, and a doll's house big enough to play in. (*Source:* Regina Lewkowicz, *The Typhoon.*)

Walraven became aware of the German persecution of the Jews at an early age. He knew that between 1933 and 1940 tens of thousands of German Jews tried to cross the border into the Netherlands. As early as 1933, his cousins Jan and Mies van Lennep Boissevain housed German-Jewish refugee children in the Netherlands. In June 1933, for example, they took in a boy who played the violin beautifully in their home. His name was Theo Olof.[284] Jan Boissevain, who then often resided in Germany and Austria for his work, helped a Jewish woman to flee Austria after the *Anschluss*. In the Netherlands he arranged a marriage of convenience for her, which presumably saved her life.[285]

Until just before the occupation of the Netherlands, Walraven's sister-in-law Emma, Gijs's wife, and Mies Boissevain were involved in rescuing young German and Austrian Jews. Shortly before the German invasion, they traveled by train to Cologne and returned with a number of children, who were then taken to Great Britain. The Germans allowed young refugees to "emigrate," provided their parents stayed behind. A soldier asked Emma during the rescue journey through Germany: "*Was machen Sie hier? Sind Sie keine Jüdin?*" ("What are you doing here? Are you not a Jew?")[286] These confrontations with Nazism and militarism and the harsh separation of Jewish parents and their children thus made the Van Halls aware of the mentality of their eastern neighbors at an early stage.

Walraven and Tilly had heard of Nazi anti-Semitism, but this did not mean that they knew in detail the fate that awaited the Dutch Jews. At the end of 1941, some reports appeared in the underground press about "pogroms» and "camps" where "young Jewish men die like rats," but no details were provided. Even in January 1942, a disastrous month for the Jews of Zaandam, little was known about Hitler's plan, formally introduced that month[287] and rendered in English as the "Final Solution.[288] Not until mid-July 1942 did the first underground newspaper write clearly about the concentration camps:

> More than a hundred thousand Dutch people will soon be taken away like cattle to be locked up in camps in a devastated environment, where a dignified existence is no longer possible and where they are exposed to the cruel moods of their criminal tormentors. (*Source: Het Parool*, July 14, 1942.)

This was six months after the Lewkowicz family was ordered to move and the day before the first Jews were deported from Westerbork to Auschwitz. A month later, resistance member Gerrit Jan van der Veen, a friend of the Van Hall family,[289] reported on the "mass murder, planned with appalling cold-bloodedness," of the Jewish deportees.

Walraven and Tilly would have been increasingly aware of reports of genocide plans, initially limited to short articles. They discussed with their Jewish
neighbors the risks of reporting to Westerbork and the possibility of escaping
deportation. They shared their knowledge to try to convince the Lewkowicz
family of the dangers that likely awaited them. Regina said:

> Mrs. Van Hall came to my mother's house one evening and made
> an offer: "We can take you and your husband to Switzerland and your
> daughter can live with us. And no one will find her." We declined the
> offer. First, my father believed the war would be over in two or three
> months. He was not fully aware of what was going on in Germany.
> And, for my part, I didn't want to be separated from my parents.
> (*Source:* Regina Lewkowicz.)

The Lewkowicz family was taken away from their home on January 17 by
a Dutch police officer from Zaandam. He tried to help them. Regina reported:

> When we came down with our stuff he said: "I have to seal your
> door so that no one breaks in. Since I will be looking after the door,
> I won't be able to see which way you go. You can go straight, turn
> left, or turn right, as you wish. We didn't understand what he meant.
> (*Source:* Regina Lewkowicz, *The Typhoon.*)[290]

The family traveled by train and reported to Camp Westerbork,[291] which
they did not know had become the gateway to the German extermination
machine.[292] In January 1944, the family was deported from Westerbork to concentration camps to the east. With a lot of luck, both parents and daughter
survived. Mother Margot and daughter survived Theresienstadt and Auschwitz, Freiberg,[293] and finally Mauthausen, where the US army freed them. In
the spring of 1945, the Russians rescued father Samuel from the Sachsen-
hausen camp. After the war, the whole family was reunited, lived in Zaandam
for a while, then moved to Amsterdam and rebuilt their clothing-workshop
business. They were lucky indeed.

Regina Lewkowicz
(The Typhoon)

Another Jewish family in Zaandam did accept Walraven's offer to place them at a safe address and they too were lucky. Isaac and Sophia Snoek ran a fabric store. One summer day in 1940, their storefront was plastered by the local NSB (Nazis) with a poster reading: "Dutch people, do not buy from Jews." Isaac reported it to the local police. A year and a half later, the same local police forced the Snoek family to leave their home for the Amsterdam ghetto. From there, they were ordered to camp Westerbork. Miraculously, the family was temporarily released, and they took this opportunity to accept Walraven van Hall's help. He placed them with Gijbertus Prast, a colleague and director of the Twentsche Bank. For 2.5 years, Gijbertus and his wife Maria hid the four lodgers from the Nazis.

Van Hall's assistance did not always end so well. In a postwar note, Tilly van Hall talked about "a little Jewish boy Aad played with. The child was betrayed. The mother had to choose: 'Hand over your child, or we will send your husband to Vught.' The child was gassed."[294] Monstrous. Tilly also referred to a contemporary of her son, Arno Salomons from Winschoten. The boy was placed with Zaandijk resistance acquaintances of the Van Halls, Hendrik and Geert Boekenoogen. Playmate Aad only knew the boy by his pseudonym, René. "In March 1944, the child was betrayed and taken with his foster mother to the Amsterdam police headquarters. Two weeks later, the Nazis transported him to Auschwitz. Immediately upon arrival, he was murdered."[295]

Nazis Invalidate Large Guilder Notes

On March 13, 1943, the Germans declared banknotes of 500 and 1000 guilders invalid. They hoped this would be a triple threat to black marketeers, people in hiding, and the Resistance. The Occupation gave the owners of high-denomination notes until March 31 to turn them in to the tax authorities. They were enjoined from paying out the equivalent in smaller banknotes unless they were sure that the money was obtained lawfully.

The measure caught the Disconto Institute for Seamen completely by surprise. Walraven called his brother Gijs, who reported that he had 212,000 guilders in the safe of his office, of which all but 12,000 guilders was in 1000-guilder banknotes. The next day, they met and decided to divide up the notes. Each would walk out with one hundred 1000-guilder notes in their pocket, looking for banks or private individuals willing to break them. It was not an easy task. The lenders had to be not only be friendly to the Seamen's Fund, but also able to justify the extra 1000-guilder notes to the tax authorities.

When the Van Halls met again on Monday, they had succeeded in converting their two "tons"[296] of banknotes into smaller denominations, and in addition they had collected promises from some institutions to exchange more, up to 93,000 guilders. However, the Discount Institute had no more large-denomination notes to exchange. Walraven remembered a bank that could not give him small denominations, but had a large stack of 1000-guilder notes that belonged to a now-banned trade union. He went to this bank again, asking if he could borrow the notes for the benefit of the Seamen's Fund, in exchange for the promise that the money would be paid back after the war (there was no need for it sooner anyway!). The bank agreed. The newly acquired thousands were then exchanged elsewhere for smaller money.[297]

This success led to further ideas. The two bankers and Captain Filippo visited their circle of acquaintances, now asking them whether they would exchange 1000-guilder notes from their own safes, or from money they managed for others, for receipts in the form of outdated securities. This paper money was then exchanged by those who could easily dispose of extra thousands at the tax authorities. Every evening, Gijs and Walraven went over their inventory of 1000-guilder notes, asking: "Were there too many or too few?" Money was collected and exchanged at a rapid pace. The Van Halls had a few tons of unusable banknotes on hand in mid-March, but within two weeks, by the deadline, they managed to convert it all to 785,000 disposable guilders.

This regulation of March 13 was a godsend for the Seamen's Fund and correspondingly a disappointment to the Germans.

To minimize risk, the initiators took the further step of informing several reliable chief tax inspectors in Amsterdam and Rotterdam. These inspectors ensured that the recipients of the Seamen's Fund notes did not encounter any problems with the banknotes. "These gentlemen later also gave their full cooperation to the National Support Fund and donated money to us on several occasions,"[298] Gijs van Hall wrote after the war. The officials in question exchanged the thousand-guilder notes without asking questions and gave the Van Halls and Filippo tips on who to turn to with their money. But a tax inspector like J. van Tilburg, for example, went further and asked Rotterdam business people to pass on their 1000-guilder notes to the Seamen's Fund, thus generating another 750,000 guilders. Over the years, the tax authorities acquired nearly 5.4 million guilders for the National Support Fund.

The relative ease with which large denominations were obtained and exchanged was related to the Allied advance. While Hitler's *Wehrmacht* made steady territorial gains until autumn of 1942, the turnaround came in November. General Montgomery pushed back Field Marshal Rommel in North Africa. In the east, the Russians launched an offensive against Commander Paulus's troops near Stalingrad. These were the first dents in the German machine. In the occupied territories they led to hope and (sometimes) to more resistance. This made it easier for the nascent Dutch Resistance to overcome its obstacles and involve neutral institutions, including banks, in clandestine activities.

The Landlubbers Fund Created

By the deadline of March 31, 1943, the Van Halls had just under twelve tons (1.2 million guilders) more cash than two weeks before. Over the entire year of 1942, the Seamen's Fund spent more than 500,000 guilders on merchant and navy families. The receipt system worked well. Gijs and Walraven were now confident they could raise much more money in 1943, so they decided to expand their financial assistance:

> Since more money was needed in other areas of the Resistance, we regretted not using the full amounts pledged for the seamen. If we gave one million in aid to the seamen's wives and received two hundred thousand in donations, we only had to borrow eight hundred thousand and still got one million back after the war. So the remaining two hundred thousand could be used for other purposes." (*Source:* Gijs van Hall, statement to the parliamentary committee of inquiry investigating the war, 1950.)

The rapid succession of anti-Semitic measures resulted in more Jews going into hiding, often with little access to money for their upkeep. Also, some of the thousands of former career and reserve officers decided to take the same step. In May 1942 they were required to report to the Occupation for assignment to work, army, or prison.

Next, in February 1943, the *Reichskommissar* decreed that all men aged 18 to 35 should be available for work. Most of them decided not to report, and instead went into hiding. The result was they could no longer work, and they lost their income.[299] First the sailors, now the landlubbers, needed help. The Van Halls took the plunge. They believed that from then on that people in hiding because of any Nazi law, and any illegal organizations, should be able to rely on the money they collected.

There was another reason to jump in. Walraven met with a Social Affairs Department official. This department managed the Special Needs Fund. Money was collected from this for people who did not fall under the regular assistance programs. From the start of the Occupation, the fund had been used for this, initially out of sight of the occupiers. It was a source of financing for the families of political prisoners. This went well until the spring of 1943, when the Germans discovered the fund, took away the money, and added it to the Nazi-run Winter Relief Foundation. This meant that an important subsidy for war victims disappeared. This development meant that quick action was needed. "In the early summer of 1943, the first loan for the Landlubbers' Fund[300] was subscribed," said a post-war report of NSF activities.[301] This date is also remembered by Ties Kruize, who had a key function in the Gooi area.[302] In June 1943, Gijs and Walraven visited him:

> I knew Gijs from working with him in the Dutch Union. I had already done some work for the Seamen's Fund, but there wasn't much to pay out in the Gooi. Then the Van Hall brothers told me that something was being done for all kinds of people in hiding. They were expanding the Seamen's Fund by adding a Landlubber Fund. I was asked if I wanted to set up a money-distribution system for the Gooi. I agreed. In the beginning I only dealt with Wally van Hall, who got money to me. Later Wally referred me to the office of Dudok de Wit (Bergsma's pseudonym), who was located on the Vijgendam in Amsterdam, on the fourth floor of the Industrial Club building. Bergsma[303] raised for the Landlubber Fund as much money as I paid over to him from the Fund. (*Source:* Ties Kruize, agent for The Gooi.)

Expanding the role of the Seamen's Fund did not go without a hitch. Abraham Filippo was opposed, because he thought the risks were too great. One of Filippo 's co-workers wrote: "We were exclusively committed to supporting sailors' families and what was related to it, the social work. Perhaps our only political aspect was that we paid no benefits to anyone involved with the Occupation."[304]

The crux of the problem was that whereas supporting the families of seafarers only mildly annoyed the Occupation, supporting the Resistance and people in hiding was a different matter entirely. Filippo wanted to defy the Germans as little as possible, so as not to endanger his supporters. So the Seamen's Fund and the Landlubbers Fund, as Walraven initially called it, were kept separate.

Other Family Members in the Resistance

Besides Gijs and Walraven, other family members were active in the Resistance, on both their father's side, the Van Halls and on their mother's side, the Boissevains. Cousin Hilda van Hall, for example, supported creative minds who did not register with the Chamber for the Arts.[305] Without an Aryan statement,[306] an artist could not become a member of the Chamber, which was created by the Germans to silence Jewish and other critical artists. Without this membership it was difficult to earn a living as an artist. Hilda van Hall, who lived in Hattem, organized clandestine art exhibitions at the homes of private individuals and at the few art dealers that did not, on principle, join the Chamber for the Arts. She was a spider in the web of the national black art[307] circuit.

Also active in the underground cultural world were brother and sister Frits and Suzie van Hall, cousins of Gijs and Walraven. Frits was a sculptor. Suzie was a co-initiator of the Artists' Resistance. Suzie assisted another sculptor, the well-known Resistance fighter Gerrit Jan van der Veen. He was the founder of a center for the manufacture of falsified Personal Identification (*Persoons-Bewijs, PB*).[308] Suzie and Gerrit had occasional contact with Walraven and the NSF in that capacity.

On the Boissevain side, the headquarters of the Resistance group CS-6 was located in Amsterdam's Corellistraat starting in 1942. The residents of this well-situated house were Walraven's cousins Jan[309] and Mies van Lennep Boissevain and their sons Jan Karel and Gideon.[310] They belonged to a group of mostly young, energetic fighters against the Nazis. Furious at the deportation of Jews, CS-6 destroyed railroad tracks, derailing transport trains heading east. The organization also set fire to a cinema on Rembrandtplein, a showroom for Nazi propaganda films. From the beginning of 1943, the group attacked Nazi collaborators. Their most prominent victim was General H. A. Seyffardt, commander of the Netherlands Volunteer Legion; he recruited Dutchmen to volunteer for the German Army. Other supporters of the German regime were killed by CS-6 liquidations.

Mies's sister Hester van Lennep also worked for the Resistance, rescuing Jewish children. With her friend Pauline van Waasdijk, she created escape routes for Jewish children waiting for deportation, in the Hollandsche Schouwburg Theater, which was used as a deportation center. Via the Hervormde Kweekschool [Reformed Trade School], opposite the theatre, they provided an escape route from the Jewish crèche. They managed to save more than eighty children.[311]

These are a few of dozens of relatives, some by marriage, who stood up to the Nazis. Many more could be added, mostly Boissevains. Most emerged from the war physically unscathed, but not necessarily psychologically. But many lost their lives as combatants in the Allied army, or as captured Resistance workers. Some were just in the Dutch East Indies at the wrong time, and were imprisoned in brutal Japanese camps. Within the Boissevain family alone, twelve to sixteen people died from the war or for their work in the Resistance.

Maurits van Hall, a cousin of Gijs and Walraven and brother of sculptor Frits, was detained in a Japanese POW camp and died on April 6, 1943 during the construction of the Burma railway line. Maurits was one of the first in a series of related Nazi victims. Several Van Halls and Boissevains died in the next two years, mostly after betrayal within their Resistance organizations. It did not stop those who survived from continuing their Resistance work.

The Occupation billeted two German officers, a Prussian and a Bavarian, on the Van Halls. Daughter Attie liked the Bavarian, but her mother forbade her to accept any candy from him. The Germans each got a room in the attic. The Van Hall family had to proceed even more carefully than before. Radio Orange could only be turned on very softly. In January 1943, the channel announced that a royal descendant had been born.[312] Attie van Hall said:

> It would have been nice if we children could hear that too. But how could that be done without arousing suspicion among the officers? Father and mother called in their maid, Iet Aproninghuis. Early

the next morning our front bell rang. Iet opened the door, there was a buzz and the door closed again, while Iet very loudly said "Thank you!" Then she ran up the stairs and shouted loudly: "Sir, madam, I just heard that a little princess was born in Canada. Her name is Margriet." (*Source:* Attie van Hall.)

After some time, the two Germans moved elsewhere, to the relief of their host family.

Help to Zaandam Resistance

Walraven van Hall was always ready in an emergency to lend a hand to the Zaan area Resistance groups. For example, local printer-publisher Gerrit Huig needed help when SS agents accused him of involvement in an attack on the Regional Employment Office in Zaandam. The office was the site of population records, which were used to conscript workers for German factories, to verify identification papers, and to identify Jews and others in hiding. During the night of May 20-21, 1943, former Employment Office employee Frans van Os and security- guard Douwe Soepboer entered the building with eighty kilos of highly flammable ashwood kindling. They made a fire-starter out of paper and turned on the gas tap. At 3:00 am they lit the fuse of the explosive and at 3:05 am the building was ablaze. The entire archive was destroyed.

Across the Zaan river, from a tree-house in their garden, the Van Hall family and their guest Iet Schortinghuis watched the Regional Employment Office explode and burn down. Aad van Hall said later:

> We were woken up at night. "Come and see, there are fireworks," my parents said. My father, of course, knew it would happen and wanted to see it, but he didn't want to leave us alone in the house." (*Source:* Aad van Hall, memoir.)[313]

Schortinghuis, whose fiancé Henk was at risk of being arrested to work for the Nazis in Germany, rejoiced at the sight of documents swirling in the flames: "Look, there go Henk's papers!" From that night on, it became much harder for the Nazis to identify young men from the Zaan area and Waterland to send to Germany.

The Huigs were on lookout duty during the arson attack. Afterwards, something went wrong. Gerrit Huig said:

> We were endangered by one of the co-perpetrators. On Mr. Soep-boer's recommendation, I contacted Walraven. It was a very delicate matter and he was the ideal person to straighten everything out—which he promptly did, with the cooperation of Mr. Buijs." (*Source:* Gerrit Huig, postwar memoir.)[314]

Huig did not say what danger loomed and how Van Hall neutralized it. But after that, the two men became good friends. "From that day on I was increasingly in touch—supplying him with newsprint, printing things, and so on. He introduced me to his cousin Suzie van Hall and to Gerrit Jan van der Veen." The Huig printing house became an important source of illegal newspapers and forged identity cards. Van der Veen's national Identity Cards Center was the country's largest producer of fake identification and other documents for the Resistance. In October 1943, another Resistance action was betrayed and Huig and his printing house employees were arrested. The staff was soon released, but Gerrit Huig was sent to a detention house.[315] Fortunately, he survived the war.

Douwe Soepboer also assisted Van Hall after the arson action. As chief of the security service at Zaandam Artillery Devices,[316] he was able to obtain weapons and explosives for Van Hall. He wrote: "Walraven asked me for trotyl[317] with fuse and percussion caps. I said I could get them and later I handed over to him several times a quantity of these goods, intended for sabotage."[318] Soepboer did not remember when he first met Van Hall. It was with Zaandam PTT[319] official Jan Westerbroek, who had known Van Hall and Jaap Buijs since the end of 1941. He had provided housing for people in hiding in the Zaan region. At Westerbroek's request, Soepboer transported explosives in 1943 or early 1944 to Van Hall, who saw to it that they got to an unnamed engineer of the Dutch Railways and Gerrit Jan van der Veen.

Walraven had developed, in just a year, from a small-sum fundraiser for a seaman's charity to someone responsible for enforcing the rules for raising and spending hundreds of thousands of guilders in a week.[320] His work helped Jewish and other people in hiding, maintained contact with the burgeoning armed resistance, and established connections among various Resistance groups.

The regional scope of his activities was expanding rapidly. This diminished his work within the Zaan region—but he never abandoned his hometown. At the end of 1942, partly on his instructions, Zaandam began building an underground telephone network. While the Germans were closing down Dutch communications networks, sixty new telephone connections were made in the Zaan region, at the service of the Resistance members, regardless of their political allegiance. It was an early sign of Walraven's search for ways to get different Resistance groups to work together.

Zaandam also created a "warning service." Jaap Buijs, the local detective Robert Pel, and Walraven decided in early 1943 to put pressure on the new Zaandam commissioner, Tonny Jansen. They warned him they had incriminating information about him and if he refused to cooperate with them, they would liquidate[321] him. From then on, they told him, Jansen would have to pass on to the two of them, via one of their new clandestine phone lines, any messages that it would be important for the Resistance organizations to know. The Commissioner gasped, but complied. Buijs wrote:

> He saved at least eighty people from the hands of the Gestapo. Moreover, his work was of enormous significance to us, because it kept us up to date. Until the liberation, the warning service functioned well—numerous Jews in hiding and wanted Resistance fighters escaped the Nazis and their accomplices. (*Source:* Jaap Buijs.)

Starting in May 1943, retired Naval Lieutenant Laurens Cornelis Weeda (*alias* Van den Brink, *alias* Brinkie) became Walraven's personal courier. On

May 7, the first group of ex-servicemen had to report for deportation as prisoners of war. Weeda did not want to be a POW:

> After a futile attempt to pretend I was physically unsuitable, I went into hiding in 's-Hertogenbosch,[322] with Louis van Bunge.[323] He told me about a group of prominent Dutchmen who had set up a support fund for all groups and strata of the population. He asked me if I wanted to be included, and I embraced the idea. At the end of May he gave me Wally's name and his address in Zaandam. When I arrived, I waited until dark and then went in to see Wally and introduced myself as 'Brink, sent by Van Bunge.' Wally was instantly on the qui vive. He was surprised, then angry, that a complete stranger was sent to him in his own home, supplied with his real name and address." (*Source:* Laurens Cornelis Weeda, postwar report.)[324]

Weeda's story illustrates the persistent naiveté of the Dutch Resistance during the first three years of the Occupation. Many activists still did not use a pseudonym and Resistance workers too readily shared information. Their information networks were sometimes too large to control, so that one arrest resulted in a chain reaction of new arrests.

Nonetheless, Walraven van Hall soon decided that this 44-year-old former naval officer Laurens Weeda could be trusted. Weeda said:

> After he got to know me, he told me that he could hire me as an assistant if I promised to carry out all assignments, no matter how dangerous. He also forbade me to disclose my location to any family member, including my wife. He told me I could never return home and never stay at one hiding place for more than a month. I agreed. (*Source:* Weeda, postwar report.)

Weeda's temporary safe houses were initially provided by Van Hall—first in Heiloo and then in Zaandam, so that he could quickly call for Weeda's services. Weeda said:

Laurens Cornelis Weeda, aka Brinkie. (Van Hall Foundation)

After a short while I was met by a son of Mr. Buijs and was shown addresses, at each of which I was allowed to stay no more than a month. This was toward the end of June 1943. From that time on, meetings were held in the evenings, as soon as it was dark, between Wally, Mr. Buijs, and me. At these meetings, we dealt with applications for support, addresses to hide in, etc. that had been received during the day. Then we prepared activities for the following day. (*Source:* Weeda, postwar report.)

The tasks he performed at the behest of Buijs and Van Hall ranged from assisting downed English pilots,[325] espionage, and care of ration cards, to bringing to Eindhoven's Resistance intelligence unit staff maps stolen from the Germans, photos of fortifications, minefields, secret telephone exchanges, and photos of persons dangerous to the state.[326]

Because the number of people being helped was growing, the trio started meeting every day. The meetings usually took place at Wally's Zaandam home at Westside 42.[327] Weeda wrote: "Our daily meetings were our happiest hours. The evenings included our so-called fireside chats. Mr. Van Hall always took time for five minutes of anecdotes and funny stories from the old days, because five minutes of laughter were required, he always said. Since the NSF[328] took care of ration cards, we often stayed to prepare receipts. Mrs. Van Hall always welcomed and helped us."[329]

Between his many meetings, Walraven paid attention to his family, sometimes in combination with his other great hobby, sailing. On Sunday, July 25, 1943, he took his children on a boat trip on the Voorzaan and the North Sea Canal. To their horror, that afternoon an Allied squadron flew over them—24 RAF bombers targeting the Fokker factory in Amsterdam North. Son Aad said:

> Father shouted out for us to lie down at once on the bottom of the sailboat and put all the cushions of the boat over us. He quickly sailed to one side. With a group of other people we sheltered under a large factory roof. (*Source:* Aad van Hall.)[330]

They heard shrapnel falling on the sugar-factory canopy, but they were not hit.

Adding the Landlubber Fund meant more work for Van Hall. He needed more help, or he had to create efficiencies. To limit the dangers and the work, he raised the minimum loan amount, which had been 1,000 guilders at the Seamen's Fund, to 25,000 guilders at the Landlubber Fund. With the same purpose, he limited to a handful the number of intermediaries he asked for money. In the early summer of 1943, the Landlubber Fund negotiated its first loan.[331] An intermediary, the former mayor of Krommenie, Jan Kalff said:

> At one of our discussions, I asked whether we could accept small gifts or loans. Van Hall was against this, as it increased our risk. I favored it, because I wanted to give a chance to those with smaller amounts to participate. Van den Bosch agreed with me, but then endorsed Van Hall's objections. In my area of operation, we continued to accept small amounts." (*Source:* Jan Kalff, former Mayor of Krommenie.)[332]

Upping the Queen's Guarantee

Unlike the Seamen's Fund, the Landlubber Fund did not have any guarantee by the Dutch Queen to repay borrowed money after the war. Few people in hiding and their families, and few Resistance workers, would likely be able or willing to repay their benefits after the war. To obtain some assurance of repayment for the lenders, Walraven visited the retired president of the Dutch State Bank,[333] Leonardus Trip, whom the Nazis replaced in March 1941.[334]

Van Hall explained about the Landlubber Fund. Leonardus Trip declared that he did not know if he would return to his old position after the war, but that he supported the Fund. He agreed to ask the government in exile to repay the borrowed money after the war and was also prepared to help convince potential lenders to make loans. Earlier, Van Hall was assured by a top civil servant of Social Affairs that borrowing the money enjoyed broad support in his department.

Although no guarantee came soon from London, the lenders to the Landlubber Fund had a little more assurance against the loss of their money. Gijs wrote that the people who loaned the money wanted assurance that they would be repaid after the war was over, and the Fund board repeatedly asked themselves whether they should ask the Queen's government for this guarantee:

> Before the war I had dealt often with [Prime Minister] Gerbrandy,[335] so he knew the business I had been involved in, and that I was used to handling large sums. We considered explaining to him that the lenders and borrowers were all "responsible citizens."[336] But my brother Walraven opposed sending a message to London because weird[337] things happened there. Time and again, the Germans seemed to find out secrets, with the only possible leak being in London. So Walraven suspected either an abundance of German spies, or people in the Dutch government in exile, who should have known better, briefing with too much detail. He had contact with the Resistance, while I was only in touch with official sources. I didn't know things that he knew.

But we talked about it all a great deal because without more assurance
it was so hard to raise new money. (*Source:* Gijs van Hall, Het Nationaal
Steun Fonds 1943-1945. Amsterdam, 1948. In Dutch.)

Walraven maintained contact with espionage groups from early in the
Occupation. The Landlubber Fund supported such organizations from
its beginning.[338] Although he could not have known about the disaster of
Englandspiel, Walraven did learn that paratrooper teams from Great Britain
kept falling into German hands, one after another.[339]

Gijs needed the Queen to guarantee repayments of loans to the Landlubber Fund. But Walraven was reluctant to send the request to London. Gijs said:

We were cautious about sending a message to London. Someone
came one time who said he could carry a message there. My brother
had an interview with him in Amsterdam, opposite Central Station.
It was quite mysterious—the man was dressed in a nurse's uniform,
which was weird. (*Source:* Gijs van Hall, to the postwar inquiry.)

Gijs knew about a second incident, which Walraven's wife Tilly remembered:

In 1943 my brother and Gerrit van der Veen had lunch with a
slim, dark man with glasses who claimed to be able to bring people to
England. My brother didn't trust him at all and this mistrust turned
out to be justified when the transfer of a professor went wrong.
(*Source:* Tilly den Tex van Hall.)

Gijs was referring to Professor Jan Coops. A serious attempt was made
through him to obtain the coveted guarantee from the exiled Dutch government. After consultation with Walraven van Hall and Gerrit Jan van der Veen,
the Vrije Universiteit (Amsterdam) professor decided to travel to Spain via
Belgium and France, and to make the crossing from there. LO[340] employee
Dirk Mulder said:

Coops left on November 15, 1943, packed and loaded with orders from the NSF. Van Tuyl[341] was faced with the difficulty that he had no government powers. He did dance around this, but ultimately there was nothing behind his appeal to London or his promises to repay. At one point someone told Coops he shouldn't go. Coops answered: 'I'm going anyway.' Van Tuyl was quite behind it. (*Source:* Dirk Mulder, LO employee.)

Ten days after his departure from Amsterdam, the England-bound messenger was apprehended at the Belgian-French border, probably as a result of betrayal. He was in possession of enough incriminating material to be executed by the Germans, including military drawings of Berlin and plans to transfer Dutch Resistance fighters to Great Britain. However, in April 1945, the Americans freed him from the Remscheid-Lütteringhausen prison in Germany. Coops survived the war. Two months after Coops' unfortunate attempt at a visit, and after Walraven's death, the NSF did receive the needed authority from the Queen, as we shall see.

Meanwhile, father van Hall had an excellent reputation in the financial world as former chairman of the Dutch Stock Exchange Association. His son Gijs played this valuable card: "Those who knew him knew us. They knew that we were not fraudsters and would not play impermissible tricks."[342] In addition, Gijs and Walraven had many banking contacts of their own through their work. It was time to take advantage of these connections.

The Landlubber Fund Borrows from Banks

Gijs proposed to his brother that they be more "systematic" in their collection of money. As he said: "A director of a company would be more inclined to grant a loan if asked by a colleague rather than an outsider. Wally agreed and therefore asked a savings bank manager friend to contact his colleagues. I did the same for directors of a large insurance company, a mortgage bank, and a Dutch-Indian[343] cultural society, and approached the banks myself.[344]

This approach worked as expected. Ten of the twelve largest Amsterdam banks approached by Gijs made fictitious loans. The registered amounts were given in full to the Landlubber Fund.

With great ingenuity, the bank managements masked their loans, each good for 200,000 guilders (two tons).[345] One placed a supply of newsprint in a large envelope, sealed it, signed the package with his own signature and that of the chief commissioner, and wrote that the contents were an "emergency rations for personnel. Opening the envelope is allowed only in case of emergency, and in the presence of the management."[346] Another director wrote:

> We agreed that extra cash from the savings bank would be kept in a separate safe deposit box at the Netherlands Bank—i.e., would be available to the NSF. That was 200,000 guilders. When the inspectors came to the savings bank, they were told: "You certainly want to check that extra cash." Promptly the agent of the Netherlands Bank received a phone call and made sure that the money arrived in the safe. As proof of its loan, the savings bank received two hundred 1,000-guilder notes. I took the money to Wally van Hall. (*Source:* Bank director.)

A loan agent said:

> A purchase of securities was feigned for camouflage. The lender thus received advice of an ordinary securities purchase. These were supposedly deposited with the securities office of Van Hall in Zaandam. The dividends or coupons were regularly settled, but in reality there were no securities at all. The amount was borrowed purely for the benefit of the NSF. (*Source:* Loan agent.)

Walraven van Hall and his Landlubber Fund colleague Iman J. van den Bosch then traveled through the country to build a network, appointing city and district representatives to connect local and regional aid organizations with the Fund. Cells functioned independently, remaining connected with one another via the local head. The Fund consisted of several sections:

1. The fundraising department, which collected donations;

2. The investigative department, which inventoried money and other organizations and individuals in need;

3. The payout department;

4. The research department, which assessed applications for (political) reliability and the existing material situation ;

5. The administration, which checked and registered the payments and support cases, issued receipts and ensured settlement with the central cashier in Amsterdam.

Standards were set for payout. If, for example, the breadwinner had gone into hiding, his family generally received a maximum of eighty percent of his salary (with an upper limit of 500 guilders). Families of Resistance workers could claim the full amount. And so on. Nine categories of recipients were identified as eligible for support.[347] The local investigators were required to make selections and determine the amount of the payment on the basis of an application document, camouflaged as an "accident insurance claim form." The form contained questions about family situation, employment, religion,[348] and age. The completed documents were sent once a month to the district head, who in turn arranged for them to go to Amsterdam. There the entire package was stored in a central, although sometimes changing, location.

In some municipalities, the aid organizations were running at full tilt from the outset. In other places pressure was needed to get the machinery going. When arrests by the Nazis were made, new contacts had to be appointed. Persons who failed to perform their duties properly were tactfully removed from their positions to avoid betrayal. In short, the pressure on the fund managers was enormous.

To keep the work more manageable, the recipients of payments from the Landlubber Fund were organized into three geographical areas. Van den Bosch, who had moved from Eindhoven to Groningen for safety reasons, switched the area he managed to the northern and eastern provinces. Eindhoven resident

Arie Voorwinde initially managed Limburg and North Brabant, but SS agents from SiPo arrested him in August 1943, and his fellow townsman Andreas Gelderblom took over this work. Van Hall took care of people in North and South Holland, Utrecht and Zeeland. Voorwinde wrote:

> The first time I attended a meeting with Van Hall in Utrecht, it was about national cooperation. That was back in 1942. In some places there was too much money, in others too little. Funding, we agreed, should be related to need. We also agreed on the division of our geographical areas of work. It goes without saying that this was not a formal agreement. (*Source:* Arie Voorwinde.)

Acquiring funds and volunteers for a working area that covered almost all of The Netherlands was initially difficult. Yes, on the one hand, the Germans were losing ground elsewhere in Europe, and the apathy that gripped the Netherlands during the first two years of the war was slowly diminishing. On the other hand, the Occupation was imposing increasingly severe punishments on captured agents of the Resistance and their families. Few people were willing to take such big risks to help their compatriots.[349]

The three, later four, leaders of the Landlubber Fund regularly visited one another, under the cover that they had to discuss matters concerning the wine trade. To be on the safe side, some applicable winery texts were put on the table before the start of a meeting. During these consultations, the committee exchanged experiences and discussed any problems. The name Landlubber Fund was changed to National Support Fund (NSF) at the instigation of outsiders, although when and how this change was made is not recorded.

From the autumn of 1943, Van Hall regularly took his confidant Jaap Buijs to the "Wine Committee." Buijs kept up to date about the day-to-day business, whereas Van Hall focused more on broader themes. "Every fortnight the top of the NSF met in Amsterdam, The Hague or Utrecht. They were Van den Bosch, Van Hall, Gelderblom, and myself. In the morning we had a meeting of the NSF, in the afternoon with the National Committee (NC)," said Buijs.[350]

One of the NC leaders, tax inspector Albert Berent Jan Prakken,[351] occasionally joined the group:

> Joint meetings of the NC and the NSF were held once every fortnight. This happened at various places, for example at Leidsegracht 13 and also at the Tax Inspectorate in Amsterdam. We were called the Wine Commission. The NC and the NSF often worked with the same people in the country. We discussed the current difficulties. One was the railway strike. I remember that Wally van Hall asked whether an illegal magazine could receive support from the NSF. Another topic was how the German conscription of labor could best be counteracted. There was always discussion about the agenda in the so-called Kern,[352] or what had been discussed there. Finally, the NC helped where difficulties had arisen in the NSF. Especially [Lambertus] Neher was the man who managed to get people to work together again when there had been a split." (*Source:* Albert Prakken.)

Prakken remembered his first meeting with Walraven van Hall. The tax officer urgently needed money to be paid to colleagues in hiding who, as former military personnel (non-commissioned officers), should have reported for detention:

> I spoke about this issue with some leaders of the National Committee. However, they decided it was not an issue for them. Instead, they put me in touch with Van Hall. That's how our collaboration started. Immediately, he understood the importance of the matter. As soon as I explained it, he asked: "How much per month is needed?" "For the time being, 40,000 guilders per month," was my guarded answer. "When and where do you need them?" was his second question." (*Source:* Albert Prakken.)

Within two days, Walraven got him the money, on time.

Both in the Wine Committee and outside it, sharp questions were asked about the accountability of NSF funds. Van Hall insisted from the outset that this accountability be demonstrable and sound, to justify government guarantees and to prevent local abuse of the funds.[353] We have already seen how lenders received numbered debt certificates, in the form of old shares and other invalidated securities. On the spending side, Van Hall required the same discipline, with all receipts—from people in hiding, or their families not in hiding—matched against NSF funding.

According to Walraven and Gijs, their administrative system was the least risky. But some groups were not convinced and were afraid of providing the Nazis with leads to Resistance workers. Several groups therefore refused to carry out the NSF procedures. The central NSF figure in Friesland, Jan Evenhuis, devised his own system based (like the NSF system) on codes that meant nothing without the separately kept name registration. When Evenhuis was arrested in July 1944, the SiPo agents obtained both the code cards and the name book through an unfortunate coincidence. The catastrophe was revealed to the Resistance and most people whose names and addresses were listed managed to go into hiding, but a few ended in prison. Evenhuis and some of his co-workers were executed on August 18, 1944. They were among 84 NSF workers who did not survive the war because of their Resistance work.[354] The exposure of the Frisian system shows that Walraven's accounting method had definite advantages. It was never penetrated by the Nazis.

5 | Resistance Banker (1943–1944)

"Resistance is not a personal hobby. It is a duty"
—WALRAVEN VAN HALL[355]

WALRAVEN WAS, BY JUNE 1943, established as the Banker of the Resistance and one of the key leaders of the Dutch Resistance. Jaap Buijs and Laurens Weeda met with him[356] every evening in Zaandam. They arranged hiding places, assessed requests for support, and planned their work for the following day. Weeda explained:

> Wally himself usually went out into the province to collect money or talk with county chiefs. Besides his exceptionally demanding work of running the NSF, Wally organized countless other new activities. (*Source:* Weeda, postwar letter to Walraven's parents.)

The Resistance Organizers

All this work kept Walraven constantly on the run. He was the only NSF[357] leader living and working in the western Netherlands, which is where most of the Resistance activity was concentrated. Because of the need for coordination, Walraven had a full schedule of meetings in and around Amsterdam. Acting primarily as a banker, he also paid out cash for counterfeit ration cards and associated stamps. Weeda said:

The NSF was issuing thousands of duplicate fake ration cards because recipients were moving around. Different organizations that helped people in hiding each added their names. Wally insisted on centralizing the distribution of these cards and his controls both improved efficiency and reduced demand by 90,000 cards in the first month. (*Source:* Weeda, postwar letter too Walraven's parents.)

Walraven also served as a coordinator of Resistance contacts and resources. For example, he was regularly communicating with the National Assault Squad,[358] high among German targets. He was also constantly in touch with the National Organization for Help to People in Hiding (LO)[359] to find hiding places and with the Personal Identity Center (PBC)[360] to obtain fake IDs.

He was widely praised for his role as a mediator among the evolving and competing components of the fragmented Resistance. Closer coordination of Resistance activities was essential because demands on the leadership were growing. The number of Jews in hiding were growing and to them were being added the large number of new men evading the Occupation's "Work Assignment Program,"[361] which sent Dutchmen as slave laborers to Germany's labor-starved factories, themselves targets of Allied bombing.

As demands for help grew, the Resistance was increasingly undermined by betrayals and indiscretions. A concerted professional effort to improve confidentiality required mutual trust, which was at first scarce. "We were terrified of any umbrella organization," said a leader of one of the underground newspapers:

> Coordination was a big problem in 1943. The human mind wants to be free. . . . The spiritual starting points of the various Resistance groups differed.[362] We also wanted to remain flexible to be able to make decisions quickly. Coordination strengthened slowly. (*Source:* Arie van Namen, "Free Netherlands," *Vrij Nederland,* a Resistance newspaper.)

In mid-1943, the ties between the LO and the NSF were strengthened. LO chief executive Hendrik Dienske urgently needed money. He hoped the

NSF would make up for the LO's revenue shortfall. He assigned another LO member, Heinrich Douqué, to contact the NSF in the summer of 1943

> I knew a certain Mr. Claus from my business. He put me in touch with Van Hall, whom I then met at the commodity exchange. We first spoke to each other under our pseudonyms. Then it turned out that Van Hall and I have known each other since our childhood. He was once a neighbor. He told me he was working on the Seamen's Fund and then the NSF. I told him what I had been doing, and I asked: "Shouldn't we coordinate these matters? We have begun working together. Shouldn't we all get together?" I then promised Van Hall I would get the leadership of the LO together in my office to meet him. (*Source:* Heinrich Douqué of LO, *Memoirs.*)

Until that moment, the LO and NSF were involved in helping both people in hiding and their relatives. From then on, NSF agreed to support new additions of families of those in hiding who remained behind at home. The LO meanwhile would continue to pay its people in hiding from its own resources. This created a clear structure for both organizations. The NSF "has a lot of money," noted LO employee Arie van Boven in his diary on December 11, 1943, so it was helpful for LO to pass on to the NSF the cases where relatives needed support:

> We filled out the NSF form [the "accident report"] and the NSF promptly paid the needed amounts. This was a great convenience and reduction of risk for LO. The cutting-to-the-bone that we were having to do to cover all the expenses damaged our reputation. The "covenant" between us was the impetus for the Kern, the first large-scale partnership among independent Dutch Resistance groups. (*Source:* Arie van Boven, *Diary,* December 11, 1943.)

Van Hall was once again the key intermediary. He connected the LO with the Personal Identity Center (PBC):

We got in touch with the PBC through Van Tuyl,[363] who arrived one day with Gerrit van der Veen, whom he introduced to Henk Dienske. From then on, Gerrit made for us the false identity cards for people in hiding and any other forgery needed for their work. (*Source: Heinrich Douqué of LO, Memoirs.*)

Walraven/Van Tuyl increasingly acted as an intermediary.[364] For example, he helped social democrat Fred von Eugen to house 1,500 Amsterdam Jews in 1942 alone, through Von Eugen's care group De Haas. Von Eugen's fellow social democrat Jan Willem Rengelink, working with his group Roelofsen (his Resistance pseudonym) was also hard-pressed for money. They both met with Walraven one morning at 695 Keizersgracht, former site of Jewish wholesale trader Bromet.[365]

The three of them discussed financial and organizational matters. Walraven was concerned about many "wild" groups moving underground and creating risks because of their fraudulent activities. Walraven asked Von Eugen and Rengelink to coordinate these groups. At the end of 1943, they created a coalition of seven groups, mostly from Amsterdam and with a social democratic orientation.

Fighting the "Work Assignment" and Z Cards

The NSF created another partnership with the LO in mid-1943 when the Occupation's Fritz Sauckel, grandly titled the General- Plenipotentiary Representative for the Work Assignment,[366] initiated the so-called Z-card procedure.[367] Sauckel planned that these cards would help him select 150,000 more Dutchmen to work as conscripts in Germany. Dutch companies were required to apply for these cards via the Chamber of Commerce and provide details of all male employees between 18 and 45 years old and the degree to which their company needed them. However, his plan failed. Only 35,000 workers went to Germany, because of sabotage by the Resistance that delayed and prevented use of the Z cards.

The first opposition to the Z cards took place in Leiden. Local NSF employee Gerard Everstijn promised to come up with a "plan to sabotage the program." Walraven liked his plan and immediately brought to Leiden Van Velsen of the National Committee and Hugo of the LO.[368] The group decided to ask the government-in-exile to call for a boycott of the Z-card program, The plan worked well. Dutch employers were instructed by London not to cooperate with the registration of the workers. Everstijn summed up: "The Z-card campaign was a Resistance success. We issued 56,000 fake Z-cards, handed out across the country. The Germans issued only 45,000 real ones."[369]

Characteristic of the role that Walraven played in aligning ideas and activities was his meeting with the Leiden district head, Rijk Keij, who wrote:

> At this first meeting, in October 1942 in the town hall in Leiden, we felt we were face-to-face with one of the greats of the Resistance.[370] The meeting lasted just half an hour, yet it completely changed our group's work. We were engaged by the NSF. His arguments and division of roles were so effective that we all felt—here is the man to follow. (*Source:* Rijk Keij, Leiden district head of NSF, postwar statement.)

A reorganization of the Leiden area and the surrounding area desired by Van Hall led to protests from some local Resistance workers. His response was to end the personal contact of these protesters with a number of people in hiding.[371] The district chief timidly tried to change Walraven's mind. In vain. "Support (of the NSF) is not a personal hobby, but a duty," he said. With iron determination, Walraven cut off contact with the protesters. Keij gave another example of Walraven's courage and devotion to duty:

> We were to hold a meeting with representatives of a large Jewish support group for delivery of ration cards and money in Amsterdam. I arrived at the appointed place an hour late, because of a train delay. Quietly window-shopping, Wally sauntered over. His face brightened when he saw me and he beckoned me to follow him. After we walked

a few blocks, he explained: "Thank goodness, this has ended well again. The house was surrounded, the meeting was called off, and the SiPo[372] were patrolling the canal. I didn't feel very comfortable staying around, but I thought I should wait for you to warn you." Despite the great danger that threatened him, he had no panic, no fear. (*Source:* Keij, cited in previous block quote.)

Armed Resistance

Devotion to duty can have serious consequences, as can be seen within the family of Walraven van Hall's mother Nel Boissevain van Hall. The Resistance group CS-6 was named after Corellistraat 6, the Amsterdam home where it was based.[373] It was the home address of Jan [nicknamed Jan *Canada*] and Mies Boissevain and their five children. [Jan *Canada* Boissevain was Nel's cousin.] The family strongly opposed the Third Reich. Jan had been angry at the Kaiser's behavior in World War I. He wrote at that time to his father, who had been Dutch Consul-General in Montreal: "The sooner this gang of thugs, which allows itself to be used for such cowardly acts, is exterminated, the better it will be for posterity."[374]

In the basement of their Amsterdam home, CS-6 made bombs for sabotage activities. Corellistraat 6 also functioned as a transit house for Jewish and Communist people in hiding. CS-6 was also involved in attacking Dutch collaborators. After having arrested several members of the group, the *SiPo* raided the house on Corellistraat on August 2, 1943. Mies and her three sons Jan Karel ("Janke"), Gideon ("Gi"), and Frans were arrested. Their father Jan *Canada* Boissevain[375] had already been arrested in 1942 for doing business with Jews; he died in Buchenwald in early 1945. A distant relative, Louis Boissevain, also disappeared into a prison cell. All but Frans were closely involved in CS-6's activities. Mies was transported to the Ravensbrück extermination camp, which she barely survived. Louis, Jan Karel and Gideon were shot on October 1, 1943 in Overveen, together with sixteen other members of the group.[376] Moments before, Gideon succeeded in smuggling a note written in blood to Louis. "Don't say anything about Zaandam," he warned in the second-last line. A reference to Walraven? We don't know. Not much is known about CS-6.[377]

Walraven's aid to Jewish people in hiding almost ended in his arrest. He worked with an Amsterdammer, Wim ("Bob") Lodeizen, who sheltered and cared for Jews in addition to other Resistance activities. On October 20, 1943, Lodeizen was arrested. Coincidentally, Walraven had scheduled a meeting with him that day, above a barber shop on the Gelderschekade. When the unsuspecting Walraven started to walk through the barber shop toward the steps, the barber grabbed him, put him in a barber's chair, and started soaping him up for a shave. His quick action prevented Walraven from falling into a Nazi trap.[378]

Meanwhile, things on the home front were not going smoothly. The Van Halls' new nanny started dating a German soldier. Walraven discovered it by chance, when he heard her summoned in German at the train station and noticed that she was met by a member of the Occupation's military. Walraven's wife Tilly managed to fire the girl without arousing suspicion.

Coincidence also played a role when German inspectors passed by the Van Hall home. They planned to requisition the Zaandam house and inspected it from top to bottom. Tilly had deposited a pile of laundry in the bathroom, which at first glance was not recognizable as such, and she heard the Germans reject their home because they believed it had *kein Badezimmer* ("no bathroom," meaning no room with a bath or shower).

Aiding Jews in Hiding

NSF funding grew, but not as fast as calls for its help. From 1943 on, many groups caring for Jews in hiding knocked on its door. Until then, the NSF had only provided assistance to individual Jewish people in hiding.

One of the first groups to arrive on Walraven's doorstep was run by Corrie Overduin.[379] She co-headed a large group that aided many Jewish people in hiding in Twente, an area in the Netherlands with a sizable Jewish population.

In the autumn of 1943, her organization ran out of money, despite support from regional manufacturers' contributing about 10,000 guilders each month. Overduin went to Amsterdam to get advice from "Uncle Jan" (Professor C.),[380] who put her in contact with Walraven van Hall. Up to that point Walraven had personally not been much involved with Jewish people in hiding. Overduin wrote later:

> We had been finding homes for Jewish people all over the country, so I knew how severe the financial distress was among the Jewish people. Several families had already surrendered to the Germans out of desperation, because of their hunger. From our experience in Twente we concluded that an enormous infusion of money would soon be needed to prevent such disasters and to keep our work going until the end of the war. With an anxious heart I presented this problem to Mr. Van Hall. What a relief when he did not respond with a "But miss, what do you want?" After some thought, he quietly said this need would be taken care of immediately. He did so by exchanging forty thousand guilders that we had and could not exchange.[381] That morning we went to a banker in Amsterdam to discuss creating a national fund for Jewish people in hiding. (*Source:* Corrie Overduin, postwar letter to Walraven's parents.)

That was the beginning of the NSF-Group J. NSF leaders concerned about accountability for funds understood that Jewish people in hiding could not risk filling out the NSF's "accident insurance claim form" or any other written receipt. However, the contact persons were required to keep monthly statements showing the size of the households to be supported, their places of residence, and the amounts paid out. The NSF randomly checked whether the funds were actually reaching their intended target group.

To limit the risks to the NSF, Group J got its own board. Its central figure was a former member of the Amsterdam Jewish Council, Abraham Krouwer.[382] Van Hall would have been better off choosing someone else, said a fellow board member:

I don't think this choice was good. I myself had never picked anyone from the Jewish Council. He turned out to be difficult to work with, self-important. (*Source:* Helena Steenbrugge.)

Initially, Herman Götzen was the chairman of Group J, but he was soon afterwards arrested. Walraven and Götzen visited Krouwer in June 1943:

Wally and Götzen were looking for someone familiar with the Jews, who knew about their persecution. Götzen had been asked if he wanted to take this on, but he was unfamiliar with the Jewish community. However, he knew me. I am Jewish and I was a member of the Jewish Council. So I knew the trials of the Jews in the Netherlands. We had a meeting with Götzen, Van Hall, Roorda, De Vries, Miss Steenbrugge, Westra, and myself. At my request, I received 50,000 guilders per month from the NSF for the entire country and I was asked to report back if this was not enough. (*Source:* Abraham Krouwer, Group J.)

By separating Group J from the NSF, a possible arrest of someone on the new board would not lead to a snowball effect that could damage the entire NSF. Jaap Buijs initially acted as the contact person between Group J and the NSF leadership. He was succeeded by Douwe Westra, who had been responsible for the Landlubber Fund in Rotterdam. However, Westra suspected the Germans were on his trail and fled to Amsterdam. Then he traveled around as an NSF inspector to Utrecht, and to North and South Holland.

A new board member from Zaandam, Remmert Aten, met Van Hall for the first time in February 1944. He didn't know Walraven, but he knew of his importance in Zaandam and his attempt to stand up to the Occupation through the Dutch Union. Aten knew nothing of Walraven's Resistance work,[383] but he knew fellow lumber trader Jaap Buijs, who introduced him to the NSF.

Soon Aten started working for Group J. Aten wrote in a postwar remembrance that Walraven and Jaap Buijs presented him with a plan to support not just all Jewish Dutch nationals in hiding, but also Jewish refugees from Germany. The NSF would take care of the money:

Remmert Aten. (Collection of Erik Schaap.)

Wally and Jaap told the five members of our local Group J we could count on the NSF getting us what we needed. Each member was to contact underground organizations in our district that supported people in hiding or Jews. Through NSF representatives in the main centers, we found suitable people to connect the new group with existing ones. All addresses of Jewish people in hiding remained secret, since both those in hiding and the hosts would be deeply concerned if they thought we wrote everything down and left them open to the risk of being rounded up at any moment. (*Source:* Remmert Aten, postwar reminiscences.)

Every month Aten went into the province under the pseudonym "De Lange" with 100,000 guilders in his pocket, double his original allotment, looking for Jewish people in hiding to support and also those helping them.

One of Aten's contacts in Amsterdam was a young man, Bob van Amerongen, who worked for the local Resistance group PP, which he co-founded.[384] Every month Van Amerongen would bring 1,000 guilders to an agreed place near Central Station, 50 guilders for each of twenty people in hiding. When Aten eventually handed Van Amerongen's task to someone else, the successor followed NSF protocol and required that the group provide the names and addresses of the Jewish people being supported. That request temporarily ended the cooperation of Van Amerongen's group with the NSF. To replace NSF funds that didn't arrive, and to alleviate their recipients' distress, they had to sell hundreds of kilograms of sugar on the black market. The group's leadership sent a letter to the NSF telling them about it. The NSF relented and restored the local group's money without their having to provide personal details. But Walraven stipulated that the group had to name a representative to account for the money after Liberation.

Rapport warmed between leaders of the two organizations. Bob van Amerongen thought Walraven was a "friendly person, very business-like, just a bit short-tempered and a bit nervous."[385] Together they philosophized about the problems created by the Landwatchers.[386] Founded at the end of 1943, this paramilitary organization, populated by members of the Dutch Nazi Party, exposed many people in hiding. The two men considered some bold plans to foil them. One was to sow panic with Resistance fighters dressed as Landwatchers. But nothing came of it.[387]

The meeting and distribution address of Group J for a while was Herengracht 368. The board met there weekly and twice a month Krouwer collected the money needed for the people in hiding from an NSF cashier who was present. From August 1944, the treatment room of a dentist in hiding, Bosboom Toussaintstraat 65, was the board's meeting place. Krouwer said:

> Everyone was to form around themselves a cell of people who would be in touch with the local connections to the Jewish people in hiding. Group J passed on the money from the NSF and in addition provided many services—ration cards via the LO;[388] if needed, false identity cards via the Personal Identity Center;[389] smaller banknotes exchanged for thousands of larger banknotes[390] that Jewish people in hiding could not use after March 1943. Group J also addressed occasional quarrels between hosts and their guests in hiding; it conducted a search for doctors in cases of illness, births, and deaths. (*Source: Abraham Krouwer.*)

In sum, Group J did far more than just provide money. It did what was needed to allow Jews in hiding to survive the Occupation as worry-free as was then possible. At first, Group J worked primarily with care groups in Amsterdam, where most Jews were living. But soon more volunteers emerged in the rest of North Holland—Limburg, Brabant, Friesland, Twente—and South Holland. An early-1943 estimate was that 25,000 Dutch-resident Jews were then in hiding. Betrayals and raids reduced the number sharply in the next two years, as "Mad Tuesday"[391] lowered the guard of the Resistance and stepped up Nazi urgency in carrying out its "Final Solution."

NSF spending on Jewish people in hiding amounted to 400,000 guilders per month. At 100 guilders per person, that would be 4,000 people helped per month. After liberation, 4,237 Jewish households (one or more persons) were being kept alive by the NSF, according to its records as of June 1945.[392] For the whole period of the Occupation, historian Loe de Jong estimated that the NSF provided funds to 8,000 Jewish people in hiding. The leader of Group J, Abraham Krouwer, estimated the number at 9,000.

> The amounts paid out per household were modest, initially 75 guilders per person, later 100 guilders per person. A post-war NSF report said: Some Jewish people in hiding were paying 300, 500, even 1,000 guilders per month for their accommodation. As long as they had money of their own, of course, we did not intervene. However, the NSF itself refused to pay such large amounts. (*Source:* NSF report on its finances, c. 1947.)

The NSF from the start established the rule that it would not cooperate with any situation where people in hiding were being exploited. In such cases, Group J tried to relocate the exploited Jews to another hiding place. Jacobus Lootsma told this story:

> In August 1943, I had a long conversation with Walraven about financial support for the persecuted Jews. In my view, something had to be done soon, and on a large scale. I told him I thought he was the

only person who could do what was needed. However, he was reluctant at first to do this, because he feared it might jeopardize his other work. He fully recognized the necessity and duty of the Dutch people in this matter, but he refused. This was the only time he ever disappointed me. Shortly afterwards, I discovered that someone had set up a large-scale support movement for the Jews. Who did it? Surprise, it was again Wally van Hall! (*Source:* Jacobus Lootsma.)

Getting a Bigger Guarantee from the Queen

The NSF spent millions of guilders in aid on its own initiative, without consulting the Dutch government in London. The Van Halls and Iman van den Bosch were *sure* that the Seamen's Fund spending would be reimbursed after the war—thanks to the promise via Radio Oranje in April 1941. But they only *expected* other expenditures to be refunded, based on the promise of former bank president Trip to Walraven.

As money needs grew for the Seamen's Fund, the Landlubber Fund, Group J, and other Resistance groups, more certainty was required. Walraven needed another official government statement, to simplify fundraising from banks and other financial institutions, and strengthen the NSF position within the Resistance. A government response came, but not quickly.

Iman van den Bosch told the Hague banker and Resistance member Charles van Houten about the Seamen's Fund in early 1943. In May 1943, Van Houten succeeded in escaping to London via Sweden. Van Houten probably told the Dutch government in London about the Seamen's Fund. In July 1943, Captain Filippo received 30,000 guilders from London for the fund. It was a just drop in the ocean. It was an indicator of how out of touch the London government was about the Resistance, what it was doing and what its needs were. Van Houten failed to convince the ministers to provide more financial guarantees or money to the Resistance.[393]

While the NSF was growing rapidly, for months in 1943 the government in exile heard nothing about it.[394] However, in October 1943, secret agent

Garrelt van Borssum Buisman sent a telegram to England. He had been in contact with a Resistance group that cared for and financed civil servants and soldiers in hiding and cabled:

> Will these amounts be repaid by the Dutch government after the war? If so, we ask Radio Orange to broadcast this message: "We guarantee the feed will be provided to the chickens." (*Source:* Garrelt van Borssum Buisman, secret agent.)

Two weeks later, London replied: "The government agrees to provide the requested guarantee, but to pay only reasonable amounts under restriction. In addition, the total amount of the payments may not exceed 200,000 guilders for the time being."[395] This minimal guarantee showed that the government had no clue about how big were the amounts being spent, and required.

Two new agents for the Resistance went to England to seek clarity from the government in exile—André Koch and Harry Linthorst Homan, former executive secretary of Philips (and in that capacity, familiar with Iman van den Bosch). They were distressed about the shortage of money, particularly for the underground press. In December 1943, Koch wrote to Prime Minister Gerbrandy:

> Resistance circles in the Netherlands are preparing plans that are desperate, including large-scale bank robberies.[396] The government should do everything possible to prevent this, otherwise public morale will sink further. I hear that the government has authorized someone to pay out $100,000 a month. That is a drop of water on a hot plate. (*Source:* Koch to Prime Minister in exile Gerbrandy, December 1943.)

Koch at that point seems to have had no knowledge of the NSF, because he wanted the money to be distributed via a secret agent to the principal underground newspapers—*Trouw, Vrij Nederland, Het Parool,* and *Je Maintiendrai.*

Only after Koch's cry for help did Gerbrandy and his cabinet appreciate the gravity of the situation. During the night of January 10-11, 1944, secret agents Harm Steen and Sjef Adriaansen were dropped by parachute over North Brabant. They had 120,000 guilders with them for the NSF. On January 15, police officer Robert Pel traveled by train to Princenhage and collected the twelve packages of banknotes, which he took to Walraven.

More important than the 120,000 guilders was a cufflink worn by Steen, which contained the microfilm of a letter signed by Gerbrandy, with the message Walraven awaited, saying:

> The Dutch government hereby guarantees the repayment of an amount not exceeding 30 million guilders, to support people in hiding, persons who have evaded the obligation to report as a prisoner of war, or as a worker in Germany, and their families—and for other purposes related to relief campaigns, at your discretion, on the understanding that you may dispose of a maximum of 10 million guilders for the time being. (*Source:* Gerbrandy to Koch via microfilm in Harm Steen's cufflink, 1943.)

London required that if the NSF wanted a guarantee for the remaining 20 million guilders, it must first ask permission. The twice-used phrase that the Resistance could "dispose of" millions of guilders led to some hilarity later between the Van Hall brothers. They tried to imagine the reaction of the Dutch Nazi Rost van Tonningen, head of the Dutch State Bank, if they knocked on his door with the Queen's order for him to "dispose of" the funds.[397]

The broad scope of Gerbrandy's letter allowed them to spend money on activities for which there were no prior guarantees. For example, until 1944, those interested in a false identity card had to pay personally for their production costs. The government commitment meant such documents could be provided free.

Harry Linthorst Homan, on a roundabout way to England,[398] believed that the government guarantee should not be released to the underground press, but only to Iman van den Bosch and his close associate M. H. J. de Wilde (whom he knew by her pseudonym Miep). Linthorst Homan wrote:

I gave Steen the names of Van den Bosch, Van Hall, and Miep. I had to use Miep, because she could travel without danger—the Dutch rail connection between the west and the north was then forbidden for men. I knew that Van Hall was an important man in the NSF, but I believed then that Van den Bosch was its leader. (*Source: Harry Linthorst Homan to Van den Bosch and De Wilde, c. December 1943.*)

In September 1943, Linthorst Homan left England for the Netherlands without finding out where Van den Bosch and Miep were located. Charles van Houten's suggestion to Steen was that he go to The Hague, to the branch office of the Dutch Trading Company,[399] which might locate Van den Bosch or Miep. Steen was strictly instructed to hand the microfilm[400] only to one of them.

Steen did visit the Dutch Trading Company, but no one there could track down either Van den Bosch or Miep. Steen had Van Hall's home address, so he traveled to Zaandam. Walraven was not at home, but his wife Tilly notified him in Amsterdam. An embarrassing situation ensued when Van Hall returned home and Steen wouldn't give him the microfilm. Steen said he was authorized to give it only to Iman van den Bosch or Miep de Wilde. Van Hall called Miep. As Miep explained later:

Wally called me in Gröningen to say I was needed, since Van den Bosch was away in The Hague, obtaining 200,000 guilders. I came to Zaandam, learned what had happened, and went straight to Van den Bosch in The Hague. We returned together to Zaandam to obtain the document from the courier, Steen. We immediately shared it with Wally, who was annoyed the courier had been instructed by Linthorst Homan to hand it only to one of us. Shortly before he returned to England, I put Linthorst Homan in touch with Wally. They met on the tram platform in front of Central Station. Linthorst Homan explained that he sent the courier to Zaandam because he only remembered Van Hall's address there and did not know where the two of us had gone. We later had a hearty laugh about the incident. It was not a big concern for Van Hall. (*Source:* M. H. J. [Miep] de Wilde, postwar memoir.)

The Queen's guarantee of repayment after the war finally reached the right people. In this way the exiled Dutch government recognized the NSF as the Bank of the Dutch Resistance. The NSF leadership gave the former president of The Dutch State Bank a copy of the government letter and informed a number of key figures within its own organization. "We regarded this letter as The Dutch State Bank regards its gold," Gijs van Hall later explained. The microfilm with the letter eventually ended up with Gijs. Walraven afterwards said the handover seemed like something lifted out of a cheap detective novel:

> We met at a certain hour in the men's room of Die Port Van Cleve,[401] a hotel restaurant not far from Dam Square. We didn't exchange a word, but stood next to each other. He put the photo in my outer pocket as he left. Then I left and waited at the Line 2 tram stop. When the tram arrived, I did not get in immediately, but jumped onto the rear platform just as it began to move. (*Source:* Walraven van Hall, probably in one of Gijs's books.)

The Kern

By the time the NSF obtained the coveted government guarantee, the professionalization of the Resistance had already taken another step. The Kern[402] was formed in December 1943, quickly growing into the first committee to succeed in coordinating Dutch Resistance activities. It was Walraven's initiative, coming out of his partnership with Lambertus Neher of NC[403] and Hendrik Dienske of LO.[404] Jaap Buijs explained it to a postwar parliamentary committee of inquiry that was investigating the early days of the Resistance:

The Kern was founded after a meeting in Utrecht between the NSF and the LO. Mr. Van Hall and I talked and agreed on the need for more communication among the Resistance groups. We felt we should include them all. Mr. Van Hall then spoke with other people, including Mr. Neher and other people from the LO. We had a meeting at the Frederiksplein in Amsterdam and decided to go ahead with the idea. Only the underground newspapers refused to cooperate, because they thought it was too dangerous. (*Source:* Jaap Buijs, Parliamentary Committee of Inquiry, 1952.)

Neher of the NC described the Kern's creation as a solution to two problems:

The first problem was to uphold the values of the Resistance and protect it from being tarnished by selfish desires. The second was to ensure that no more ration cards were issued than necessary, because in the long run our food supply would run out. (*Source:* Lambertus Neher, Parliamentary Committee of Inquiry, 1952.)

Within the Kern, Van Hall got on well with Lambertus Neher, who was more than sixteen years younger. They had a shared disappointment. Like Van Hall, Neher had aspired to be in the merchant marine as a young man and had to leave after a few years because of poor eyesight. This shared career blow, Neher's technical skills, and his social-democratic inclination helped strengthen his bond with Walraven during the year following their first meeting.

At first, the Kern was intended primarily to coordinate NSF aid to people in hiding, but in January 1944 the three leaders got a large number of organizations to meet together to expand their agenda. Their objective was practical cooperation. However, the first two meetings did not go so well. Buijs called them "wild:"

Walraven in wartime. (Collection of Erik Schaap.)

There was no mutual understanding. I had a conversation with Van Hall and I said: "We should talk about this. There must be guidance." (*Source:* Jaap Buis, Parliamentary Committee of Inquiry, 1952.)

The outcome was that Buijs was asked to chair the Kern meetings. Gerrit van der Veen announced to him: "Good. We have a job for you. When you make a proposal, you get to do it."[405] The Kern met weekly from February onwards, with Buijs in the chair. Over time, ten national Resistance organizations participated.[406]

Every Thursday morning the talks in Amsterdam were about general matters and determining the next direction of the Resistance. In the afternoon, members of the Kern filled in the details. The agenda items varied, but were often related to the tens of thousands, later hundreds of thousands[407] of people in hiding in the Netherlands—for example, forging identity papers and ration cards, bringing in money, acquiring food, stealing goods, and obtaining official cooperation. They also reviewed sabotage and elimination[408] activities. Neher said after the war

Jaap Buijs.
(Van Hall Foundation)

Politics, the constitution, or the question of what should happen once the Netherlands was liberated, was never discussed. None of the older people present wanted that. (*Source:* Neher, Parliamentary Committee of Inquiry, 1952.)

His NC[409] colleague Van Velsen wrote:

The Kern was a place for Resistance practitioners. They handed out ration coupons by the thousands and exchanged names of hiding places.[410] They worked on Resistance papers and discussed possible offensive actions. Politics was not part of the discussion. Members of the Kern didn't have to disclose what political group they belonged to. The non-political middle group had the initiative. (*Source:* Van Velsen, NC.)

This way of working fit Van Hall's character. He did not wish to exclude any clandestine organizations. He pushed for common goals and his view was that political positioning only diminished the chance of achieving those goals. His opinion was partly based on experiences with earlier, failed attempts by third parties to coordinate or direct the Resistance. However, serious discussions did take place within De Kern about the status of the Resistance after liberation. At the beginning of 1944, the Kern played an important role in the formation of ideas about the postwar tasks of the Resistance, which subsequently resulted in the Foundation 1940-1945.[411] As Walraven wished, the members of the consultative body decided that the Resistance should play no political role after the war.

> Although his friend Buijs acted as chairman, Van Hall was the linchpin of the fast-growing Kern. The two Zaandammers decided where the weekly Amsterdam meetings would be held. Security was tight. Buijs said: The Kern was never tracked by the Occupation, because only Van Hall and I knew the place of the meeting. We agreed on this procedure: "Stand in front of the Binnengasthuis. As we walk past, we will tell you where to go." It averted a betrayal, because the address was only given out half an hour before the meeting. (*Source:* Buijs, Parliamentary Committee of Inquiry, 1952.)

The Kern and the NSF provoked pushback from some Resistance groups—partly because they had to sacrifice some independence to follow uniform procedures and partly because of Walraven's strong character as the person enforcing the procedures. Adolf Rüter in his book *Riding and Striking* describes Walraven as "a great man," "honest, selfless, willing to sacrifice, energetic and intelligent."[412] These positive character traits and others ("powerful personality, own vision, strong will") show that Van Hall knew what he wanted, went straight for his goal, and did so magnificently.

However, a few people confused his directness with a desire for power within the Resistance. The Ration-Card (TD) group[413] was the most opposed to centralization. The TD mantra was: "The goal should be to create not a power apparatus, but a Resistance apparatus." The underground press was also wary of the Kern because it was too apolitical or conservative for most of them. With the exception of *Trouw's* Care group, they remained outside the Kern.

The TD group mainly focused on resistance within the Dutch civil service and in time became more amenable to the Kern's guidance. In December 1943, two TD leaders—Gerrit van der Veen and Henk Dienske—discussed with Van

Hall possible cooperation. When Van Hall asked the TD group to join the growing coalition, it first reacted without enthusiasm and clung to its independent identity. Later, it decided to support closer ties. This led to the TD group receiving 50,000 extra ration cards for people in hiding. Walraven van Hall later also ensured that the TD group received money, despite the group's refusal—to his regret—of his proposal that it join forces with the much larger LO.[414]

Van Hall promoted coalitions with increasing success. He tried to create a smoothly organized counter-movement, urging small Resistance groups to accept being absorbed into a bigger picture. However, the smaller groups had difficulty with this. Rüter correctly concludes:

> The simple desire for independence in the Resistance derived from differences of opinion about tactics, differences of a social, political and personal nature, and sometimes just a natural urge of individuals to assert themselves. (*Source:* Rüter, *Driving and Striking*, cited.)

This makes Van Hall's achievement more remarkable. He managed to persuade almost all egos to move in a single direction, in service of a common goal. In the end, only a small minority refused to cooperate with the Kern or the NSF. Everyone else recognized, sooner or later, the qualities and inspiration of the two coordinating organizations.

In 1943, the NSF Divided the Netherlands

In 1943, the NSF divided the Netherlands into 23 districts.[415] Van Hall, Van den Bosch and Voorwinde (later Gelderblom) appointed as district heads people they knew—friends, acquaintances and business associates. This reduced the dangers of infiltration. These heads in turn appointed local leaders responsible for getting financial support to people in hiding. Everyone worked with Resistance pseudonyms. Each group had couriers who distributed money and documents. Eventually the NSF counted nearly 1,900 permanent employees,[416] most of them on the disbursement side.

Because of this *top-down*[417] approach, most employees knew few contact persons, often only one. District chiefs knew the names of the local leaders in their region, but not who functioned under them as background checks or payers of people in hiding. They didn't know who the NSF leaders were. They would have known the Resistance name "Van Tuyl," but not that this was a pseudonym of Walraven van Hall. The triumvirate at the top[418] provided instructions and the necessary finances via couriers. Gijs van Hall gave as an example a monthly distribution system to a man in Dordrecht.

> Once a month, a lady from Amsterdam whom he did not know came to him with a pack of banknotes. If the man was arrested in Dordrecht, he had no information to reveal, even if he wanted to offer something to his interrogators. At most, he would have said that a lady he called "Miep" came to bring him money. That ended the trail. As it happened, this man was in fact eventually arrested,[419] and did not say anything. He was shot, but there were no further consequences to the NSF. (*Source:* Gijs van Hall.)

Sometimes things went wrong with the money distribution. Like the time a courier set off by bicycle to Wieringermeer with half a million guilders hidden inside some rags. When she saw a checkpoint in the distance, she hid her bicycle in the bushes and looked for a place to stay the night. She found it at a farmer's house. But when she went to find her bicycle the next day, it had disappeared . . . with all the money.[420]

Incidental losses of money did not prevent the NSF's guilders from circulating through the Netherlands at a rapid pace. Thousands of receipts poured in to Gijs's office, the central cashier, at Vijgendam 2 in Amsterdam. By collecting the receipts in one place, double payments to people in hiding or their families were prevented. Walraven and his courier "Brinkie" Weeda brought in money almost daily, which then found its way to the needy. Gijs's cupboards soon overflowed with receipts. As the strength of the Resistance increased, more and more people appeared at the Vijgendam office. This increased the chance of betrayal of the address of the cashier. The NSF spread out the risk by adding new cashiers, each responsible for a specific target group. Among the newcomers were several colleagues of Walraven.

The Dutch stock exchange during World War II was an excellent cover for all kinds of prohibited activities. Hundreds of people walked in and out every day without requiring permission from the authorities. It was easy to make contacts and there were numerous niches and hiding places in which people could retreat for awhile. Van Hall also knew many people there, because of the nature of his work. For example, a securities broker took on part of Group J:

> Wally van Hall asked me at the stock exchange if I wanted to participate. On March 8, 1944 I received a Turkish pass[421] from him. With this I had to go to the fountain on the square in front of the stock exchange. There stood a gentleman with the other half of this pass.[422] I received from him 25,000 guilders, which I started with. (*Source:* Stock broker.)

Another stockbroker, Willem de Ranitz,[423] distributed money to the Resistance intelligence services. Walraven asked him to act as a cashier, which he did at his office on the Herengracht. Walraven would introduce him to people who came to collect money.

> For example, on the stock exchange square (Beursplein) a gentleman called "Music Association Ben" was to receive 25,000 guilders per month. I had to remember his face. I did not receive receipts for the amounts I gave from any of my groups. It all went on the face. Wally decided on the amounts that could be given per month. I had a phone number in Amsterdam I could call if I needed money. After a few times I figured out who was behind that number. After the railway strike began, this person could no longer be reached—he left his home. I looked for Wally at the stock exchange, and he sent me a courier with money. (*Source:* Jonkheerh Willem de Ranitz.)

After 1943, there was not much to do on the stock exchange trading floor.

Prices were frozen and virtually no trading was taking place. The Occupation did not like the way the traders reacted to war news. "Everybody was cheering at Stalingrad and other Russian successes, so prices rocketed up," said a broker.[424] After Mad Tuesday the markets were shut.

Wanted by the SD: Walraven van Hall

January 1944 was the last time Walraven and Tilly were together for any significant stretch of time. Gijs van Hall was visiting Twente to put together a fictitious bank loan, and told the Van Heeks that it was high time that his brother took some rest. So the Van Heeks invited Walraven and Tilly to stay with them in Twente. The Van Heeks were happy to do so, but the host commented: "The quiet rest was imaginary. For Wally, it was not a reality."[425] Every day, the NSF leader engaged in talks with Resistance members in Enschede and the surrounding area. He directed,[426] begged, assisted where possible. The Van Halls stayed one week and then returned to Zaandam. Nico van Heek summed it all up: "Wally regained his strength in a relatively safe harbor. But he was driven to go back to the stormy sea, to achieve the great goal he had set himself."[427]

Walraven meanwhile had reason to believe that the SD had targeted him. He was in hiding in Amsterdam, constantly changing addresses to avoid detection. He could no longer come back to his home and family in Zaandam. Weeda said:

> Our time in Zaandam ended suddenly. The trackers were on our trail. That was a terrible punishment for Wally, because he was so attached to his wife and children. But the sudden raid on his house, during which the depraved attackers[428] smashed the large mirrored window in their dining room as they stormed in, was a warning. He was forced to flee. Fortunately, Wally never stayed overnight at home, so the attackers caught nothing.[429] Mr. Van Hall first went to the Gooi[430] for a fortnight to recover somewhat, as he was totally overworked and overtired. Together with Mr. Buijs I went there a few

Walraven and Tilly. (Amsterdam City Archives)

times for needed meetings, but, as we might have expected, the break was short. Mr. Van Hall was back at work well before he announced. (*Source:* Weeda, postwar memoirs.)

Geert Mak wrote:

His daughter Attie at the time obviously knew nothing about her father's double life. He wasn't home much, that's for sure. From this period she remembered only the many people who visited their house in Zaandam. A well-known Resistance leader came—but for Attie he was not the man in charge of the successful attack on the Population Register at the Plantage Kerklaan, but instead was a "nice artist" who came to eat once and was given a precious half-wheel of cheese by Wally. *Source:* Geert Mak, *Een kleine geschiedenis van Amsterdam,* "A Little History of Amsterdam" (Amsterdam, 1999).

That "nice artist" was the boyfriend of Walraven's cousin Suzie, Gerrit Jan van der Veen. On May 1, 1944, she took Gerrit Jan in at the Amsterdam publishing house De Spieghel, where she was co-director. The sculptor, who was also the founder of the Personal Identity Center (PBC), was seriously injured early in the morning in an attempt to liberate prisoners from the SD.[431] In the corridor of the House of Detention on the Amsterdam Weteringschans, where the liberation attempt was taking place, he was hit by two bullets. Van der Veen managed to escape and reach De Spieghel, located at Prinsengracht 856. Suzie and a few other aid workers took care of him as best they could. When the SD discovered where the long-sought Resistance leader was hiding, a raid followed on May 12.[432] Van der Veen, Suzie van Hall, and two others present were arrested. Van der Veen was shot a month later by a firing squad. Suzie first went to Ravensbrück,[433] then to Dachau. She was liberated from Dachau in the spring of 1945.

According to NC representative Arie van Velsen, Walraven played an important role in the restart of the PBC[434] after the death of Van der Veen, who was the undisputed center of the smoothly functioning forgery factory. "No one at the PBC could get things going again. Van Tuyl did it, laboriously and avoiding pettiness, and the PBC started up again."[435]

NSF Grows, Resistance Strengthens

In the spring of 1944, NSF spending increased almost daily. More and more Resistance organizations were discovering the Resistance Bank.[436] The Van Halls looked for additional money. The Netherlands Trading Company had managed labor camps for the unemployed on behalf of the Ministry of Social Affairs and this gave Walraven an idea. He wondered about creating one or two new, fictitious labor camps, charging the costs to the Ministry. Walraven approached an acquaintance, a top civil servant at Social Affairs, with this idea. The acquaintance thought it had merit, since Dutch people in hiding were indeed likely to be unemployed. In the end, the plan fell through. During a meeting in Utrecht between an NSF representative and the director of the Heath Society,[437] a robbery occurred. This immediately made construction of the camp too risky.

Cooperation among the Resistance groups was increasing. The demise of Nazi Germany seemed imminent after June 6, D-Day, when the Allies captured some Normandy beaches. On June 8, the government in exile sent a telegram from Queen Wilhelmina to secret agent Dré Ausems who had parachuted into the Netherlands. The telegram for the second time urged more unity and coordination of the Resistance groups. The first attempt, which went as a message via Ausems, failed. It is important to elaborate why it failed, because it shows why uniting the Resistance groups was so difficult. It also provides a picture of the valuable role the government ascribed to some Zaandam Resistance fighters and their organizations.

Ausems had lived in Zaandijk since 1938. He worked in Schiphol at the Fokker airplane factory[438] and since the Occupation had been sabotaging his employer's repair orders for the *Luftwaffe*. In 1942, Fokker's German managers discovered his obstruction. Ausems went into hiding, got deeper into the Resistance and decided to flee to Great Britain, taking with him a report on the emerging Council of Resistance.[439]

In December 1943 he arrived in London after a roundabout and dangerous journey through Nazi-controlled countries. There he handed over the information from the Dutch government. The government saw him as a reliable messenger and ask him to return to the Netherlands. War Minister Piet Gerbrandy and his cabinet decided the Dutch Resistance was too fragmented and they wanted more coordination. They prepared guidelines, "19 points," for Ausems to deliver to the underground groups. The points, with Gerbrandy's signature, were in a microfilm hidden in a matchbox for Ausems. He was dropped by parachute near Breda[440] on the leap-year night of February 29 to March 1, 1944. The next day he traveled with his wife Pauline by train to Zaandam for an evening visit with his friend Jan Hendrik ("Hein") op den Velde and his wife Fien.

Radio technician Op den Velde was chief of the technical service of the OD[441] and contact man for, among others, the Intelligence Bureau in London, the department under the government in exile that supervised Dré Ausems. Op den Velde set up a radio center in his workshop at 140 Westzijde in Zaandam. From there he sent and received messages relating to the Resistance.

*Andreas W. M.
Ausems (Collection
of Erik Schaap.)*

When Ausems and his wife Pauline entered the Op den Velde home on March 2, 1944, they were met by three men from SD, the Nazi investigation agency.[442] The reason they were there was unclear, but the Germans had Op den Velde and his transmitter in their sights. A raid was in process. Dré and Pauline knew how to play dumb. They said they came by for a *rendezvous*[443] with the befriended couple. After the war, Dré Ausems reported:

> I was searched. After I had emptied all my pockets, I stood with outstretched arms with a matchbox, in which were the microfilm, under a handkerchief in my hand. A wallet was in a raincoat in my suitcase, so when I opened the suitcase, I took the coat myself and held it up, and let the *SiPo*s rummage in the case. (*Source:* Dré Ausems.)

The Ausems couple were allowed to leave the house as free people. However, Hein and Fien op den Velde were taken away. The radio man was killed, a few months before liberation, in a concentration camp. His wife survived the war.

Both Ausems evaded capture. So did Jan Eikema,[444] a pastor who, like Van Hall and Op den Velde, lived on Zaandam's West Side. Eikema arrived at Op den Velde while the SD was still searching the house. He had come with a number of coded messages in his pocket, intended for transmission to England. He succeeded in convincing the Germans that he was making a home visit to the Op den Veldes as part of his pastoral care. He was allowed to

walk out of the house and was therefore able to warn other Resistance members—including Walraven, who was "fortunately recognized on his way to Op
den Velde in the dark and thus escaped,"[445] according to a postwar report by
Zaandam Resistance leader Johann van Marle.

Ausems decided to burn all the information he brought from Great Britain in the stove that evening, including the matchbox and the microfilm with
the 19 points. The couple went into hiding for several weeks, Dré wandering
through the Netherlands, his wife Pauline staying in Goirle.[446] Only after a
few weeks did Dré contact the Resistance again; first the Council of Resistance and then the Kern. At that time, the Kern included organizations such
as the National Organization for Aid to People in Hiding (LO), the Personal
Identity Center (PBC), the National Knokploegen (NKP), the National Committee of Resistance (NC) and the NSF. Ausems drew up statements based
on his memory of the 19 points and tried to win the Kern over to them. "As
the designated Kern contact, I am fully in accordance with the wishes of the
government," he added.[447]

However, since Ausems was in German hands for several hours, the
Kern distrusted him. He was not invited to the weekly Kern meeting. Before
responding to the Queen's wishes, the Kern wanted to see the actual 19 points.
Ausems requested a copy from London. He was told that it could only be
smuggled to the Netherlands the following week, the night of May 7-8. When
the message finally reached the Kern, it was not well received because information in it was outdated and some relationships within the Resistance were
incorrectly described.

On June 8, as mentioned earlier, the government sent a coded
telegram to Ausems on behalf of Queen Wilhelmina. Where she used
to talk about her hope that cooperation would arise within the Resistance, her telegram was stronger. Through Ausems, she "required"
the coordination of "all underground groups." The Resistance
should "appoint a group of leaders," who in the event of a vacuum,
are instructed to designate one or more persons to act as temporary
representative(s) of the government to maintain order and peace; to

prepare for the arrival of the ministers to be sent ahead, who can be regarded as quartermasters; and to prepare for the Military Authority. Another task of these leaders should be to advise the government in the initial period after liberation. (*Source:* Message from Queen Wilhelmina, Prime Minister Gerbrandy, and the Government in exile.)

Three days after it was sent, Ausems had the decrypted text in his possession. [By then, the D-Day invasion of Normandy had taken place.] But he could not read it until the June 23, 1944, weekly meeting of the Kern. In the following days, government orders were distributed among other Resistance organizations and magazines.

Mutual discussions, even within the Kern, did not immediately lead to a consensus on how to act. It took a while for the Resistance to absorb the new message. Not until July 3, 1944,[448] did more than twenty organizations come together in an office building on the Amsterdam Singel, accounting for two-thirds to three-quarters of Resistance activity. During the meeting, those present noted that the organizations represented views on the left, the middle, and the right.

- The left sector included the Council of Resistance (RVV) and the magazines *De Vrije Kunstenaar, Christofoor, Katholiek Kompas, Ons Volk, De Vrije Katheder, Het Parool, Vrij Nederland, De Waarheid,* and *Je Maintiendrai*.

- The middle sector included the NSF, the National Committee of Resistance, the Student Resistance, the Seamen's Fund, the Medical Contact, and the PBC.

- Organizations on the right were *Trouw*, the Protestant Christian School Resistance, the LO, and the LKP. But the Ordedienst (OD, in the person of Catharinus Caljé) and the Fatherland Committee (Willem Drees) remained aloof.

A Contact Committee for the Resistance was chosen from the three movements. The Committee consisted of *Parool* man Jan Meijer on behalf of the left, Siewert Bruins Slot (*Trouw*, School Resistance) on behalf of the right, and Lambertus Neher, who alone represented the middle groups. The Contact Committee was supplemented by Drees and Caljé. This meant the majority of the Resistance was united for the first time in four years of occupation. However, this coordination in the last year of the war still did not mean unanimity about doing battle against the Occupation. New tensions kept surfacing about the ideas and activities of other groups.

The Queen Loses Contact

After secret agent Steen handed over the government authorization to the NSF at Walraven's home in January 1944, London waited for a response. But the transmitter that Steen was expected to use for this was silent. Steen did contact Jan Hendrik op den Velde in Zaandam via Pauline Ausems around January 13, but that also did not lead to a message to the government. In mid-March, a collaborating policeman recognized Steen, who worked for the Hague police before he left for Great Britain. Steen was immediately arrested. Four months later, he was shot.

So the Dutch government in exile did not know what was happening with the NSF. It did not know whether Gerbrandy's message was in the right hands or whether the guaranteed amount of 10 million guilders was being spent usefully. Telegrams went back and forth between London and the Resistance, only sometimes reaching their addresses. In any case, the telegrams did not reduce the confusion. The government was therefore puzzled as to whether the 20 million more guilders that the government had guaranteed (on the condition that the NSF first asked permission to spend it) were ready to be released.

Some Resistance leaders opposed having the NSF credit released. Two of them were Ludo Bleijs, a Roermond priest[449] who fled to Great Britain in the spring of 1944, and his Limburg colleague G. J. Kuiper, a bank manager from Maastricht. These LO employees had great difficulty with the NSF methods, partly because of the so-called "accident insurance claims forms" used as receipts. As early as 1943, NSF methods had created tensions in Limburg. The

LO had survived financially in the province for a long time without Amsterdam interference. However, LO leader Ambrosius[450] also did not like working with receipts or debts and did not get along with Walraven van Hall. LO's chief executive Teus van Vliet said: "Ambrosius was always at odds with Van Tuyl. They couldn't see or smell each other. Yet both were men of excellent character."

NSF representative Andreas Gelderblom had been negotiating with the Limburg Resistance for months to arrive at a form of financing and accountability that everyone supported. It was in vain. "The NSF leaders later reproached us, through Van Tuyl, that, despite the broken cooperation, we still cheerfully borrowed money in Limburg on their guarantee," Kuiper complained after the war. He called the accusation ("already remarkable in itself among Resistance brothers") incorrect. It is certain, however, that until April 1944, Roermonder H. L. van Hooydonk, working under Bleijs, received about 100,000 guilders from Gelderblom for regional aid. In addition, Van Hooydonk borrowed large sums of money on behalf of the NSF in the vicinity of his hometown.

To take the chill out of the air, the NSF leadership eventually traveled to Nijmegen in May 1944, where they met with Hendrikx and Kuiper, among others. Van Hall was committed to promoting cooperation. He was willing to accept the Limburg *modus operandi*. This leniency was ultimately the deciding factor in the LO decision to start working with NSF money in Limburg.

Their agreement did not prevent Father Bleijs from giving the government a negative report on the NSF, written by his Limburg LO colleague G. J. Kuiper. It was in the summer of 1944, months after Bleijs had left for England in April. So Bleijs did not know about the agreement between his own LO and the NSF. His introduction to Kuiper's complaining report was tentative, but overall negative:

> I know that Mr. Van Dijk has formed a committee with Mr. Van Tuyl and Mr. Van den Berg[451] to finance the Resistance. It is apparently mainly led by Mr. Van Tuyl—and so we refer to it in the following as the Comité-Van Tuyl. I have a strong impression that this committee has good patriotic intentions. Otherwise, it is still unclear

to me. The Van Tuyl Committee has made far-reaching claims, at least to the province of Limburg, through Mr. Van Dijk but has never shown any evidence. (*Source:* Father Bleijs.)

In his gold-standard work on the Dutch Occupation, Loe de Jong explained the report as follows:

> Kuiper thought that in that province [Limburg], financial support was generally well organized for people in hiding and the families of Occupation victims. For that reason, he did not think he had any need whatsoever for supervision by gentlemen from other countries or parts of the country. Besides, he doubted their ability, their expertise, and readiness for Resistance work. He also doubted the authenticity of Gerbrandy's letter, which had been communicated to him at the end of March or the beginning of April by Gelderblom (who had gradually become impatient with Kuiper's obstruction), but which he had never seen. Kuiper was of the opinion that the NSF (there was no Catholic in the leadership!) should be placed under the supervision of a National Financial Committee, to which he would like to give a "compartmentalized"[452] character and in which he also included several senior officials of Finance. He wanted it on the record that the Committee should also ensure that persons with Communist sympathies receive no aid. (*Source:* Loe de Jong, *History of World War II in the Netherlands;* in Dutch, 24 volumes.)

It was strong language, jeopardizing NSF's guarantee. Another Resistance fighter who escaped to England, the former *Parool* editor, and Gerrit Jan van Heuven Goedhart, who rose to minister in London, refuted the criticism of Kuiper and Bleijs. He urged Gerbrandy to authorize the NSF to borrow the 30 million guilders. A telegram from the Netherlands supported his plea. "Very well-functioning support organization present," reported the Chief of Staff of the OD (Ordedienst) on July 4 about the NSF.

For a moment, André Koch threatened to throw a wrench into the works.

On July 24, 1944, the London-based officer of the Bureau of Intelligence noted that no "application for the second 10 million guilders" had yet been received. Unfortunately, the Resistance case for the larger guarantee did not reach the Dutch Government in exile. Koch again recommended supporting the Resistance through some of the underground magazines.

The Government again opted for a compromise. On August 2, 1944, Gerbrandy signed a second authorization "to proceed with the withdrawal and distribution of the remaining 20 million guilders." The letter advised the Resistance to use existing support (that is, the NSF) and hiding (that is, the LO) organizations. It also advised that the Medical Contact and the distribution apparatus of the underground press should be involved. A central body was also to be charged with distributing the funds. It was a typical letter composed by a committee, a "polder letter"[453] in which the opinions of Bleijs and Kuiper, as well as Koch and Van Heuven Goedhart, can be read.

Secret agent Robert de Brauw was charged with getting the microfilm with the second authorization to Jaap le Poole, leader of the espionage group Dienst Wim. The reason for the change in recipient was that London had been in the dark for so long, after the first authorization was destroyed by secret agent Steen. The Government in Exile thought it would be easier to restart via Le Poole. De Brauw parachuted in over occupied territory during the night of August 7-8 and managed to get the second authorization to Le Poole, who wrote later:

> I immediately told De Brauw that I was the least suitable person to act as an intermediary with the NSF, certainly with a message asking for more accountability. People in London clearly lacked any clue about what had grown up in the Netherlands in the system of financial support. I suggested he contact the NSF leadership directly, which he agreed to do. Shortly afterwards, I met with Wally van Hall and gave him the microfilm to read. (*Source:* Jaap le Poole.)

After reading it, Van Hall was *not amused*.[454] He was angry that the government did not contact the NSF directly. The requirement that the first 10 million guilders must be accounted for via De Brauw and Le Poole was unacceptable (Van Hall to Le Poole: "Nothing will come of this."). The message that the NSF would be placed under the government's so-called "central body" was annoying. Le Poole wrote:

> He wanted to accept the document without further ado in view of the commitment to increase the appropriation. But he stated that his accounting for the spending of the first tranche was obviously impossible then. I objected, at least as far as the authorization was concerned. I suggested it be subject to the approval of the Chairman of the Contact Committee, and that he should propose this. (*Source:* Jaap le Poole.)

The chairman of the Contact Committee for the Resistance was Willem Drees, who later became prime minister. He quickly decided who should get the second authorization—Walraven van Hall. Finally, the NSF had an agreement covering activities and expenditures of the past and for the future. It occurred just in time—the first 10 million guilders was spent and the need for money was now urgent. Meanwhile, it was the late summer 1944 and the battle for the Netherlands, and with it the role of the NSF, had reached a seemingly new, decisive phase.

Resistance-Group Tensions Persist

Van Hall continued with his coalition-building efforts without a pause. He was annoyed by the discord and that joint efforts sometimes took second place to personal gain. NSF district head Willem de Clercq marveled at how keenly Walraven understood everyone:

> Those who worked with him remember his typical sayings, his postulate of "discipline accepted voluntarily," his regretful remarks about the "little kings"—the leaders of small groups who, for fear of becoming less important, do not want to join a bigger picture—and his sarcastic remark about "secret ambition"[455] when he saw through

the outer appearance to the inner reality. (*Source:* William de Clercq, NSF District Leader.)

The three armed underground forces in particular were now at odds with one another. The armed Amsterdam gang LKP, the *Landelijk KnokPloeg*, was Orange-minded[456] and denominational. The same applied to the Ordedienst (OD), the main difference being that the OD was politically conservative and militaristic. For the Council of Resistance (RVV),[457] the employees were mainly secular, civilian, and often Communist. The officers in the OD leadership did not rule out the possibility that the Communists might want to carry out a revolutionary coup d'état during the power vacuum surrounding the liberation. In addition, the OD, in contrast with the other two groups, could hardly be regarded as a Resistance organization. Since its foundation in 1940, its intention was to keep the OD members passive until liberation and then have them act as body guards and enforcers of the re-installed royal government.

Division and envy were evident among the groups within the Resistance. Chris van der Heijden drove this point home in his book, *Gray Past*, in which he pointed out the difficulty of understanding what was happening and then asserting authority when communications were weak:

> It was an unclear situation to begin with, and it became even murkier because the three groups had no firm agreements among themselves. The "legal government" (Queen and cabinet) soon claimed authority over the Resistance, and yet they were divided. The disintegration of the country meant that local Resistance organizations did not have to heed the "orders from above" if they didn't feel like it. Further confusion was created by the fact that the orders were often unclear. Finally, because of poor communication systems, the orders rarely got through properly. (*Source:* Chris van der Heijen, *Grijs verleden,* "Gray Past,"[458] 1954, in Dutch.)

For example, when disagreement among the three main groups representing the armed Resistance became an annoyance to the government-in-exile in

London, they issued a decree. The Royal Decree of September 5, 1944 established the Domestic Forces,[459] designed to bundle together the KP, OD, and
RVV. Prince Bernhard was named the Commander of this underground army.
That September 5 is also known to history as *Dolle Dinstag*, Mad Tuesday,[460]
the day celebratory emotions got the upper hand throughout the Netherlands.
The madness stemmed from premature reports that the occupied Netherlands
might be liberated at any moment. Twenty-four hours earlier, Allied troops
had conquered Antwerp[461] and it seemed to everyone that it would be a matter
of days before the entire Netherlands would be liberated.

So, on September 6, the commanders of the OD, KP, and RVV met in
Amsterdam at the police headquarters. They all expected the Allied armies to
be moving soon towards the capital and they wanted to be of service when the
time came. At the time of the meeting, however, the three organizations in
Amsterdam commanded no more than about forty armed men—not a number
that would impress either the Germans or the Allies.

The combat groups realized that to be of any value, they must gain strength
quickly and bridge their differences. To that end, they turned of course to Walraven van Hall, the self-proclaimed oilman.[462] He consulted and mediated,
with a good result. Four days after the proclamation of the Royal Decree, the
Top Triangle was a fact, including all the three armed groups. Van Hall provided accommodation for the national headquarters at Nes 25, in the premises
of wholesaler Facentra Welners Zilver. He was also involved in the construction and staffing of the office, and provided access to the clandestine telephone
network.

> To spread the risks, new Domestic Forces quarters were created at
> various addresses. For example, at Van Hall's instigation, office spaces
> were created in the director's residence of the Maritime Training
> School (Prins Hendrikkade 189), in a house (Keizersgracht 533) and at
> the NV Wholesaler in Electrical and Radio Articles Ph.J. Schut (Keiz-
> ersgracht 584). Marie Renée Boissevain, a secretary for the Domestic
> Forces, said: In those September days you hustled, sparing no effort to
> get things going. For the NSF's new offices, you selected people who

knew the Resistance's complicated and careful ways. You approached —under your own name, which was a dangerous experiment in itself, as any word or name mentioned among friends could lead to discovery and arrest by the SD—stock-exchange friends to get them to give up office space. As an agent for the oilman you were everywhere at once, giving courage and getting rid of the rigidity of this new machinery. (*Source:* Marie Renée Boissevain, daughter of former alderman Walrave Boissevain, who was one of the secretaries for the Domestic Forces.)

Amsterdam LO member Dirk Mulder wrote:

Then Van Tuyl comes to me: "Dirk, I need you, because I'm sitting here with a bunch of guys who know nothing about Resistance work." I had to arrange telephone and postal addresses, a few offices, and a whole security apparatus. I was able to draw from my different groups and then I pulled out some addresses for the rural Delta, with telephone numbers and so forth. That had to be done within two days. Van Tuyl always required anything to be done within a certain amount of time. You accepted his deadlines, because he worked from early morning to late evening. Everyone accepted his timetables. (*Source:* Dick Mulder of the LO.)

One of those present remembered how Van Hall showed how he visualized the Domestic Forces using as props an ashtray, a matchbox, and his pipe:

"Look," he said, "This ashtray means the six joint commanders— they are together as much as is necessary and possible. That Lucifer matchbox[463] means the incoming office. So that has to be in another house. And the pipe, the office for outgoing messages, has to go somewhere else. Since then, the command center has been commonly referred to as Ashtray, the second desk as Luci,[464] and the third as Pipe. Van Hall got to work and in a very short time Luci and Pipe were functioning smoothly. (*Source:* "One of those present.")

Looking back, the impression Walraven gave of a smoothly functioning team was a bit misleading. On September 13, Van Hall spoke with Johannes van Bijnen, who had been unilaterally appointed National Sabotage Commander three weeks earlier by the LKP leadership. The Top Triangle decided "to act as an intermediary for the entire country between the Domestic Forces and the commander of those forces," Van Hall informed LKP's Van Bijnen. He explained that a main office in Amsterdam had already been set up, and that the BS would be organized from there throughout the Netherlands. Van Bijnen and his RVV colleague Jan Thijssen thought the construction was "a monstrosity from a military point of view." Together they sent a letter of protest to the Contact Commission of the Resistance, while Thijssen also protested to the government in London.

In Amsterdam, the joint efforts nevertheless continued. Through Van Hall's mediation, the armed Resistance accepted that it would have to lose some independence and would be absorbed by the Domestic Forces. The Top Triangle changed its name to Delta Center, abbreviated Delta C. On September 16, the "KP, OD, RVV, and all other underground organizations and their regional and local branches" were notified that they should function just like the national partnership. Calls were made to "rapidly form regional, district and local triangles," subordinate to Delta C.

A second communication was addressed to the top of the KP and the RVV. Thijssen and Van Bijnen, who were both temporarily in Rotterdam, were invited to join the Amsterdam Domestic Forces leadership. They refused. The Allies were on the march and they didn't want to leave their posts near the front to become part of "a discussion group in the capital that would probably have trouble getting off the ground" (in Van Bijnen's words).[465]

Van Hall also had no time or need for jawboning. They must be ready to fight, even more fiercely than before. A few days after Mad Tuesday, he called Jan Rot (alias De Boer) to meet:

> He instructed me to obtain offices, postal addresses and telephone
> contacts for the espionage service. "It takes effort." Things had gone

smoothly with the postal addresses and telephone contacts, but not so well with obtaining office space. That prompted Van Tuyl to express himself in bitter terms about Amsterdammers who were very patriotic, but who did not dare risk anything. "But we go ahead, right, De Boer?" (*Source:* Jan Rot, alias De Boer.

In the afternoon of September 19, eighteen leaders—of Delta C, RVV, OD, LO, LKP and several other Resistance organizations—met to shape the BS structure. Van Hall was among them. The choice of a general commander was difficult. In the end it was Colonel Henri Koot from The Hague. It suited Koot well that Van Hall set up headquarters in Amsterdam, without having consulted him. He said: "The Hague is such an awful chatterbox, I know that from experience. I wish to blend in with the crowd and Amsterdam doesn't know me." But the choice of Koot did not sit well with Thijssen and Van Bijnen.[466] The new Domestic Forces leader had a lot of work to do with them for the next month and a half.

Clueless in London

In England, the government in exile understood little of the power struggle going on within the Resistance. The London-based Intelligence Bureau sent a message to the Netherlands on September 18: "It is incomprehensible who is now in command. Is it the Triangle or Delta Center? Or are the Triangle and Delta Center identical?" This confusion on the other side of the North Sea lasted well into October. By that time, the Domestic Forces in the still-occupied Netherlands had grown into a fragile partnership tying together 6,800 armed fighters—4,000 with the OD, 1,800 LKP'ers, and 1,000 RVV members.[467]

Although the Domestic Forces were a paramilitary organization, civilian Van Hall remained involved in its design. Behind the scenes, Henri Koot regularly asked him for advice.[468] They discussed policies to be followed to negate all kinds of German financial measures and go through the underground press and Domestic Forces logistics. Once again it showed how much trust Van Hall managed to inspire in his work environment, and how much people wanted his advice.

Problems arose again about control within the triangle, this time the local chain of command. OD commander Wibo Boswijk made several attempts to become commander of the Amsterdam Delta. The two other groups were not in favor of this:

> LKP and RVV do not wish to be pushed aside by an OD clique late in the day," said LKP leader Philip Vermeer. LKP does not accept the new OD leadership. LKP and RVV want to continue with the armies to the front. (*Source:* Loe de Jong.)

Boswijk withdrew his candidacy on September 30, but no alternative candidate was immediately available. On October 2, in the presence of Van Hall (Loe de Jong assumed that this happened at the insistence of Koot, who hoped that Walraven would bring about consensus) two possible candidates for the vacant post were discussed, but without agreement.

Van Hall was the one who again broke the impasse. He was not hostile to the OD, but found Boswijk reactionary and arrogant. Walraven supported, steered, and cemented a consensus. In a surprise to those who were not in the inner circle, the Delta staff presented a new candidate, nominated by Walraven and named by Henri Koot with Delta C's approval. From the Delta minutes:

> Since none of the three members of Delta C could put forward a suitable candidate for the post of commander, the Bureau is announcing someone who can be considered highly suitable for the job and was recommended by the "oilman." The three members will inquire about this person and then give their answer. (*Source:* Delta C minutes.)

The candidate was a Reserve Major in the infantry, Carel F. Overhoff, chairman of the Association of Stockbrokers and a four-year OD member. Van

Hall recognized that his old acquaintance Overhoff would play a more moderate and less prominent role than Boswijk and for that reason might be acceptable to all parties. Moreover, the new candidate had time to spare, as a result of the trading ban on the stock exchange that was introduced a few weeks earlier.

However, the RVV and LKP were not easily convinced. At the first joint meeting, where Carel Overhoff was present, both Resistance organizations deliberately showed up half an hour after the agreed starting time. Overhoff reported:

> The first meeting was decidedly unpleasant. The LKP and RVV leaders saw in me a representative of the "kind" they did not want. They found it hard to accept a Reserve Major, someone who worked at the stock exchange and was its chairman, someone who had been with the OD, and they openly showed this. LKP waltzed in half an hour late with a "Morning, lazy!" and also behaved "independently" with the feeling of "We'll see how that goes!" RVV did the same. (*Source:* Carel Overhoff, *Reminiscences of War*, Amsterdam, 1949, in Dutch.)

Overhoff did his best to get everyone present on the same page. As proof of his goodwill and obliging nature, he decided to call himself within the Domestic Forces by his long-time Resistance pseudonym "Knecht." In his *Reminiscences of War*, he wrote:

> After only very few meetings, the mood changed visibly and it is true that in the end we worked together in great harmony and a great deal of mutual appreciation was established regardless of the distance between us. (*Source:* Overhoff, *Reminiscences.*)

As soon as the Domestic Forces were up and running, Van Hall withdrew. He had no need to come to the fore, despite the fact, noted his secretary Marie Renée Boissevain, that:

Actually, the entire attendance came through our contacts. They often had to call Walraven for help, especially when security issues required a new venue. Our original plan was to distribute the unavoidable meeting risks, as much as possible over several addresses, with a locked headquarters for mail and telephone messages. We had to a minimize the number of people who knew the address of the meeting. You adapted quietly to the limited options. (*Source:* Marie Renée Boissevain, Walraven's secretary.)

American Airmen Given Up

The Domestic Forces were less than a week old when Van Hall had a conflict with one of the Zaandam leaders over the handling of a group of airmen in hiding. On September 11, 1944, the American bomber *Betty-Jane*[469] flew from England to Hanover with ten crew members on board. Near the intended target, German anti-aircraft guns hit an engine of the aircraft. The pilot tried to turn the wobbling aircraft to its base in Norfolk, but slowly lost altitude. Flying above the Zaan river, the distance to the ground was less than three hundred meters. Captain Merrill Olson[470] ordered his crew to parachute out of the B-24. The pilot was given permission to try to reach England with the lighter aircraft, which proved to be successful. The nine other airmen landed at various locations in the Zaandam region. The majority managed to go into hiding with the help of the Zaandam Resistance. The SD[471] searched for them in vain and then demanded that the Resistance give up the crew. They threatened to execute four people if the Americans were not handed over quickly. The threat did not cause Olson's men to emerge.

Two days after the Allied drop, the Germans shot four people dead on the Leeghwater Road in Zaandam. That was not the end of it.[472] Occupation Police Chief Hanns Albin Rauter threatened to have eighteen arrested Zaandammers executed the next day if the airmen were not produced. If his demand was still not heeded, he says, then 100 to 150 random civilians would be shot from moving cars. The Zaandam area commander of the Domestic Forces, Johann van Marle, was ready to meet Rauter's demand.

> "I had a debate about this with Walraven van Hall," he told the local newspaper twenty years later. He said: "I am against giving in to the demands of the Germans. When you resist, you go all the way." I told Van Hall that I did not want to take responsibility [for more reprisals]. (*Source:* Johann van Marle, in Zaandam newspaper.)

Van Marle carried the day. Six Americans ended up in German hands and experienced the end of the war in a POW camp. The other three were kept hidden by the Resistance. The eighteen hostages in jail were released.

So far as is known, Van Hall had no contact with the stranded airmen. In at least one earlier case, according to his courier, he did. In a postwar letter, Weeda wrote that Walraven would often put aside his own interest and be ready to do the most dangerous jobs himself:

> It was always: "Brinkie, I have dangerous fireworks again tomorrow, don't you think it's better if I do it myself?" Or: "Say, some English pilots have to be picked up and taken away tomorrow. Shall I do it?" (*Source:* Lt. der zee L. C. Weeda, Resistance pseudonym van den Brink, postwar letter to Walraven's parents, reprinted in Michael C. Van Hall, *Three Centuries,* 2018 edition, 105.)

The Germans carried out another act of reprisal at the end of September. The sabotage department of the Domestic Forces disabled a railway bridge on the border of Wormerveer and Krommenie. As reprisal, the *Grüne Polizei*[473] set fire to two houses on the Zaanweg in Wormerveer. Johann van Marle, who was in hiding nearby, had to find another hiding place fast. The debate with Van Hall about the American air crew ended without animosity, because Van Marle stayed with Walraven's wife at Westside 42. He was Tilly's guest for several weeks.[474]

Van Hall Hunted (Reprise)

No one knows for sure when the Germans first suspected that Van Hall was involved in Resistance activities, but it had to have been early in the Occupation. Historian Loe de Jong said Walraven had been "wanted for several years by the SD." Gijs van Hall concurred:

> They were looking for my brother for years. He was once raided in Zaandam, because the Germans suspected he was the financier of the Resistance. They were then led off the scent. The Germans had known for a long time that a Mr. Van Tuyl in the Netherlands was actively involved in financing matters, along with a Mr. Van den Berg. In fact, Mr. Van den Berg was Van den Bosch and Mr. Van Tuyl was my brother. Before Mad Tuesday,[475] we obtained access to files concerning financing cases, in which Van Tuyl was a leading suspect and was wanted. The Occupation also had a clue that Van Tuyl was probably a Mr. Van Hall, which is why they raided the Zaandam house. But on Mad Tuesday, the SD[476] left Amsterdam and burned their own archives. Then Ohlschlägel was shot on the Apollolaan.[477] He was an incredibly clever anti-spy, who knew the business. With the files burned and Ohlschlägel dead, we thought we could safely get back to work. (*Source:* Gijs van Hall, The National Support Fund 1943-1945.)

Gijs van Hall's story is supported by Johann van Marle, who said that the SS had searched for Van Tuyl in Amsterdam several times and not found him, but one day they came to his home in Zaandam and searched it:

> The SD confiscated a photo that they incorrectly identified as him. When someone from the NSF was caught, he of course shifted all the blame to the mysterious and untraceable Van Tuyl, because he was sure that the Germans would then reach a dead end. The incorrect photo was a large photo of Tilly 's American girlfriend and her

husband.[478] But the SD believed it was Tilly and Walraven. (*Source:* Johann van Marle.)

Daughter Attie van Hall confirmed the story. She said the SS shouted to her mother: "That's you and your husband and now that we know what he looks like, we'll find him!"

And mother thought: "Then you can search for a long time." The raid on Westside 42 in 1944 happened the night before the "lazy party."[479] When I went out with my girlfriends in the morning, we saw that a window next to our door was broken. We thought it was from "lazy partying."[480] But later I heard from my mother that in the middle of the night the Germans came in and entered my mother's bedroom. They said she had to come. My mother then said: "I insist you let me put on my dressing gown in peace." My father was not there and my mother realized that there was a pile of illegal newspapers on the floor. She said she wanted to go to the bathroom first. She hid those newspapers under her bathrobe and a moment later pushed them deep into the toilet drain, because there was too much to flush. The Germans found nothing and no one, but they said they would come back. (*Source:* Attie van Hall.)

The Amsterdam banker Henri ter Meulen, who acted as a general banker for the NSF, recalled another incident that shows the risks that Walraven took routinely. Her Meulen had worked with Walraven from the beginning, at the Seamen's Fund,[481] and Walraven would often hold a meeting in his office, although it was not ideal, because it lacked a back entrance through which to retreat. Ter Meulen reported:

In August 1944, Wally had just arranged a meeting with me on the street in front of the *Algemeen Handelsblad*. We then noticed that a man was following us with interest.[482] So we got off and boarded several trams independently, after we had agreed to meet at Dikker and Thijs.[483] In the hotel bar, the gentleman who had been following us to the tram stop in front of the Handelsblad also appeared. He offered me a drink, which I immediately declined. He was apparently looking for Wally, because he asked me: "Didn't you just talk to Mr. Van Hall?" I was then able to warn Wally, so that he continued on the tram. After that, no more meetings were held in my office, because that man could have heard the address. (*Source:* Henri ter Meulen.)

Something similar happened to another acquaintance, Kees Ingwersen. He had an appointment to meet with Walraven one evening at 6 pm in the autumn of 1944, at the tram stop for lines 1 and 2, in front of the *Handelsblad*. Walraven thanked him for being on time and suggested another meeting at his office the following week:

We agreed on a date and talked some more about all sorts of things in front of the Handelsblad, until we came up with the idea of having a drink together, to get rid of a man who seemed to be circling us to try to hear what we were saying. We decided to each board a different tram, meeting up in the Zeeland Corner.[484] I got on Line 1. Wally followed a few trams later. When I got to the establishment, I did not see a soul other than the waiters. I ordered a drink that they were unable to bring to me, and was suddenly addressed by the man we believed was following us at the *Handelsblad*. He introduced himself unintelligibly and immediately inquired about Mr. Van Hall, with whom he had seen me talking at the tram stop. What did he do? Did I know his brother Gijs? I answered meaninglessly and quickly left, since the drink I was interested in having was not available anyway. On the street, Wally was just getting off the later tram. I was able to inform him in a few words what had transpired. We postponed the drink and Wally acted immediately, saying: "No meeting at your office next week—and be careful." (*Source:* Kees Ingwersen.)

The Four Suitcases Ransom

At the beginning of September 1944, the NSF had collected about nine million guilders. Thousands of receipts, accounting for the use of the money, were in the office of Gijs van Hall for a while, and then were moved to a somewhat more spacious storage place on the Rokin. They finally ended up at the textile wholesaler De Vries van Buuren at Waterlooplein 1-13.[485] An accountant took seven suitcases full of documents there and deposited them in the office safe. When, a short time later, a house search was reported to be imminent, the receipts were moved again, this time to the attic of De Vries van Buuren. They were thought to be safe there. However, Rotterdam police inspector S. van der Wind, brought to Amsterdam by Walraven to advise on[486] the Resistance investigation, expressed his concern.

> I remember I once heard people talking at the office of the NSF, Leidsegracht 25, about putting away the papers of the NSF. I asked: "Are those papers kept safe?" To which Van Tuyl answered more or less paternally: "Don't worry about that, man. It's fine." (*Source:* Van der Wind.)

When the suitcases disappeared at the beginning of September, it caused great panic at the NSF. Van der Wind continued:

> I might have forgotten all about this conversation, if I hadn't bumped into Van Tuyl and Brinkie on the Nieuwendijk in Amsterdam the day after Mad Tuesday. They called out to me, "Dude, where have you been? Everyone has been looking for you. The papers of the NSF have been stolen!" (*Source:* Van der Wind.)

The seven suitcases were stored on the fifth floor of the Waterlooplein, in a locked room. Someone broke the lock and took four of the suitcases. On September 6, the day that Van der Wind encountered the two NSFers on the Nieuwendijk, the NSF had received a blackmailing letter sent two days earlier:

In our possession are 4 suitcases with papers that are seriously compromising for you and many other prominent persons. We hereby send you some of these as proof. If you would like to receive these suitcases with their full contents back again, we ask for a ransom of ƒ50,000 (fifty thousand guilders). We expect your answer to this: Mr. Van Rietschoten must be in The Red Lion[487] Café tomorrow, Tuesday afternoon, at 3 o'clock (alone) and tell the porter at which table he is located in order to meet our negotiator there. If you do not meet our conditions, we will hand over the suitcases with the name and surname of your co-perpetrators to the appropriate German authorities.—"The Four Suitcases." (*Source:* Letter to NSF from the then-unidentified thief-ransomer.)

The man to whom the letter was addressed, the director of De Vries van Buuren, didn't receive the message until the day after he should have appeared in The Red Lion Café. So there was a chance that the thief had already taken his prizes to the SD. Van Hall asked Van der Wind to take action. Van der Wind wrote:

Messrs. Van Hall and Weeda told me that their dismay was acute. This was understandable, since if the SD started searching these papers and acting on the information in them, they could make a lot of arrests, greatly impeding the work of the NSF across the country. (*Source:* Van der Wind.)

Because of the theft, NSF activities at the headquarters stagnated and the leadership had to go into hiding. Police inspector Van der Wind called in some reliable Amsterdam police officers to retrieve the stolen goods as quickly as possible. He faked a break-in at the company on the Waterlooplein, which gave him an excuse to have the police search the homes of possible suspects of the suitcase robbery. He himself arrested a few candidates, who turned out to be innocent. No one else was arrested. The police officers Van der Wind had involved decided there was no point in continuing to be involved in the case.

A few days later, another ultimatum arrived by mail. This time, underlining the ransom demand, a letter was attached that related to a woman supported by the NSF. The Germans put her husband to death after an insignificant incident. His wife was left with seven children and no income. Gijs van Hall wrote:

> The form[488] was sent in by that man, and he said that if the 50,000 guilders ransom was not paid, the case would be reported to the Germans. So there was a risk that the woman would no longer receive her money. (*Source:* Gijs van Hall, *The National Support Fund 1943-1945.*)

The unknown sender ordered the requested ransom be handed over that day at two o'clock in the afternoon at the corner of Rijnstraat and Jozef Israels quay.[489] These were stressful hours for Van Hall and his Resistance employees. They decided to face the thief, bringing an empty envelope and planning to overpower him at the critical moment.[490] But at two o'clock no one showed up at the agreed place to receive the envelope. However, a former employee of the company where the suitcases were stored was spotted in Rijnstraat. That same evening, Van der Wind and two colleagues arrested this man, posing as police officers working for the SD. A tough interrogation in a hastily arranged cellar produced a confession. Van der Wind:

> During his interrogation I hinted that it was very stupid of him that he had not immediately handed over these suitcases to us, the German police, and that he had been very foolish to try to use them for blackmail to seek his personal enrichment. To which the man said that he "would like to work for us." (*Source:* Van der Wind.)

The suitcases turned out to be hidden on the Nieuwezijds Voorburgwal,[491] where they were picked up. The detainee, still under the impression that police working for the Germans had arrested him, was released with some threats (Van der Wind: "I couldn't bring myself to liquidate this man just for the sake of convenience."). According to Gijs van Hall, he was "an ordinary worker from Amsterdam, who with a few friends had committed a burglary in the shop where he worked." The suitcases with NSF receipts were moved for the umpteenth time, this time to the convent of the Redemptorists at 220 Keizersgracht. There they remained hidden until May 1945. After liberation, the Special Court sentenced the thief to a prison term of five years.

Luckily, the suitcase robbery ended with a fizzle. That was not the case with another attempt to extort money from the NSF. In his book on the NSF, Gijs van Hall devoted one long, bitter sentence to it:

> In the only case where we contributed to a ransom[492] at the request of official authorities, it promptly ended up in the hands of the notorious fraudster Wreszynski. (*Source:* Gijs van Hall, *The National Support Fund 1943-1945.*)

Siegfried Wreszynski was a master con artist. Before the war, he extorted 19.5 million guilders from the Amsterdamsche Bank, among other victims. During the war, this Jewish schemer went into hiding in Amsterdam. Even so, he extracted money from countless gullible people. In the last year of the war, he extorted hundreds of thousands of guilders from relatives of ten imprisoned Resistance fighters in exchange for his promise that he would free them or at least prevent their execution. In one case, the NSF guaranteed the ransom. Wreszynski's claim that he could rescue anyone through his "good connections in high German circles" turned out to be worthless. Nine out of ten of his victims did not survive the war.

Hanneke Eikema Signs Up

In 1944, Hanneke Eikema was a 19-year-old student. She lived in Amsterdam, but regularly visited her parents in Zaandam. Her mother and her father, a Protestant minister whose services the Van Halls occasionally attended, were up to their ears in the Resistance. Their home at 134 Westside was a hive[493] of Resistance activity as well a place to stay for people in hiding. Her father, Jan Eikema,[494] worked closely with Jan Hendrik op den Velde until his arrest, translating coded messages intended for the Dutch government in exile.

Hanneke found her way into the center of the Resistance. On a September day in 1944, she was approached in Zaandam by Jaap Buijs. "If you want work, follow me to Amsterdam tomorrow morning for a new job. Your name will be Miep," said Buijs. At half past eight the next morning, Hanneke followed Buijs to Amsterdam. They stopped at Leidsegracht 5. She remembered:

> A man was waiting for us and I was introduced. He was called Mr. Van Tuyl. He was slender and had a fascinating, strong face with piercing eyes that, to my surprise, could occasionally be kind. "Hello," he said. "You will be my new courier. One of your main tasks is to find different meeting places in Amsterdam where we can go every Friday morning at nine o'clock. Also see if you can heat the place a bit and provide us with some food if possible. You'll be doing a lot of shopping for me the rest of the week, so you'll have to be around all the time. Tell me if you need money and I'll get it. And it would be good if you keep changing what you wear, because you might be followed by the SS.[495] (*Source:* Hanne Eikema, *Memoirs.*)

What the pastor's daughter did not yet know is that Jaap Buijs had her shadowed by his son for the previous six weeks in consultation with Van Hall and that he had examined her *curriculum vitae*. Buijs described his actions, in a postwar letter:

> In mid-August 1944 she asked me if she could be deployed with the NSF. Before using her services, we inquired about her. These investigations showed she had taken care of Jews and people in hiding the year before and that she had done an excellent job. (*Source:* Jaap Buijs, postwar reference for Eikema.)

After her appointment, Hanneke Eikema searched weekly for a suitable meeting place for the leaders of the Dutch Resistance. Every Friday morning, nine of them met somewhere in Amsterdam. One time in a room behind a greengrocer's shop, the next in a classroom of a private school, the basement of a launderette, or a back room in the house of Walraven's mother-in-law. The owners of the meeting places rarely knew who their temporary guests were. Week after week, plans were being made, for the near future and into the months that would become the postwar period.

Walraven's charisma stood out in Eikema's story. First, her interpretation of Walraven's gaze, which she described as "piercing eyes" that can also "be kind." Other Resistance workers also mentioned Van Hall's eyes. "I stay most with his eyes, often tired, but with that familiar, beautiful glow of a benevolent and persevering person, who knows that he is called to something,"[496] wrote a member of the underground. "His bright eyes and his barely controlled urge to forge people together," said NC chief executive Arie van Velsen.[497] Jan Rot: "How wonderfully he could laugh and how expressively his eyes could twinkle."[498] And a fourth was powerfully drawn to Walraven by his eyes: "With his short, sure explanation and with the compelling power of his strong eyes he was irresistible to me."[499]

Second, Walraven's soft but compelling voice was regularly mentioned as a characteristic, as was the tranquility he always radiated. He knew how to put things into perspective with a joke, but also to put people on edge with a single word of warning.

Other qualities of Walraven that stood out, according to Hanneke Eikema, were his professionalism and speed of action. These skills were frequently talked about. His fellow Zaandam townsman Remmert Aten occasionally visited Van Hall at home:

> Often, however, after fifteen minutes he graciously ushered me out the door, because others were already waiting or telephone calls had to be made. He then inquired if everything was going well. He would not listen to details or ordinary difficulties. He left that to us. He briefly discussed the broad outline and the changes in guidelines that sometimes took place, but then preferred to speak of something else, to switch his mind for a moment to something new. (*Source:* Remmert Aten.)

Hanne Eikema
(Wikipedia)

Arie van Velsen wrote:

> When you entered his house, he was all charm. He slapped you
> on the shoulder and you felt a little as though he was overdoing it,
> treating you like a long lost son. But later, when he knew you better,
> and those expressions were no longer necessary, he hardly looked up,
> gave a somewhat short greeting and you sat down and then you spoke
> to him in all simplicity and all confidence. (*Source:* Arie van Velsen.)

Walraven's Work Life

When NSF employee Willem de Clercq had a letter to deliver to Walraven at
his Westside home, things were handled in a friendly but firm manner. He said
he was ushered in to a large room with a bright fire, surrounded by two men
(Walraven and Weeda) and the lady of the house, Tilly. He was invited to join
the other three by the fire.

While one of the two men read the letter quickly, I looked around and saw on the mantelpiece the portrait of an old gentleman with a beard, whom I recognized as a personal friend of my father. A quick comparison with the master of the house's face and I knew whom I had in front of me. Wally discussed the letter with the other man in the room, then threw it into the hearth. Then he gave me some verbal instructions and I already had observed how fast Wally works, with head and hands. I am then quickly pushed out the door, because the bell of obedience is already striking. And that's how it always went. Some arrests were made in Haarlem. Wally got a call. He immediately appeared on the scene. He was in a huge hurry, but he managed to restore order and give instructions within five minutes, and then he vanished as quickly as he came. . . . A friendly organization disagreed with the NSF. The NSF individuals requested authority from Amsterdam. Wally came, saw, and conquered. Quickly and clearly he identified the problems and solved them. (*Source:* William de Clercq, postwar letter to Walraven's parents, reprinted in Michael C. Van Hall, *Three Centuries*, cited, 105-106.)

Despite the immense workload and the inevitable, ever-increasing tensions, Van Hall managed to maintain his optimism and hospitality. Weeda wrote that he wanted to do everything himself and was always afraid of giving someone too much.

In addition, he always had the worry that someone else was not getting enough rest and food. For example, if I came back late at night, it was direct: "Have you already eaten and are you not tired? Come on, let Brinkie have a cup of coffee first." In fact, it has happened more than once that I came in at dinner time and he slid half his piece of fish onto my plate. Always take care of someone else. (*Source:* Weeda.)

Gerrit Huig, Walraven's friend and a printer of Resistance work in Zaandam said: "He always had an open ear for my difficulties and plans. His concern for my well-being was remarkable. Every time I was with him, he warned me to be careful."[500]

Arie van Velsen said that he found Wally to be the greatest figure in the Resistance.

> Wally was a rare pure human being, who achieved an incredible amount. Even in the most serious conversations he kept his sense of humor and could suddenly laugh heartily. In my opinion, he presented himself most as he was towards Buijs and the chief courier Van den Brink. When we came, he would say, "Dude, it's great to have you here. Sit down. Would you like a cup of coffee? Tell me." With Buijs and Van den Brink, however, he just kept up the work. They were his two most trusted comrades. (*Source:* Arie van Velsen.)

NSF member Dirk Vos de Mooij experienced Van Hall 's generosity as a blessing. He was arrested in connection with activities for *Vrij Nederland*. After six and a half months in prison, the Germans released him. Vos de Mooij said that immediately after his return, "Wally was there, one of the first to shake my hand. I can still see him standing in front of my door, carrying a large fruit basket."[501] In passing, Van Hall arranged for Vos de Mooij to catch his breath for a few weeks in Sinderen in Gelderland.

Someone from a completely different socio-political orientation, the Communist worker and RVV representative Gerben Wagenaar, is also full of praise for Walraven:

> Wally van Hall was one of the rarest characters I have ever met. I couldn't guess his occupation in our conversations, but assumed he had been a machinist. He was a man of broad insight and broad views. He had an incredible knack for dealing with people. He was great at improvising and also very honest and sincere. I didn't think he was conservative. He had progressive ideas and I thought his views on social issues went a long way in the right direction. Above all, he was also a very practical man. (*Source:* RVV representative Gerben Wagenaar.)

Walraven's moments for contemplation were rare. Only in the evening, during curfew, was there an occasional opportunity to catch up. At his Amsterdam hiding place, Walraven then talked to his Resistance friends about home, the fear of being separated from his wife and children, post-war politics and religion. The strict Reformed Corrie Overduin said:

> He always said with some pride that he was originally a Calvinist and that he was still attracted to it, although circumstances led his life in a different direction. He was aware of the religious conditions in our country and liked to talk about them. (*Source:* Corrie Overduin, postwar letter to the parents of Walraven van Hall, reprinted in Michael C. Van Hall, 2018, 106-107.)

The conclusion cannot be drawn from Overduin's remark that Van Hall was ecclesiastically oriented. Both before and during the war, frequent church attendance was not a regular part of his life, although he and his family did occasionally visit the services of "Resistance preacher" Eikema. His daughter Attie attended catechism with Eikema, and son Aad attended Sunday school. However, Walraven's affinity for religion stemmed more from a sincere interest in visions of life than from a strong inner urge to believe.

Van Hall was busy day and night with the Resistance. He undertook this work in addition to his work for the banking and securities firm Wed. J. in Veltrup. The continuous commitments and responsibilities were exhausting, but Van Hall kept going. The great Dutch war historian Loe de Jong said:

> He possessed inexhaustible energy, a sharp insight and great organizational talent, but he was first and foremost a warm-feeling person; the tensions of his Resistance life and the fears associated with it never prevented him from feeling exactly how much the other Resistance worker who asked him for advice (or money) could bear. A conversation with Van Tuyl was always something special. He was a man who combined great gifts with great charm; a warm interest for everyone personally. (*Source:* Loe de Jong.)

When the hunted De Koster, leader of espionage group Peggy, knocked on Walraven's door in the autumn of 1944, Walraven knew exactly what was needed.

> He said, "You should sit in a very quiet place with good people for awhile. I know you as calmness itself and you don't give me that impression now. I can give you an address where you can go. It's in this Zaandam area. Come to the Leidsegracht tomorrow." I said that I didn't have a bed for the night. He said this would also be arranged. I was particularly impressed how well the Amsterdam Resistance was now organized. (*Source:* De Koster, leader of the espionage-intelligence group Peggy.)

The Zaandam group provided him with a false identity card in the name of Pieter Cornelis Willink. It then arranged a hiding place for him as well. De Koster said:

> That night I slept in an empty room near the Leidsedwarsstraat. Then I got the address Walraven had promised. I cycled along the winding water of the Zaan river. You almost always think you are cycling against the wind. Past the factories of Verkade, oil mills and remnants of rice mills, I arrived in Zaandijk. The chemical engineer of this company, Boekenoogen, lived just past the Duyvis factory, married to Geert, without children. It was an ideal address. Not a word too much was asked or said. They were circumspect and completely reliable. (*Source:* De Koster.)

These were the daily achievements of the gentle man who came to lead the Dutch Resistance. But his greatest achievement of all was still to come—the bank heist under the Nazi noses of the managers of the Dutch State Bank, which unknowingly funded the Resistance in the darkest days of the Netherlands.

6 | The Railway Strike and Bank Heist (1944–1945)

"Versteeg's children can go to bed'
—DUTCH GOVERNMENT IN EXILE[502]

SUNDAY, SEPTEMBER 17, 1944 was a fateful day for the Dutch. On that day, Allied paratroopers[503] dropped behind German lines, near Arnhem, Eindhoven, and Nijmegen. The 30ᵗʰ British Army Corps then departed from the Belgian Albert Canal, with a plan to make speedy crossings over the bridges to Arnhem.[504] The Allies would then attack Germany in its heartland, where they would join the paratroopers and attack the industrial Ruhr valley area. The German army in the west would be isolated and the Allies would then strike a final blow there. The *cognoscenti* on both sides were sure the end of the war in the Netherlands was weeks away.

The Queen Calls for a Railway Strike

At around seven o'clock in the evening that same day, the OD (*OrdeDienst,* Order Service) decoded a London telegram with the text: "Versteeg's children can go to bed." It was a strike call. Versteeg was the Resistance name for Dutch Railways[505] President-Director Dr. Willem (Wim) Hupkes. The purpose was to stymie German travel through and in the Netherlands—and thereby support the Allied effort. Several times during the evening, author A. den Doolaard[506] announced on Radio Orange that "an important message from the Dutch Government" would follow. The message was:

In response to a query from the Netherlands and after consulting with the Allied Supreme Command,[507] in connection with Dutch operations that started today, the Government has decided that it is a good time for a railway strike,[508] to hinder enemy transport and troop concentrations. (*Source:* A. den Doolaard, Radio Orange, September 17, 1944.)

A large portion[509] of the more than 30,000 Dutch railway employees responded to the call and went into hiding. Staff in Zaandam, two hours after Den Doolaard sent out his call, left the platform and took with them a station cashbox full of strike money. In the days that followed, more railway workers left their jobs.

The Dutch Railways management was taken by surprise,[510] but initially assumed the strike would not last longer than a month. President Hupkes even guessed that the Netherlands would be liberated within two to three weeks.[511] Earlier in 1944, the management had built "invasion greenhouses" in many places to bridge the food needs of those first weeks of liberation.

The tension among the railway workers was acute. Striking was punishable by death and it was unclear how the Occupation would respond. After hours passed, it became clear that the Germans' priority was to defend the front. However, State Commissioner Seyss-Inquart decided on a reprisal—he banned further food transports to the populous western Netherlands. He would starve the Dutch.

Meanwhile, the Allied military initiative, called Operation Market Garden, did not go as planned.[512] Failure is too weak a word. Allied troops were mired in the south of the Netherlands and did not advance as swiftly as the planners of the operation had expected.[513] Valkenswaard was taken on September 17 and Eindhoven on September 18, more or less as expected. But then the Allied advance faltered. The government in London had no reason yet to tell railway workers to end their strike, and the prestige of the Government in Exile was at stake. They decided to continue the call for the strike. It sounded strong for them to say: "The strike must and will succeed." However, given the response of Seyss-Inquart, blocking food transport to the west, shutting down the railway had less impact on the occupying troops or transport to concentration camps than it did on the ability of the Dutch people to eat or get fuel.

> After a few weeks, the German railway officials,[514] with thousands of employees sent by the Reich Railway,[515] put part of the railway network back into operation—but now for German use only. Despite this, the strike call from London on Radio Orange was repeated on October 6, this time from Prime Minister Gerbrandy himself. He said the Dutch government was confirmed in its conviction that the country's interests would not be served by ending the railway strike. So the watchword is: persevere across the board despite all difficulties until the enemy has been cast out of our country with God's help.
> (*Source:* Prime Minister Gerbrandy, Radio Orange, October 6, 1944.)

In December, Seyss-Inquart ended his blockade of food transport to the west, but by then it was too late to prevent a famine. Temperatures were below freezing and much vital water transport was now impossible. The western Netherlands faced the *HongerWinter*, a Hunger Winter with dire coal and food shortages. The appeal to "the little children of Versteeg" therefore heralded the war's most difficult period for the Dutch people. Although the south was liberated, the north—especially the northwest—had at least six murderous months ahead.[516]

The NSF Supports the Strikers

The NSF moved to support the Dutch Railways strike, but their resources were depleted. Van Hall and Van den Bosch ordered the district and local heads to provide additional funding to ensure that the strike would be successful. But this was an impossibly huge new burden. A strike by the largest employer in the Netherlands was on top of support for existing people in hiding and other Resistance needs. The dwarfed previous support efforts. The NSF managed to carve out 100,000 guilders for the Amsterdam strikers on September 21 or 22. Elsewhere in the country, where a strike fund had not been set up or was inaccessible, the NSF helped. In Almelo, Zutphen, Haarlem, Alkmaar, and many other places, the NSF promised financing to, or at least made contact with, strike leaders by the end of the month.

For example, Van Hall contacted Amsterdam LO worker Willem Viersma after the strike call. He told Viersma that the NSF would finance the strike and that the Dutch Railways would provide lists with the names and addresses of the personnel for this purpose. However, Viersma noted that the NSF had set up no distribution network in the Amsterdam, and he suggested using the LO for this. Van Hall agreed and, on the same day, he sent Viersma the first NSF advance.

Although Amsterdam Central Station had its own invasion budget, it took a week and a half to obtain it. The station master there, Antoon Dirk Cupéry, left the money in a safe-deposit box of the *Associatie Cassa* (the Cash Association, a bank founded in 1806),[517] and then went into hiding. When Cupéry was found, he said he did not want to hand over the money. When he finally came around to cooperating, the key to the safe was missing at Central Station. Finally, Van Hall, accompanied by a reliable Dutch Railways employee, entered the office of the *Associatie Cassa* where, after a long and difficult conversation, he had the safe opened. The two men left with 450,000 guilders in strike money.

These NSF finances enabled the Resistance and the strike to carry on. But the Dutch Railways[518] was not grateful. The president-director of the Dutch Railways had long regarded the Resistance leaders as risk-taking adventurers who could not agree on anything. Wim Hupkes tried for four years to keep the German occupiers away from his operations by alternately giving in to German demands and being unruly.[519]

To his credit, he succeeded in excluding Dutch Nazis[520] from the railway management and in protecting most Dutch Railways personnel from the Work Assignment.[521] His trains ran for the Dutch, which meant they could travel as passengers (subject to German laws) and bring back food.

However, his trains also continued to run for the Germans—who used them to transport Jews and other prisoners to concentration camps[522] and move weapons and troops for the German Army. Hupkes believed his job was to keep the trains running for everyone until the Queen told him differently.

The probably last photo of Walraven van Hall, with daughter Mary-Ann in front of his home on the West side of Zaandam (1943). (Van Hall Foundation)

That call came on September 17. Although not informed in advance, Hupkes was loyal to the Queen and allowed the strike to shut down the railways.

But President Hupkes did not welcome NSF support as a way to make the strike a success. Although the NSF offered help at once, at first Hupkes avoided accepting their help. The Labor Council, which worked closely with him,[523] expected the Netherlands to be liberated within a month. Hupkes argued that this brief period should be bridged with accumulated strike funds.

When it became clear that the war was going to continue for months,[524] everyone understood that the strike money was too small a fund. Then the question arose: "Who will finance the strikers?" The Dutch Railways leader was willing to let the NSF pay, but he wanted to keep handling the payroll and receipts. This would enable Hupkes and Labor Council chairman Gerrit Joustra to claim credit after the war for the railway strike and for maintaining support to the workers. In postwar assessments[525] of who was "right" or "wrong" during the war, such evidence could be decisive. The NSF and the LO were reluctant to accept this approach and wanted the NSF, LO, and the Dutch Railways to cooperate via local committees. The LO would ensure that benefits reached the correct people in hiding, while receipts became NSF property. Both Resistance organizations also wanted to keep payments to railway personnel in line with payments to other people in hiding.

A stalemate ensued, although B. H. de Jongh, the NSF district head in Utrecht, discussed the strike problems with Hupkes weekly. They could not agree on a working method—some disagreements between the NSF and the LO, and between the NSF and the Staff Council, were insurmountable. On October 7, Walraven consulted with G. Koot, at that time representative of the Staff Council. Koot reported that Walraven suggested he could now speak on behalf of the Dutch Railways management as well as for the NSF, but Koop did not respond. Walraven's assistant Weeda also tried to reach an agreement with the Staff Council in Haarlem on October 20. In vain.

To break the impasse, on November 1, Walraven and De Jongh together confronted the Labor Council chairman, Gerrit Joustra, and H.C.A. van Eldik Thieme, who represented railway President Hupkes.

On November 19. Walraven and Gijs van Hall traveled with Douwe Westra—who then lived in Hilversum—to Bilthoven, where Hupkes himself and Joustra were waiting for them. Gijs van Hall wrote that Walraven stayed with him near Hilversum and on Sunday they left together on bicycle for Bilthoven.

> Westra was to meet us in the woods of the Lage Vuursche. He was there, but a bomb had fallen on his house during the night and he had to return immediately to find another place to live. So Wally and I went alone. (*Source:* Gijs van Hall.)

At Hupkes's hiding place, deep in the forest, things came to a head. Gigs later wrote that the NSF refused to agree to withhold support from railway workers who were political enemies, notably the Communists. "We flatly refused to remove certain people[526] from local committees simply because they opposed the Labor Council." The Labor Council's chairman, Mr. Joustra, had incidentally angered some railway people because he had traveled to Germany to see what the Nazi "Strength through Joy"[527] program for workers was achieving.

> Joustra tenaciously complained, not for the first time, that some strike money in Amsterdam and Haarlem was going to Communists, who opposed his union. He demanded the NSF stop supporting them. Walraven answered decisively: "No. It is the NSF's duty to support[528] the strike. It is not our duty to support feuds of the Dutch Railways management or the Labor Council." Walraven ordered that all Amsterdam and Haarlem strikers be paid. Our job was in making the railway strike a success. After that, Mr. Joustra finally kept his mouth shut and we had a pleasant conversation with Hupkes about what the NSF would do. (*Source:* Gijs van Hall.)

Hupkes repeated his wish that he handle the payroll payments himself. Gijs and Walraven van Hall agreed to that. One reason was that they were quietly worried about how they would get the money to pay for the strikers. It was a huge leap of faith, because the NSF's money on hand would last for just two more weeks. Any solution was still just an an idea.

Unfortunately, the minute the NSF acceded to Hupkes's wishes, he walked back on his agreement. He was probably worrying about about how little cash the Dutch Railways had, and the likelihood that the Occupation would stop payments to the strikers.[529] Ultimately Hupkes agreed only that (1) the NSF would finance the strike and (2) the Labor Council would remain involved.

According to one of the NC leaders, the two sides of the "pleasant conversation" on November 19 were anything but pleasant, and it was a failure.

> Both Van Hall and Hupkes were authoritarian figures who cut off others from speaking. Hupkes argued that the Dutch Railways

should handle payments and should not have to promise to provide any kinds of receipts. (*Source:* Marie Anne Tellegen, leader of the NC, *Nationaal Comité.*)

Another NC leader had similar memories of the November 19 conversation between Hupkes and Van Hall. It was not a success:

> The two personalities clashed. Hupkes spoke from his lofty position as president of the Dutch Railways. Wally usually never put himself in the foreground and was never at all ambitious, but in this situation he was grandiose.[530] He stressed that the NSF was providing the finances for the workers and thereby enabling the strike. Wally insisted that the NSF's role meant it had to retain accountability for funds. I was absent, but Hupkes informed me afterwards that, contrary to what I had assured him before the meeting, he found the conversation unproductive. Wally in turn said to me about Hupkes: "His eye was on a lot of moolah for him!"[531] That wasn't fair, but Wally could be just as acerbic as Hupkes. (*Source:* Arie van Velsen, representing the NC.)

The author Adolf Rüter, in his book on the railway strike, said:

> Mr. Prakken remembers that Mr. W. van Hall once said to him about Hupkes: "Such a big man in such a small box. He thinks he has something to say, but he doesn't." (*Source:* Adolf Rüter, *Riding and Striking*, previously cited.)

Not until early 1945 did the Dutch Railways management and the NSF agree how to handle payments to the striking railway workers. Van Hall kept up the pressure. In a letter to Dutch Railways President Hupkes, Van Hall referred to their agreement of eleven days earlier:

When we talked, I made quite clear that the NSF could only do its job if it has total responsibility for financial reporting. (*Source:* Walraven van Hall, letter to Hupkes, November 30, 1944.)

Van Hall believed that the Labor Council[532] had "not sufficiently informed" Hupkes about the full extent of NSF aid to the strikers up till then, and that Hupkes was also "not properly informed that railway officials had issues with the Labor Council."[533] He asked Hupkes to confirm what they had agreed on November 19, that the NSF would be fully responsible for both the checks and the receipts. To add emphasis to the letter, he asked an NC leader[534] to urge Hupkes to grant the NSF's wishes. The NC man did so and he summarized the dispute between the two men as a question of who would keep the receipts:

The NSF wanted receipts and Hupkes refused to give them. On behalf of the NC, I told Hupkes, "Under normal circumstances, the easy solution would be to create duplicate receipts. But in this case, I can see that would be unwise. So I suggested the receipts be stored at a neutral address." At first he said no. But then I told him that if he didn't agree, I would end my participation. He said he needed time to think about it. In the end, he agreed to depositing the receipts at neutral addresses. However, by then it was nearly Christmas. (*Source:* Lambertus Neher of NC, letter to De Jongh.)

The outcome was that the NSF agreed to pay the full wages of railway workers, while keeping support in line with that of other people in hiding. The NSF agreed to involve the Labor Council. On January 7, 1945, they agreed with "what Mr. Van Tuyl wished for in Haarlem,"[535] namely storing receipts at the Dutch Trading Company[536] until liberation.[537] Van Hall prevailed.

Unions Opposed Support to Communists

Van Hall was fully aware, from the start, that some within the Resistance resented the Communists, especially union leaders like Gerrit Joustra on the Labor Council. Their resentment was rational, because the Communists opposed the unions. Van Hall had an early taste of this back on September 26, 1944, at an Amsterdam meeting with a representative of the Labor Council, W. Brouwer. After a postponed morning meeting,[538] Van Hall offered Brouwer NSF support for striking railway workers, as well as an office for handling payments. At the meeting, the OD representative,[539] who as usual worked closely with the NSF, said he would organize delivery of money to railway employees. Van Hall's only condition was that Brouwer's organization should not "exclude dissident workers,"[540] i.e., Communists. Van Hall believed the Resistance should be as inclusive as possible. Adolf Rüter, in his book on the railway workers' strike, noted that Brouwer then dismissed Walraven's proposal:

> Brouwer said: "We and the Dutch Railways will pay our workers.[541] We don't need charity from the NSF." The OD representative told Van Hall that in this case he would leave the meeting, since if the NSF is not needed, he would have nothing to do. However, Van Hall asked him to stay, because he explained that Brouwer was inexperienced with Resistance work and other things. (*Source:* Rüter, *Riding and Striking*, previously cited.)

Brouwer finally realized he had to accept Van Hall's conditions. He agreed. Brouwer would pay all striking railroad workers, including those whose opinions he disapproved of. Unfortunately, Brouwer broke this agreement. A month and a half afterwards, he wrote to Joustra from his 30 Amstel office that Van Hall had arranged for him:

> I did not ask what they meant by dissidents. That became an issue later on. I thought it was more important that the Labor Council

continued to hold the purse strings, so that decisions about who was paid were centralized through me. (*Source:* Brouwer.)

Brouwer succeeded in excluding Communists and other opponents of the trade union movement when paying the 4,600 Amsterdam striking railway employees.

The Central Bureau's Railway Office,[542] which Brouwer set up, was operating improperly in other ways. Many strikers got their money late or not at all. Lists of names circulated without enough care, putting the LO especially at great risk. The Labor Council caused some chaos because it was more concerned about building its reputation for postwar political purposes than with forming a coalition. After the war, Jacobus Lootsma said about Brouwer:

> He was acting not to serve the NSF, but to serve his own interest. This is precisely what Mr. Van Hall repeatedly warned against at meetings when he said: "*We serve.* Not, *I deserve.*"[543] (*Source:* Jacobus Lootsma.)

Van Hall discussed Brouwer's independent behavior with an NC representative, who said:

> Brouwer was such an impossible man to work with. He would sail under no one else's flag.[544] Van Hall said: "We have to work with Brouwer. Let's just work it out with him." Lootsma was instructed by Van Hall to "keep things together." If cooperation was impossible, Brouwer would have to leave. But the railway management and the Labor Council did not want this. (*Source:* NC Representative Albert Prakken.)

Unsurprisingly, the people Bouwer eliminated from his payroll were furious and called on the NSF leadership to help.

On October 9, 1944, it all came to a head. Leaders of the "free railway groups"—the NSF, the LO, and the Dutch Railways Central Bureau—held a meeting in the Prins Hendrikkade. Van Hall sat at the head of a long table. He began by announcing that the meeting was called to investigate allegations against Brouwer, who was present. Van Hall honed the edge of the discussion by stating outright that "someone here has behaved in a dubious way, to say the least. If he did not have a history of going about his work with good intentions, he would not leave the meeting today alive." The Communist railwayman Leo ter Laare, who was also present, later remembered what Van Hall said next: "We have our eye on you, Brouwer." At that point, Ter Laare said, "Mr. Brouwer collapsed like an old man."[545]

During the emotional meeting, Van Hall saw that the problem was not just idiosyncratic behavior by Brouwer, but deep-seated distrust among people with different political allegiances. He realized that just pushing Brouwer aside would not clear the air. Ter Laare said:

> In that meeting, Van Hall's position was that Brouwer was not the enemy. For the time being no judgment should be made about accusations against him. These accusations would be dealt with by a tribunal after liberation. (*Source:* Leo ter Laare, Communist railway worker.)

Van Hall made a plea for cooperation based on trust, as the only way to move forward. So, for the time being, Brouwer and his Central Bureau remained in place. The independent railway groups were given the task of tracking down strikers who had received little or no money until then and remedying the situation.

Frictions nonetheless persisted that placed demands on Walraven's empathy and negotiating skills, in part because President Hupkes[546] continued to support Brouwer. The controversy ended only in December 1944, when Brouwer was arrested. After that he no longer had the Central Bureau "in his own hands,"[547] and the problem seemed solved.

However, it was still not over. Walraven was advised of payment problems in Haarlem. Once again, distribution of funds was affected by the presence of Communist on local committees. The rift was closed only through great mediation efforts by Van Hall.

Overall, the payments to the strikers, Dutch Railways pensioners, and companies affiliated with the railways proceeded without major issues. The 33,553 railway payroll employees in 1944 received their money every month.[548] In December, NSF even paid a Christmas bonus demanded by the Labor Council. Nearly 60 percent of the required finances of 63.4 million guilders was provided by the NSF,[549] with the rest supplied by the Dutch Railways and by contributions from private individuals.

The key fact to understand is that without the NSF's regular stream of payouts, the Occupation probably would have broken the strike. Railway employees were not all Resistance fighters. With every hiccup in pay packets, some "disadvantaged persons" threatened to return to work. In Groningen, 190 Dutch Railways employees refused to strike unless assured of a monthly salary in advance, with another month's wages set aside as "security" at an institution they would designate. The NSF refused their ultimatum and also didn't budge[550] when the driving staff demanded mileage money.[551]

Finding the Money

All the local groups understood the importance of raising money to pay the striking railway workers. The National Assault Gang[552] hunted for money for the strikers in months when NSF money did not fully fund the payroll. Two successful fundraising moves and one unsuccessful one are especially worth citing, all occurring around September 1944:

- *In Utrecht, a success.* The Resistance cracked the safe of the Utrecht Dutch Railways headquarters. The proceeds were 1 million guilders, which the NSF kept.

- *In Olst, Nijmegen, and Rotterdam, successes.* Gangs succeeded in capturing more than 1.3 million guilders. Part of the money went to the NSF, which kept it.

- *In Almelo, success and then failure.* A regional National Assault Gang in Almelo, in the eastern Netherlands, was tipped off that about 130 million guilders in cash was headed to the local branch of the Dutch State Bank[553] from its headquarters in Amsterdam. Nazi Commissioner[554] Arthur Seyss-Inquart ordered the move so money could be more quickly transported to Germany in the event of an Allied breakthrough. On November 15, a group of eight local Assault Gang members raided the Almelo branch and removed more than 46 million guilders—the largest bank robbery to that time in Dutch history. The Almelo haul was largely destined for the NSF, but the money never left the city. After a few weeks, during a street check, the Nazi police arrested a motorcycle courier with forged papers. Through him, the Germans tracked down some of the bank robbers. To prevent more arrests, the local Resistance revealed where the money was hidden and returned it all. Most of those involved did not survive the war.[555]

The Resistance leadership was not sorry the Almelo money was returned. According to a surviving report from the Kern, they deeply regretted the robbery and requested those receiving the money to refuse it. The Kern condemned armed bank robberies because:

> Such robberies lead to local stresses and to unsavory individuals attempting them in the name of Resistance, while likelihood of success is remote, because the numbers of stolen banknotes are recorded, and a watch is put on them. (*Source:* Kern report.)

While the Resistance leadership said they disapproved of stealing from banks, Walraven van Hall went on to steal even more from the Dutch State Bank than the Almelo gang. But his theft was more sophisticated and was astonishingly successful. It funded the NSF indefinitely. The brilliant theft of Treasury bills from the Dutch State Bank—which earned Walraven the title of "Banker of the Resistance"—was never discovered by the Occupation. How did Walraven do it?

G. C. M. Smit, who began helping the NSF in 1943, argued that the

Germans were just careless and failed to take enough interest in the NSF. The Occupation cared about the organizations with armed agents, the illegal press, the escape line through Belgium for refugees. These were the German targets, not the organization that funding everything:

> The Germans did not realize that the NSF was the financial bed-rock of the Resistance. Everyone in the Resistance had to be paid. make a living. All one smart German had to do was to figure out how someone who sat at home without a job was paid. Enough Dutch Nazis[556] were around to find and report such people. A guard posted at the house could intercept a courier bringing money. Following back the money would have brought them to the NSF. Breaking the Resistance would then have been simple. Fortunately, the Occupation overlooked the obvious. (*Source:* G. C. M. Smit, in Gijs van Hall, *The NSF,* previously cited.)

Smit's theory might reasonably describe the first two years of the Occupation, but certainly not the years 1943-1944, when the an active and unsuccessful hunt for the mysterious Mr. Van Tuyl was under way. The main reasons the SD[557] was unable to track the NSF after Mad Tuesday[558] were that NSF methods were good at ensuring secrecy, in the absence of betrayal, and the Occupation was distracted by slow-but-steady Allied advances in the Netherlands.

The NSF managed to do what the Queen ordered, fund the strikers. But, sadly, the order had more impact on the Dutch people and the Resistance itself than on the mobility of the German Occupation. A few thousand German railway[559] workers posted in the Netherlands got part of the railway system operating again within a few weeks, and they were able to meet Germany's railway needs. The public and the Resistance, however, no longer had rail service and by then had hardly any other way of getting around. The few cars still in use during the fourth year of the Occupation were generally under German control, and gasoline was so expensive few could maintain a car in any case. The bicycle remained, but those in reasonable condition were a favorite prey for the German Army and Landwatchers.[560]

The Germans showed little interest in the source of the illegal flow of cash to people in hiding. The bank account of the Dutch Railways was not frozen until November 22, 1944. By then, it was too late, as payments were moving through other channels. In a letter to Seyss-Inquart, Dutch Nazi Meinoud Rost van Tonningen, head of the Dutch State Bank, apologized: *"We have temporarily put off examining the question of how this strike is financed."*[561]

By then, postponement meant never doing it. Despite arrests of dozens of NSF employees, the work of the NSF itself was never interrupted. The arrested leaders remained silent, and the few who were forced to speak up had too little information to pause the NSF's activities. Its many precautions were effective.

Based on full documentation, the organization supported at least 150,000 individuals in its last year, after the Dutch Railways workers were added. The NSF had committed itself to supporting all these people without nearly enough money on hand. Even before the railway strike, the NSF was supporting 45,000 people in hiding and their dependents[562] and 6,000 seamen's households.[563]

On September 17, 1944, the NSF had 1.5 million guilders left, *about one week's cash flow.* The Queen's call added nearly 30,000 striking railway strikers. Walraven had to find the money for them and their dependents, a 60 percent increase in the burden.

This was the challenge Walraven wrestled with in September 1944. He was on the edge of desperation and could safely discuss it only with his brother Gijs and his courier Weeda.

This new heavy burden for the NSF from the Queen was accompanied by another one. The Dutch Nazi director of The Dutch State Bank,[564] Rost van Tonningen, on Mad Tuesday, September 5, 1944, prohibited any bank withdrawal of more than 100 guilders, except for salaries, pensions, or redundancy benefits.[565] The Mad Tuesday[566] celebrations were disastrously premature. More money was urgently needed to keep the railway strike going—lots of money, five to six million guilders per month, almost the entire amount the NSF had spent up to that point.

The Big Banks Pony Up

Serendipitously, that day Walraven had a previously scheduled meeting with a fellow banker.[567] on September 17, the day that the Operation Market-Garden disaster began and a few hours before the railway strike was declared. The banker said:

> Wally had asked me if I would visit him that Sunday. We spent an entire afternoon talking at his aunt Den Tex's house about his plan to appeal to the banks for more support.[568] (*Source:* Henri ter Meulen.)

Within two weeks, the Van Hall brothers had approached ten Amsterdam banks[569] for loans to be paid from their cash reserves; eight of them agreed. Since it was entirely illegal, it was a major risk for the banks. Bankers revered the law, because the Wall Street crash and bank panics made it essential to show the public they were trustworthy, and to restore depositors' confidence. Bank owners and their employees rarely confronted the Occupation or joined the Resistance for fear of Nazi reprisals.

Despite the risks, the Van Halls went ahead. On October 1, 1944, Walraven visited Carel Overhoff, chairman of the Association for the Securities Trade. Walraven explained he needed 1.7 million guilders within five days. Overhoff wrote later:

> Walraven was at his wit's end. He asked me to meet with bankers to obtain the needed fund. Credit was not what he needed, but actual cash. The NSF had decided to approach Cornelis Collot d'Escury, the director of the Dutch Trading Company.[570] That Sunday the three of them met and prepared a plan for a larger meeting, inviting high finance.[571] (*Source:* Carel Overhoff.)

Overhoff made the phone calls. They brought representatives of the eight Amsterdam banks that agreed to meet around the table the next day; only two refused. At the meeting, Walraven explained the problems to them with such clarity and conviction that within half an hour he had commitments from the banks for 3.5 million guilders. That gave the NSF one month's breathing space. Overhoff said: "It was no small success. It was one of the most remarkable meetings I have ever witnessed."[572]

The banks used various pretexts on their ledgers to justify (i.e., camouflage) the illegal outflow of aid money. For example, the Netherlands Trading Company pretended to have sent 500,000 guilders to the agency in Eindhoven just before the liberation of the southern Netherlands. They reported that because communications were broken,[573] no receipt was received back from Eindhoven and the bank created fictitious correspondence with the local branch to serve as the necessary paper trail for the transaction.

The problem was that only the Dutch State Bank had enough guilder notes to meet the NSF's longer-term needs. The Van Halls had to figure out how to transfer some of these guilder notes to the eight Amsterdam banks that were cooperating in the NSF financing. The idea was, if that worked, the NSF might get access to some of this money.

Gijs van Hall began his begging tour at the Twente Bank. He met with director Herman van Leeuwen, a friend. He knew Van Leeuwen was stung[574] by the Nazis—a Landwatcher had just shot his son on Mad Tuesday. The conversation went something like this:

Van Hall: "Would it not be difficult if bombs were to fall on The Dutch State Bank, blocking access to the banknote vaults? Would it not be a sensible measure to create a separate emergency fund? It could then be kept in a safe deposit box, with the key in the hands of the management, to be used only in an emergency."

Van Leeuwen: "I never thought of that! An excellent idea!"

Van Hall: "Listen. First, I have no interest in whether or not you can pay out your customers' withdrawals. Second, of course, a bomb will never fall on the Dutch State Bank. That's why you probably think it's a bit strange that I propose this to you. Still, I would like you to form that cash reserve. But I want you to put the money in the safe in theory and in practice to give it to the NSF."

The administration of the National Support Fund.
(Dutch Institute for War Documentation)

Van Leeuwen: "I have to discuss that with my colleagues first. How much do you want?"

Van Hall: "Half a million a month from each bank." (*Source:* Conversation recreated by Erik Schaap, 2014, 124.)

Van Leeuwen's colleagues agreed to the plan.

To carry out the plan, the Twente Bank went to the Dutch State Bank's Cashier General Cornelis Wilhelmus Ritter for a large quantity of banknotes. Ritter explained to his employees that the special arrangement had been agreed upon by the State Bank's management, i.e., Nazi leader Rost van Tonningen. Of course, management knew nothing about it.

From then on, Twente Bank pretended to add 500,000 guilders every month to its cash reserve. In fact, Gijs van Hall entered the head office on Spuistraat monthly, put the plastic-wrapped[575] five tons—five thousand 100-guilder banknotes—in a suitcase and, leaving behind some old securities as IOUs, walked out. The Amsterdam Bank accounted for its monthly half-million guilders by selling diamonds and postponing booking profits until after the liberation.

It was a huge step for the bank executives to participate in these illegal NSF operation, not just because of the visibility of the gigantic sums being moved around, and the consequent dangers to those involved, but also because banking protocol was being defied.

Few places in the country followed rules as strictly as the Dutch State Bank. Work clothes, the wording of letters and memos—everything was pre-scribed to the last detail. For example, when someone left the board room, the etiquette then was that staff should shuffle backwards, as with royalty. Follow-ing the rules was everything. In this environment, any monkeying with the bank's guilders was unimaginable.[576]

Nevertheless, other banks followed the Twente Bank's bold move. The Incas-so-Bank had a different approach. Director Reinier Koole realized it was not only the Dutch State Bank that could be bombed, but his own bank's head office. Part of the bank's cash supply should therefore be transferred to branches. In the following months, chain-smoking Koole handed over to the NSF the 500,000 guilders in cash that he picked up every month from the bank's headquarters. Instead of guilders, he carried to branch offices emptied cigar boxes, wrapped in paper and sealed. He deposited the packages, giving branch employees the impression that cash had been transferred to their safe. Koole enjoyed the game:

> "You know, Van Hall, what I have found to be a problem for me?" he told Gijs: "When I enter a branch with a large package, the branch manager immediately asks: 'Let me carry that for you, Mr. Koole.' But of course I can't let him do that, because it weighs nothing!" (*Source: Reinier Koole.*)

Through these various banking games, the NSF had access to more than eight million guilders, enough to cover its payments in November and Decem-ber 1944. But the banks using the reserves coverup had to stop after those two months. The Nazi managers of the Dutch State Bank eventually found it dubious that these banks were increasing their monthly reserves when the local economy was barely functioning. The NSF was forced to find another source of money.

Meanwhile, on January 10, 1945, the good news was that the Government in Exile increased its maximum guaranteed repayment from 10 million to 30 million guilders. This guarantee limit was swiftly reached in support of the railway strikers. On December 2, the NSF informed London that the remainder of the initial 30 million guilders would be spent within a month and asked if the limit could be raised.

The Queen guaranteed repayment of 5.5 million guilders per month, but only for the first three months of 1945, clearly not enough money. The Board[577] asked for an increase to 80 million guilders. One month later on February 13, 1945, the increase was granted, with the reassuring message: "Pledged credit for NSF is now a total of eighty million."[578] This meant the guarantee gap had been eliminated for the time being. But, once again, a guarantee was not the same as cash.

Planning the State Bank Heist

Where would the NSF find the cash? Gijs van Hall came up with an ingenious idea. He remembered a bank fraud from the 1930s that generated millions for its creator, the Swedish match manufacturer Ivar Kreuger.[579] Kreuger borrowed money from an Italian bank using counterfeit bank promissory notes as collateral.[580] Gijs van Hall wrote later:

> I heard this story in detail, because I worked then for a bank very closely affiliated with the banker for Kreuger and Toll. From A to Z, I heard how the man had done it. My idea was—what Mr. Kreuger could do, we could do, but with counterfeit Treasury bills. (*Source:* Gijs van Hall.)

The Van Halls realized that it was not possible with available tools to produce perfectly forged Treasury bills.[581] The risk of discovery was too great,

Forged treasury bill, 1944 (Dutch Institute for War Documentation)

because the details of the securities were by design hard to copy. Treasury bills passed through countless hands. Moreover, the economic consequences could be serious if counterfeit Treasury bills were still circulating after liberation. Therefore, circulation of these Treasury bills had to be kept to an absolute minimum. The Van Halls' brilliant solution was to exchange the forged Treasury bills for real ones in the vaults. Then the real bills could be removed and sold safely, for the benefit of the NSF. After the war, the government would repay the banks that loaned money based on the counterfeit paper.

The substitution trick was ingeniously simple. However, its implementation was dangerous and definitely not simple. One question was whether the Resistance could generate a plausible forgery of a Dutch Treasury bill. Walraven took the challenge to the Personal Identification Center,[582] with which NSF had worked closely, having by then paid the PBC nearly 450,000 guilders for fake IDs. Forging Treasury bills, nicknamed "lottery tickets," was a huge counterfeiting challenge.

   1. To begin with, the paper the Treasury bills were printed on had embedded blue, green, purple, and red hairs. Such paper was not for sale anywhere and therefore had to be counterfeited. This was achieved by an offset book-and-art

Cornelis Ritter's room at De Nederlandsche Bank. (Allard Pierson Museum)

printer in The Hague, Mouton & Co. An employee of the Personal Identification Center came up with the idea of covering a glass plate with red lead and making scratches on it to represent the hairs. By applying a new cliché,[583] in turn, for each of the four required colors, the printer created sheets of paper that suggested embedded hairs. Each sheet was large enough to make two Treasury bills.

   2. The second step was to create three clichés. This took place in Warmoesstraat,[584] Amsterdam. The Union Cliché Factory created three more clichés for further printing—one for the text, one for the gray background (containing the coat of arms of the Netherlands), and one for the border. Each cliché was then taken to Spin & Sons at the New-Side Front-Bastion Wall,[585] where the different colors of the Treasury bill were printed on a simple stepping-platen press. It was hard work, but the printers didn't complain. "It warmed you up a bit in the cold," said manager Willem Keet of Spin & Sons.[586]

3. The third step was the manual application of the text that the State of the Netherlands undertook to pay 100,000 guilders to the bearer. The date of issue and the expiry date were affixed with a stamp, which had been separately prepared. Then the signature of the acting agent of the Ministry of Finance and the name of the Government Postal Savings Bank,[587] the owner of the coveted Treasury bills, were filled in by hand.

4. In the fourth step, another printer, Monopole in the Govert Flinckstraat, filled in the numbers from the genuine Treasury bills due for redemption. Before the finished Treasury bills were handed over to Walraven van Hall, master forger Ab Oeldrich spent three nights perfecting them. Only after the war could Oeldrich tell his worried wife where he spent those nights.

5. All this painstaking forgery work would have been for nothing if the cashier general of the Dutch State Bank, Cornelis Ritter, refused to cooperate. As head of the vault department, Ritter had to exchange the forged Treasury bills for the genuine ones deposited with the Dutch State Bank. A Dutchman, he had previously helped when reserve funds were transferred to banks in favor of the NSF. Gijs van Hall easily convinced Ritter of the plan, but Ritter's condition was that he first obtain a green light from some board members who resigned in 1941. He got it. Preparations were ready. The largest Dutch bank heist in history was underway. It may be the largest documented bank heist in world history.[588]

Addressing Sexism in the Resistance

No sooner had this huge challenge been met, than Walraven van Hall had another to face.[589] Opposition to the Resistance one day, conflicts within it another day—he was constantly running the gauntlet. This time the internal conflict was between the leaders of Group 2000 and those of *Vrij Nederland*. After dozens of employees of the underground magazine *Vrij Nederland* were arrested in the spring of 1941, the leader of Group 2000, Jacoba van Tongeren, thought it wise to cut loose her group's close ties with it and go into hiding. Group 2000 handled the care of, 4,500 people in hiding.[590]

Three years later, members of Group 2000 and *Vrij Nederland* tried to resume cooperation. However, a major hurdle was that the leaders of the two organizations couldn't stand each other. Van Tongeren compared the editor-in-chief of the Resistance magazine to a German potentate. The editor, Henk van Randwijk, in turn later called her "that person from 2000 who adds more misery to my life than the Gestapo." Van Randwijk's idea for resolving their differences was to absorb Group 2000.[591] Walraven van Hall's task was to bring these characters and their important groups together, in such a way that one did not outshine the other.

At the end of September or the beginning of October 1944, the representatives of the two groups gathered in the Central Bureau for Social Work at 520 Herengracht. After the war, Jacoba van Tongeren wrote her impressions of that emotionally charged meeting. Everyone was there on time, except for two people.

> At a quarter past the hour, Henk van Randwijk and [Assault Gang leader] Sjoerd Gerbrandy arrived together, with heavy footfalls.[592] No one said anything, but Mr. Van Hall's look at his wristwatch spoke for itself. After a short word of welcome to those present, I handed the chairman's gavel to Mr. Van Hall, but with a courteous gesture he returned the chairman's gavel to me. "Today we are the guests of 2000," he said, with a meaningful look at his friend Van Meer. (*Source:* Jacoba van Tongeren.)

After listening to both parties present their views, Van Hall gave, according to Van Tongeren, "a magisterial speech" in which he filleted the "petty-bourgeois," narrow-minded quarrel for priority within the ranks of the Resistance." He took sides in favor of Group 2000 and against the annexation attempts of *Vrij Nederland*.

> Once Mr. Van Hall finished speaking, no one wanted to say anything. The facts were clear. The two distinct groups, Vrij Nederland and Group 2000, could not merge. (*Source:* Jacoba van Tongeren.)

Jacoba van Tongeren, the only female leader of a Dutch Resistance group, revered Walraven van Hall as the man who stood by her side when she was under attack.[593] During the break in the meeting she gave him "her stammering thanks."[594] Van Hall responded:

> Don't thank me. Here today is the place and the time to speak these words of fitting tribute to the daughter who will have a hard enough time, I fear, with such ambitious fellow Resistance members. (*Source:* Van Hall is quoted by Van Tongeren.)

The meeting continued according to Van Tongeren's wishes.

> When everyone had left, I retreated to my room for a while and to my surprise found Messrs. Van Hall, Van Meer, and Van Tongeren in a debriefing. I wanted to leave without being noticed, but Van Meer was already approaching me: "No, no, no, we are the burglars here." Mr. Van Hall was attentively contemplating the copper engraving on the wall. "I suppose," he said, "this is your lofty chamber, with open windows to Jerusalem. The great in the Resistance is verily a prophet in Israel." (*Source:* Van Tongeren.)

The 1940–1945 Foundation

Friday, October 13 was a memorable day for the Resistance. Not far from Walraven's parental home at 567 Keizersgracht in Amsterdam, the Foundation 1940-1945 was established.[595] Twenty-one organizations showed up. A *Vrij Nederland* worker wrote:

> It was the most worrisome meeting I had ever attended during the war. You didn't know who was who. There could be a provocateur among us. We could be ambushed. I had absolutely no idea where it would be. I had received the message that I had to be at the

Rijksmuseum at half past nine in the morning. A guy would pick me up there. I was given a piece of paper. He had something like that too. Those two pieces had to fit together. They called it a Turkish pass. It worked. (*Source:* Arie van Namen, *Vrij Nederland.*)

On behalf of the NSF and Natura,[596] Jaap Buijs took a seat on the first foundation board. The founding meeting of the 1940-1945 Foundation was the provisional final piece of earlier consultations about the post-war future of the resistance fighters. At about the same time, within the Resistance, the decision was made to develop an aid plan in which the people in hiding in particular and the affected citizens in general would be central. It is clear that even after the liberation they would not be able to return to their old lives at once. Central roles in setting up this plan were reserved for the LO [for people in hiding], the Domestic Forces, and the NSF.

On November 1, Van Hall discussed the plan that had now been worked out with the organizations involved. He and his fellow combatants realized that aid to war victims was largely a government task, but they also believed that the civilian population should be given an important role. They expected that the post-war social distress would be so great that the civil servants would not be able to cope with the problems. Charities should not go back to the religious pre-war approach, with the organizations working independently of one other. One semi-government institution headed by a government commissioner with extensive powers should assist the thousands of people in hiding, deportees, and evacuees, efficiently and decisively.

The name of the new organization was the National Recovery Committee. After the liberation, the name became the Dutch People's Recovery.

The Dutch People's Recovery arose from a dialogue between Wally and me, originally about the return to society of Jews and Jewish children in hiding. The concept for such an institute, which was first given a different name, was set up by both of us and worked out by me. (*Source:* Lambertus Neher.)

After some discussion, the Kern agreed to the new organization on November 3. In addition to the LO and the NSF, all kinds of assistance, welfare and health care institutions were taking part. On November 16 their cooperation was confirmed,[597] and a day later a telegram was sent to London:

> **November 17.** Insert: . . . Provide training to organizations generally helping those affected by war. Ensure cooperation among government, church, private initiatives, and the Resistance." (*Source:* Telegram from the Kern to London government in exile.)

This was added, and eight days later, the government-in-exile gave its consent. The National Recovery Committee was a fact, and the initiators sent couriers throughout the country to inform the district heads about the plan to form local and regional committees. From May 1945, the organization assisted the government to:

> Help the Netherlands out of its first postwar difficulties as quickly as possible. It addressed the material needs of the plundered Netherlands: housing, clothing, furniture, stoves, pots, and pans. Help came in wagonloads from everywhere, even from America. We dealt with its distribution. (*Source:* Deputy director Frida le Cosquino de Bussy,)

Van Hall's name was linked, possibly without his knowing, to another organization—the Central Financing Foundation.[598] Its charter was drawn up on November 20, 1944 at a notary in newly liberated Eindhoven. Its creation culminated months of negotiations between, in particular, the NSF leader in the south, Andreas Gelderblom, and various Domestic Forces officials reporting to Prince Bernhard. On September 26, it stipulated that

> The National Support Fund will act as the central agency for financing of all expenditure by the Domestic Forces in the liberated areas and wherever else this should be necessary. (*Source:* Regulation on the Financing of the Domestic Armed Forces, under the auspices of Prince Bernhard.)

In other words, from then on the NSF was responsible for paying the salaries and clothing allowance of tens of thousands of Domestic Forces employees. This new financing entity was renamed the Central Financing Foundation to avoid drawing the attention of the Germans to the NSF in the still-occupied part of the Netherlands.

Gelderblom and others were appointed to the board on November 20. Five days later, a secret statement was added to the foundation's incorporation, listing Iman J. van den Bosch[599] and Walraven van Hall as co-directors, to be represented—"as long as said persons are prevented from exercising their administrative functions as a result of the war"—by Eindhoven NSF members N. A. J. Voorhoeve and J. Wijsman. This was the only Resistance activity to which the born *trouble-shooter*[600] Van Hall's name was attached that did not require him to do any work.

Van Hall helped create another entity from which he then withdrew—the Commission for the Restoration of the Port of Amsterdam. Tonny Eggink explained later how he had fled Arnhem when it was attacked by the Allies and was temporarily living in Bussum. He received a request from his friend since childhood, Van Hall, to come to Amsterdam. Eggink wrote:

> We met in the American Lunchroom and here he confided in me: "Tonny, you must help us. The Krauts have destroyed some of the harbor cranes.[601] More will follow—we have their destruction plan in our hands. The port of Amsterdam must remain open. The English must be able to come here with food and other aid." In the afternoon he gave an introductory speech to some insiders, explaining what had to be done, that the technical work was beyond his experience, but that he would stay in touch and get whatever we needed. He followed through on all this. He brought us into contact with numerous authorities. He handled it like a general in his staff quarters. He never lost himself in details, he listened during the evening when I reported and he indicated with a few lines in which direction further work should go. For us, what Wally said was law and we worked hard. We elected him a member of the board of directors of what soon grew

into the Port of Amsterdam Recovery Committee. He thanked us for the kind gesture, and said he would like to decline the honor. "I greatly appreciate your gesture, but I work for a good cause and not for myself. Since I'm not technical, I see this as an honorary job and I don't want that." (*Source:* Tonny Eggink.)

Van Hall therefore did not join the Port Commission board, but in other respects he violated his own rule that limited to a minimum his participation in non-NSF Resistance organizations. He feared that too much involvement would enable a domino effect after an arrest, so that the Germans could easily attack one organization after another. He was not only aware of the danger himself, he warned others about it. He made an exception for himself, guided as he was by an irrepressible inner urge to do things. His skills were valued and he found it difficult to say no. He was the spider in too many webs.

Van den Bosch's Capture and Execution

In mid-October, 1944, the NSF sustained a heavy blow: the arrest and killing of Iman van den Bosch. His last message to Walraven was written, in stages, on October 15-16, 1944. He wrote about a scheduled money transfer. Early in October, to fund the northern provinces, Walraven sent two female couriers— one to Groningen with 400,000 guilders and one to Leeuwarden with 300,000 guilders in their pockets. Normally, all money traffic for the north goes through Van den Bosch, who was in hiding in Groningen. He did not like resources being delivered directly to Leeuwarden. Friesland was an unruly province that initially refused to obtain the receipts required by Van Hall. Van den Bosch managed to get the chauvinistic Frisians to comply with the receipt system, but Walraven's delivery of money threatened to disrupt his hard-won agreement. According to the courier Jetske (pseudonym of Henriëtte van Styrum), who had been sent to Groningen, "Van den Bosch was outraged. He said he would so inform Van Hall, but he did not give me a letter." As already mentioned, his last messages were sent in pieces, and in code. Here are a few lines from the long epistle:

October 15, 1944. Your niece[602] arrived the day before yesterday and handed us the welcome gift. It is a pity that she and her friend did not turn to me first, for I fear your gift for Leeuwarden may fall into unauthorized hands. It must make a strange impression there that gifts are suddenly laid out before them, behind the back of the leadership they accepted! I sent your niece back to Leeuwarden with the request to collect the gift deposited there and bring it here, so that I can provide from here what is needed. You know that Friesland, in particular, likes to handle its possessions in a self-willed way, using them for purposes we do not consider a priority.

October 16, 1944. What I feared yesterday has happened. The Friesland district has detached itself from us "by authority directly from Amsterdam" and are going their own way! I do not agree to this and have sent Miep to Leeuwarden with my inspector's emissary to save what can still be saved. Your niece is expected back in Groningen tomorrow. I doubt she was able to get the money back. They appeal to you, and where does that leave me? Look at it from my point of view![603] (*Source:* Van den Bosch to Van Hall.)

On October 18, Van den Bosch was arrested, with his courier "Miep" de Wilde, the NSF district head Fré Legger, and Assault Gang commander Henk de Ridder. The four had planned a meeting about the Domestic Forces branch to be formed in Groningen. De Wilde wrote:

That afternoon we were caught by the SD. I had gone to an address on Parkweg,[604] where we would meet, because I wanted to speak to another worker beforehand. I arrived with him. I didn't trust the address, but he thought that was silly. With the words "on your responsibility," I rang the bell. We walked right into the arms of the SD. We were standing together in the front room when I saw Van den Bosch coming. I signaled him. Unfortunately, our guard saw that and shot through the window, hitting Van den Bosch in the shoulder. (*Source:* De Wilde to Van Hall.)

Van den Bosch managed to reach a nearby bicycle shop and hand over some incriminating documents to a staff member there. The SD then found him and arrested him. He was bandaged in a hospital and then locked up. In the days that followed, he remained silent to his interrogators, who at first did not know exactly who he was. After a few days his identity was revealed by a betrayal. With the approval of Van Hall, the NSF in Groningen attempted to buy his freedom with payment of 100,000 guilders. In vain. The Germans placed Van den Bosch on a list of death row inmates.[605] NSF employee Andreas Gelderblom wrote:

> After some painful interrogations, which he endured bravely without revealing anything, the ring was closed around him. The sentence was carried out in Westerbork on October 28. Standing straight and fearless, he awaited the bullet of his assassins, and with the cry of "Long live the Queen" one of our most distinguished Resistance fighters, one of our noblest men, fell for his fatherland. (*Source:* Andreas Gelderblom.)

How Hard It Was to Travel in 1944–1945

With Van den Bosch dead, and Gelderblom out of reach in liberated Eindhoven, the NSF leadership was now completely in the hands of Gijs and Walraven. Their superhuman task was made much harder by the railway strike and the lack of communication with the liberated Dutch south, since few telephone connections remained. The Allies bombed the roads on which the couriers transported NSF money to the district chiefs. Raids took place repeatedly. In addition, men of the age of Walraven and Gijs were arrested under the Work Assignment law. It was increasingly difficult to find meeting addresses. The food was slowly running out. Any bike that still looked even at all usable was taken. The same had long before already happened with most civilian cars.[606] Trains, buses, and trams were no longer running because of strikes and fuel shortages.

The situation that this led to became clear from the story of courier Jetske. In October, with great difficulty, she transferred the 400,000 guilders from Walraven van Hall to Iman J. van den Bosch, and traveled back to the capital to report Van den Bosch's arrest. She was then sent back to Groningen. Jetske wrote:

It was very difficult to find a boat. The Lemmerboot was full of evacuees from Arnhem. Thanks to the river police I got to the boat. But this boat hit a wreck at the Oranjesluizen and sank. We were able to get to the side via an attic barge with iron beams. Then we went again with the Lemmerboot and arrived in Lemmer. From there with a German tug to Groningen. I was on the second barge with a German and a Dutch boy who was transferring penicillin. The German gave me his bunk for the night, but after that I had trouble keeping him out of my hut. (*Source:* Jetske, pseudonym of Henriëtte van Styrum.)

The couriers, and also Gijs and Walraven themselves, cycled back and forth with "rye sandwiches," money packages with five hundred notes of 100 guilders (half a "ton"). It was possible to transport only a limited number of sandwiches per bicycle, hidden in a bicycle bag or in a potato bag. Traveling with dilapidated bicycles, often fitted with solid tires, they crossed the country distributing money. The local Resistance had to take care of breaking the hundred-guilder notes into smaller denominations. It was impossible to distribute large packages of 10- or even 50-guilder notes from Amsterdam without being noticed.

Swiping T Bills from Under Nazi Noses

The railway strike therefore presented numerous new obstacles. But the main obstacle was still the same—acquiring sufficient income. The Treasury bills were intended to solve the acute financing requirement. Just to pay the 30,000 railway strikers, 5-6 million guilders were needed every month. On top of that immense amount, the obligations before September 17 remained, and they also cost millions of guilders per month. The first Treasury bills were ready and approved in November 1944. The counterfeiting process was therefore functioning as planned, but this was not the end of the road.

The NSF and cashier-general Ritter needed to get the genuine Treasury bills out of the vaults and substitute the counterfeit ones. They agreed that someone should regularly visit The Dutch State Bank with forged bills. The bills were there, on the Rokin, under lock and key in the cellar vaults. To exchange the forged bills, Ritter needed the help of the cellar masters. It was quite unusual for the "lottery tickets" to leave the vault. Among other things, Ritter used the excuses that "there was something wrong with the Treasury bills from the State Postal Savings Bank"[607] or that some German official ("It's really something for those Krauts," he complained to the cellar masters) wanted to check some promissory notes, since there might be counterfeit copies in circulation. Again and again, the cellar masters provided the requested securities to Ritter, who in turn signed and returned a receipt. Ritter then walked to his room with the loot. That's where Gijs van Hall waited. Together they compared the real and fake promissory notes by numbers, dates, and other characteristics. As soon as everything was found to be in order, an exchange took place and Gijs van Hall left with the original copies. Ritter in turn ensured that the imitations ended up in the safe, where the cellar masters compared the numbers on the securities with the numbers on the receipt signed by Ritter. From November 1944 on, the transfer operations took place about fifteen times and amounted to 51 million guilders.

No one noticed anything wrong with the promissory notes during those months for two reasons. First, the forgeries were of a high quality. Second, the lighting in the area of the safe was poor. Because of the wartime destruction, the electricity was not working and work on site was done by candlelight. Nevertheless, it almost went wrong once. A bank employee discovered a wine-colored shine on one of the securities in the presence of the Nazi director Jan Robertson. Cornelis Ritter prevented the bank employee's curiosity from snowballing out of control. He saved the NSF from a disaster by reacting quickly.

Gijs van Hall attributed the willingness of a law-respecting man like Ritter to assist the NSF to the apparent death of two of his sons as a result of the German actions.

> One had just joined the Dutch air force when the war broke out. He had gone to England with the remaining aircraft and all the personnel. Mr. Ritter understood that his son had become a pilot there, and because many were killed in the RAF, he was convinced that his son was no longer among the living. His second son was involved in

Resistance work and had been betrayed, arrested, and sent to a Nacht-und-Nebel camp in Germany.[608] Whoever went this route was usually dead within a few months. Therefore, Mr. Ritter never expected to see either of his two sons again. He was sure that they had sacrificed their lives for the fatherland and he felt he should do what he could himself. We could always count on him. The good thing is that both his sons returned after the war. They survived. (*Source:* Gijs van Hall.)

Operation *Tante Betje*,[609] the code word for the exchange of promissory notes, took place with the knowledge and consent of the Government Postal Savings Bank,[610] the owner of the documents. Even before the counterfeiting started, the director arranged for the NSF to have access to the necessary numbers and dates of issue of the original promissory notes. No difficulties were therefore to be expected at this bank during the exchange of the securities. But other financial institutions would be surprised if RPS promissory notes suddenly appeared on the market in such large quantities—first, because this bank never sold promissory notes; second, because it was not logical that millions worth of recently issued securities were on the market.

This problem was also solved. The Kas-Vereeniging, an Amsterdam bank,[611] managed 180 million guilders in Treasury bills that were freely negotiable. The management was willing to exchange its own promissory notes for RPS papers—on condition that the government in London gave its approval via Radio Orange. The requested permission came in the form of the cryptic statement: "Let brown pull." By then it was April 12, 1945 and the occupation of the Netherlands was within a month of ending. The Kas-Vereeniging didn't take it too seriously. From the start, they cooperated without complaint in what was the largest bank fraud ever in the Netherlands.

Exchanging the Treasury bills for cash was the last stage in a long series of steps in the execution of the fraud. Director Rost van Tonningen of The Dutch State Bank decreed on September 5, 1944 that issuing cash would be limited to 100 guilders per week, unless salaries had to be paid. The Treasury bills, each with a value of 100,000 guilders, could not therefore be submitted to any random bank.

Gijs van Hall remembered an annual report from the chocolate factory Kwatta. The Occupation ordered the company to transfer its profits to the Fund for Closed Companies, administered by the Main Group Industry.[612] The Fund was created to provide severance payments to laid-off employees of companies closed because the war disrupted their supply chains. Fortunately, the Main Group Industry chairman was Frans den Hollander, former chairman of Artillery Installations[613] and manager of the Incasso Institute. Den Hollander had already tried to thwart the Occupation. Now he was ready to help the Resistance:

> Walraven van Hall: "Mr. Den Hollander, does the Fund for Closed Companies have much money?"
> Frans Den Hollander: "Not a penny. Everything was paid out."
> Van Hall: "Is that widely known?"
> Den Hollander: "No. How would anyone know?"
> Van Hall: "So there could be a lot of money there?»
> Den Hollander: "If they had any money, it would have to be paid out immediately." (*Source:* Conversation recreated by Erik Schaap.)

The two of them came up with a plan. The Fund would report it had invested its income in Treasury bills. But because of the Allied advance, it unexpectedly required more money for redundancy pay. Some Treasury bills, therefore, had to be sold. For this they opened an account for the Main Group Industry.

Frans den Hollander and Gijs and Walraven van Hall then approached five major banks with their nonsense story,[614] allowing bank directors to explain their involvement (though they knew it was invented). All five boards were alerted to the plan. From January 1945 on, the NSF provided 400,000 guilders worth of "lottery tickets" to each bank every week. The banks then each wrote a check for that amount to the Dutch State Bank, for the benefit of Den Hollander's Fund, marked "For wages and salaries." The Dutch State Bank then paid out this amount in cash. Every Friday, Van Hall returned to his office with several million guilders.

Finding money for the strikers, people in hiding, and Resistance organizations was a problem no longer. The NSF could now pump immense and increasing amounts of money around the country. But strange new problems arose. One was the labels on the packages of money. One of the distributors wrote:

> The money was in packages, wrapped in plastic, of five hundred 100-guilder banknotes. Each package had a label on it from the Dutch State Bank reading "500 banknotes of 100 guilders." The people who had received these bundles to distribute liked the labels so much, they kept them. Then their kids played with them in the street! Next time, we removed the labels. (*Source:* Distributor.)

Another problem was the crispness of the notes. Utrecht student C. J. van der Lee[615] remembered the day NSF distributor Peter Plantenga walked in with 1.2 million guilders in his pocket—all brand new and therefore conspicuous. Plantenga admonished those present: "Go outside for a walk in the grass and the dirt and then come back inside with dirty shoes. *Don't wipe your feet.*"[616] When the residents returned, the floor was covered with thousands of hundred-guilder notes. They walked over the bills a few times, after which the "used" notes were ready to be exchanged for smaller denominations.[617] Van der Lee wrote upon the local NSF accounts in a notebook with the masked heading: "Insulin Units Dispensed to Patients."

Some Traders Sold Shares Stolen from Jews

Most large Dutch banks helped the NSF, but the record should show that they also cooperated in misappropriating[618] Jewish property. Financial institutions like the Twente Bank, the Dutch Trading Company,[619] and the Amsterdam Bank loaned millions to the Resistance, but also traded securities they knew were stolen from Jews.

Right after the invasion, the original Jewish owners were required to hand in all their money, securities, and other valuable assets to Lippmann, Rosenthal & Co., a bank in Amsterdam's Sarphatistraat.[620] The Occupation confiscated Jewish property worth more than one billion guilders, and the "Liro securities," about one-third of the total loot, were sold on the Amsterdam stock exchange.

The proceeds financed deportation of Jews and the operation of Dutch camps Vught and Westerbork. At the time, tens of thousands of Jews were being deported to concentration camps.

Radio Orange warned against trading in Jewish possessions. The government-in-exile's campaign complicated robber-bank Liro's selling of the securities. It had to lower the sale price and raise brokers' commissions. But with these incentives more than one-third of the specialists[621] and brokers at the stock exchange eagerly traded the securities. "Of the 375 stock-exchange members in 1942-1944, almost 140 bowed to Mammon."[622] Chairman Carel Overhoff of the Association of Securities Brokers[623] defended handling the stolen goods on the dubious basis that the securities would thereby at least remain in Dutch hands.

Did the banks assist the NSF out of patriotism or altruism, or did they hope to hedge their bets on the future, and wash their hands somewhat clean, by helping the NSF? No one knows.

Walraven and Gijs van Hall undoubtedly knew about the trading of Jewish shares. Walraven worked as a commission agent at a stock exchange firm, and Gijs worked at an office that administered portfolios. Their father was chairman of the stock exchange until 1941. His successor Overhoff was well known to the family and worked with the Resistance.

A postwar letter from the Utrecht Mortgage Bank[624] shows that in 1943 Walraven himself became an owner of Jewish securities. The Utrecht Mortgage Bank bought Jewish shares that Lippmann Rosenthal & Co. had acquired. The Occupation viewed Lippmann Rosenthal as a Jewish company. The bank would be taken over by the German caretaker unless an Aryanization Permit[625] was obtained. To get this permit, the Liro shares had to be sold to non-Jews at short notice. A trick was devised to prevent appointment of a caretaker German manager.[626] Walraven explained it in a letter to his wife Tilly:

> Some of my business friends "bought" as many shares of Lippmann Rosenthal as they were allowed, given the statutory maximum of thirty shares per person. They borrowed money from our bank to buy the securities. The shares were transferred to their name, but

stayed in our safe—the coupons were not even cut. (*Source:* Walraven van Hall, letter to Tilly van Lennep van Hall, 1943.)

He sent her this letter because in the early summer of 1943, Walraven had 28 Jewish shares of the Utrecht Mortgage Bank, at 75 guilders each, in his name. The intent was clear that after the war, if Walraven should not survive, Tilly should return the shares to the original owners.

Walraven's and Gjis's father, Adriaan van Hall, also had access to Jewish property. As executor of the will of a Jewish man living in Belgium, Adriaan managed a life insurance policy taken out around 1900. The man was a musician at the Palace for Industry[627] and left for Belgium after his contract expired. When Lirobank requested the annual insurance premium of 10,000 guilders, Adriaan van Hall devised a stalling tactic. He responded that he would like to pay the premium, but he did not know whether the Belgian complied with Dutch legislation. If not, the money should probably be deposited with "a Belgian Lippmann Rosenthal."[628] A few years later, Adriaan was advised that the Belgian authorities had agreed to the transfer to the Dutch Liro. Adriaan asked for a copy of this decision, which was not finalized until 1944. By then, the Belgian civil administration was replaced by a military one. Adriaan asked: "Do the new commanders agree with their predecessors' decision?" Lippmann Rosenthal did not answer. In this case, Jewish property survived the war without having changed hands.

Father Van Hall also chaired the Supervisory Board of the Leer factories in Oisterwijk. The Jewish owners escaped to the United States at the start of the war. Van Hall dealt with the day-to-day affairs of the factories with the caretaker the Germans appointed for this Jewish property. Various German institutions were trying to get their hands on these immense factories, and Adriaan skillfully played them off against one another. He even used his deafness as a weapon. Van Hall claimed all verbal communications were unclear and repeatedly demanded written responses, which took a long time. None of the German institutions took control, and ownership of the factories ultimately remained in the Netherlands. After the war, Adriaan van Hall transferred the company back to the original Jewish owners.

The NSF Paid Out 50.9 Million in 1944–45

Money from the NSF kept most Resistance activities going. Walraven and Gijs van Hall were called upon from all sides. They were increasingly able to meet the demand for cash. Johann van Marle wrote:

> Large amounts were borrowed, especially by Wally. He would then tell someone casually that he had come back from Twente, in the eastern Netherlands, with one million guilders—mentioned as if he'd said that he had bought back a cigar. After the September days of 1944, Wally was Prime Minister of the entire Resistance. Financially, all of the major Resistance institutions were brought under the NSF. Through the Kern, the NSF had brought together the LO (the major Resistance group for people in hiding), Trouw, NBS, and NC, and created one central point, radiating out, from which every Resistance group could be organized. (*Source:* Johann van Marle.)

SPENDING BY THE NSF,
MAY 1944 TO APRIL 1945, GUILDERS

RECIPIENT	AMOUNT	PURPOSE
Religious Groups	800,000	Relief
Natura	800,000	Food, Clothing
Artists, Non-Nazi	250,000	Income
PBC	420,000	Identity Cards
Espionage Groups	965,000	Intelligence
CS-6, LKP, OD	6,000,000	Armed Resistance
Group J	4,700,00	Aid to Jews
Dutch Railway Strikers	37,000,000	Continuance of Pay
TOTAL FOR YEAR	50,935,000	

Translator's Note: The total of 50.9 million guilders was equivalent to $484.5 million in 2024 dollars at the immediate prewar exchange rate of $0.56 per guilder. By the end of the Occupation, the NSF had paid out 83.8 million guilders and had 22.5 million on hand, for a total raised of 106.4 million guilders. At the immediate prewar guilder exchange rate of $0.56, the 2024 value of what the NSF raised (the 1945 dollar is worth 17 times the 2024 dollar) was $1,009 million in 2024 dollars, a little more than $1 billion.[629] Most of that money was raised and spent in the last year.

In the last year of the Occupation, more than 800,000 guilders[630] went to the confessional[631] Resistance organizations. Natura, the food and clothing organization headed by Jaap Buijs, received approximately the same amount. The NSF spent about 250,000 guilders on artists who refused to become members of the Nazi Kultuurkamer.[632] It spent 420,000 guilders on forged identity cards and other documents for hiding and other Resistance activities.

NSF earmarked 965,000 guilders for intelligence/espionage, more than 6 million guilders for armed resistance, and 4.7 million guilders for the J Group, assistance to Jews. But most of the NSF money went to the Dutch Railways strikers—more than 37 million guilders.

Special NSF Projects

"Small" Resistance ideas and activities were not ignored. For example, in 1944 the draftsman Jan Rot wanted to create a new underground social-democratic trade union magazine. He wrote:

> I had several conversations with Van Tuyl about supporting the illegal magazine Paraat. I found out he wasn't ready to go skate on thin ice.[633] My request was not smoothly resolved. I thought Paraat was entitled to recognition and said so, perhaps ad nauseam, to Van Tuyl. I always came to the address Leidsegracht 5 in the afternoon, until Van Tuyl finally invited me to come "tomorrow at 3 o'clock." The next day, standing in the corridor, he said to me: "Ready. I recognize

you. What do you need?" There was something in his voice that gave me the assurance that Van Tuyl was happy when he was able to make others happy. (*Source:* Jan Rot.)

Walraven van Hall was not entirely enthusiastic about the subsidy for the new magazine, which appeared for the first time in August 1944. He wasn't the only one. The illustrated periodical, one of the few of its kind during the war, was widely criticized for its party-political character and its Johnny-come-lately founding date.

The NSF supported another, smaller effort by Amsterdammer Anna Marie le Cosquino de Bussy, a Walraven acquaintance. During World War I, she helped German soldiers interned in the Netherlands. After the war, she was awarded a German decoration for her kindness. More than twenty years later, she used the decoration in her rescue work—starting before the Occupation, when she transferred German-Jewish children to Great Britain. After May 1940, she used her deception to help camp victims.

> She called herself, enterprising as she was, "International Red Cross Sister," and pinned on herself a Red Cross. She invoked her German decoration and pushed herself through to various offices of the SD. (*Source:* Louis de Jong. SD stands for *SicherheitsDienst*, Secret Service, the bloodhound investigators of the SS.)

Cosquino de Bussy tried to provide food to prisoners in concentration camp Vught. When Lower Commander Karl Chmielewski refused her entry to the camp, she wrote to Commissioner General Hanns Albin Rauter on January 17, 1943:

> About fifty people die here every day. Here people suffer like never before anywhere in the Netherlands. In the name of humanity I ask you as an old, harmless mother: Let me do for my countrymen what I used to do for your country, let me help prisoners. (*Source:* Louis de Jong.)

Rauter changed direction.[634] A few days later, the so-called Red Cross Sister reported to the camp gate with three trucks full of food and medicines. She continued to help camp victims in the Netherlands and Germany for the next two years. Much of the food she brought was paid for by the NSF. "Particularly from the Zaan region, a lot came from Resistance circles. Van Hall, head of NSF, was my great friend."[635]

Even the neutral Red Cross benefited from the NSF. The Germans were beginning to object to blood transfusions, afraid that "Aryan" blood would get mixed with "non-Aryan" blood. Money for transporting blood started to become scarce. The NSF provided the blood transfusion service with money for gasoline, so that cars carrying blood plasma and flasks of fresh blood could continue to transport them. In exchange, the Resistance received blood where necessary and the Red Cross trucks carried NSF remittances to the north and east of the Netherlands.

Three Resistance Women Arrested

At the beginning of December 1944, a courier and two Domestic Forces[636] secretaries were arrested at the Rijksmuseum. One was a niece or cousin of Walraven van Hall, Louise (Lies) Boissevain. Walraven had recruited Lies (known as Elizabeth) and her sister Roos for a job at a branch office of the Domestic Forces a few months earlier. After a short time, the sisters arrived at headquarters. Van Hall's assistant, Weeda, was one of the first to learn of the arrest of the three women and was concerned:

> When Elizabeth Boissevain was arrested, she carried the key to Delta C, the headquarters of the Commander of the Domestic Forces, General Koot. (*Source:* Laurens Weeda, letter to Walraven's parents, cited in Michael C. Van Hall, *Three Centuries*, 104-105.)

Weeda did not know that on the night of Lies Boissevain's arrest, she had managed to flush the key down the toilet—so he alerted Van Hall from the

NSF office at Leidsegracht 48. Walraven was hiding in the adjacent house at number 46 and in response he climbed over the fence and took action to prevent the headquarters of the Domestic Forces from being emptied by the Germans. In the house annex was office space where the names of many Resistance groups and lists of their members were kept, as well as a stock of weapons.

Van Hall called the head of the Assault Gang teams,[637] now part of the Domestic Forces, via a secret telephone line. He directed them to bring the then-sick Domestic Forces General Koot to safety. He also called an Assault Gang deputy head, Reineveld Goedkoop, requesting him to come immediately. Weeda said: "We couldn't get in touch with one of our armed squads, and yet the place had to be emptied before the SD got there." Weeda explained that they had to secure the Domestic Forces inventory of weapons and papers. They reviewed the options. Then:

> Walraven decided to take the plunge. "We must do it ourselves," he said. The three of us went in the dark, at 5 a.m., to Keizersgracht 533.[638] The big unknown was whether or not the Germans were already inside. We briefly debated who would open the door first and go upstairs. Wally said, firmly: "I will do that myself." Only at his signal should we approach. We protested, but he at once entered the house alone, unarmed, knowing that the SD could be waiting for us. We waited outside. Thank God, Lies Boissevain[639] must have been silent about the location. We got the all-clear signal and emptied the desk quickly, undisturbed. I removed the weapons. Van Hall and Reineveld Goedkoop took out most of the files. An hour later, we returned with a cargo bike and carted the remainder to a hiding place. (*Source:* Laurens Weeda, letter to Walraven's parents, quoted by Gijs van Hall, *The National Support Fund*, in Dutch, and by Michael C. van Hall, *Three Centuries*, 104-105.)

As usual, Walraven did not ask for volunteers. He was the first to take on the biggest challenges, the most dangerous work. His bravery would catch up with him.

7 | Betrayal and Execution (1945)

> *"Just a little while and it's done."*
> —WALRAVEN VAN HALL

DURING THE HUNGER WINTER, Walraven van Hall was working to his limits, and beyond them. His friend Jaap Buijs commented how often he noticed that Van Hall came to a meeting exhausted:

> [Walraven] had previously complained to me he was almost unable to cope with the work. Yet when he met comrades who were depressed, either because close friends had been arrested or shot, or because the work had not been going right, then with never-failing energy he helped them through their doldrums[640] and gave them the courage to continue. (*Source:* Jaap Buijs, *Diaries.*)

Walraven's Exhaustion

Buijs was not the only one who noticed this. Walraven's courier and relative, Marie Boissevain, said that one cold Monday morning she was in the office with other Resistance workers. Outside the building the wind was biting, and the office had only a small stove that did not begin to heat the large room. Then Walraven (Van Tuyl)[641] stood in front of them—covered in snow, but cheerful and full of energy, wearing bottle sleeves[642] tied around his ankles to protect himself from the cold and snow, since he had to leave before dawn to bicycle from Zaandam to the office:

Immediately, he took off his dirty but much-loved old hat, from which he was never separated. It was a cheery symbol for us. He filled the hat to the brim with more coke, and brought it to the underperforming stove. If anyone else had tried this, the heating source would no doubt have given up with a sigh. But the stove couldn't resist Van Tuyl's attention. It was red-hot within ten minutes. With both people and things he had the same magical touch. His contagious zest for life got everything and everyone going. When Wally came in, everyone was happy in five minutes. He could still joke in the worst of times. If an emergency heater would not light up when needed, it was a disaster. A lot of people would try and fail, but when Wally fiddled with it, it worked again. (*Source:* Marie Boissevain, Eulogy at Memorial Service, *Walraven van Hall, 10 februari 1906–12 februari 1945,* 43.)

But Marie Boissevain noticed that "his appearance was getting worse. He was getting thinner, with deep circles under his eyes," and in her *Memorial eulogy* to Walraven, in her grief she addressed him posthumously with a sad accusation:

You didn't spare yourself. In those last months you became unhealthy because of the long, cold bike rides, lack of sleep, skipped meals, too much worry, and the grief of losing friends who fell into German hands. You didn't set aside time to unwind and stop working! We often saw, with amazement and concern, how in recent days you lived entirely on willpower and strength of mind. Driven by the distress of these days, you never allowed yourself a moment's rest. (*Source:* Marie Boissevain, Eulogy at Memorial Service, *Walraven van Hall, 10 februari 1906–12 februari 1945,* 43.)

It was true. Walraven had long-standing back problems and headaches resulting from a fall. His rapidly declining condition was noted by others. Corrie Overduin, for example, coordinated aid to Jewish people in hiding in Twente, and maintained frequent contact with Walraven, her "adviser and navigator." She commented:

I still see him in my mind, waiting at the third-class waiting room, or at the exit of the Central Station. Always kind and courteous, but always, around his eyes, dark shadows that showed the weariness he tried to hide. (*Source:* Corrie Overduin, Eulogy at Memorial Service, *Walraven van Hall, 10 februari 1906–12 februari 1945*, 43.)

Corrie was worried about him and shortly before his arrest, she spoke to him about it. It would be the last time she saw him. She went to a meeting on the Leidsegracht.[643] After she entered, she took one look at him and became anxious about his health the same way as Marie Boissevain:

I asked if he had taken a turn for the worse.[644] He said no. Was his current hiding place uncomfortable? No, he said, again. Then, despite my young age, I remonstrated with him. I earnestly reminded him of his wife and children, and of the families of those who worked with him. He laughed a little. Becoming more serious, he said, "You're right. We have become too accustomed to the dangers. We won't stay here much longer. It's such a dangerous place." (*Source:* Corrie Overduin, Eulogy at Memorial Service, Walraven van Hall, 10 februari 1906–12 februari 1945, 43.)

Johann van Marle wrote that Walraven visited him most Wednesdays at his office for lunch, sharing the difficulties he faced with human nature and with issues of honor. They also talked about the future, including the 1940-1945 Foundation.

He enjoyed a chance to review his problems with me, despite the unlikelihood of my being able to help him. He was by now not in good health. He appeared unwell and sometimes was actually sickly, but his tremendous energy and vigor[645] carried him through. (*Source:* Johann van Marle.)

Opposing the New Forced Labor Campaign

At Christmas time 1944, Walraven made one of his last visits to his home on Zaandam's Westside. Even during the holidays, he was forced to do Resistance work. Before Christmas 1944, posters announced the final German measures for a new round of recruiting Dutch labor for German factories.[646] The next morning a response placard from the Resistance was pasted next to the posters of the Germans.[647]

That response was the result of crisis Zaandam consultations led by Van Hall and including Jaap Buijs, Robert Pel,[648] and August Sabel. On Christmas Day, the four of them drew up a text urging noncooperation with the new call for recruits.[649] The publishers of the Zaandam Resistance magazine *De Typhoon* printed many posters with the appeal for noncooperation.[650] On the night of December 25, these posters were pasted over the German ones, which resulted in only a small percentage of Zaandam area workers participating. None of the employers applied for the ID cards.[651] In the following weeks, the design of the Zaandam posters served as a model elsewhere in the Netherlands.

Provincial LO/LKP leader Kees Kraay, who lived a few dozen yards from the Van Hall family, wrote that he was called in by Van Hall because of the December recruitment announcement:

> We drew up a proclamation ordering destruction of all population registers in the Zaandam region. That is what happened. In one night everything was gone. On December 25-26, the Resistance stole and hid the population registers of nine Zaandam area municipalities. (*Source:* Kees Kraay.)

The official representatives of the Queen and the Government in Exile joined in the Resistance appeal for noncooperation. On December 27, the Board of Confidential Officers[652] rejected use of the corporate ID (*Ausweis*) exempting "indispensable" employees from deportation to Germany for forced labor. On December 31, the commanders within the Domestic Forces asked the Queen for instructions and on January 2, 1945, the Queen—and on January 9,

Prime Minister Gerbrandy—openly called for rejecting the labor program. Of men called up, only eight percent reported. This was a great success, led by Van Hall.

Despite the exhausting demands on him, Van Hall managed to make some time for his family. His daughter Mary-Ann wrote that at Christmas time 1944, or not long after, her father and her brother Aad made an igloo out of snow for the family in the garden: "A snow slide was also constructed for us on the stairs of the 'air house,' the tea house in the back of the Zaandam garden, where we could go sledding."[653]

Jacobus Lootsma, who got to know Walraven early on during the creation of the Seamen's Fund, saw Walraven around Christmas that year:

> I and my family suffered quite a bit from that harsh war winter. He probably saw how despondent I was. Otherwise it would be hard to explain his last words to me. As I was leaving, he said: "Hold on just a little longer. Don't let them catch you. Just a little while and it's done!" A few days later, the bloodhounds got him. (*Source:* Jacobus Lootsma.)

Gerrit Huig had preceded Van Hall to prison, having been caught making clandestine printed materials. He was imprisoned until liberation. Van Hall's involvement with his fellow combatant remained as great as ever. On New Year's Day 1945, he visited Huig's wife to encourage her.

It was cold. In Amsterdam, people collected fuel by prying loose the wooden ties between the tram rails. To fill the stoves for heat and cooking, trees were stripped of their branches or, if possible, were cut down completely. Famine had taken hold. In January, about 1,200 people died from lack of food. The number of deaths increased each month.

Walraven Battled Favor for the Resistance

Although the NSF had millions of guilders at its disposal, little flowed to their own organization. After the war, Jaap Buijs told RIOD[654] historian-researcher Adolf Johan Corn Rüter:

> The NSF always held that they did not work to enrich themselves and that ration cards should be handed out free of charge. When it appeared that Resistance workers were being favored in getting food, Wally van Hall fiercely opposed this practice in the Kern. (*Source:* Jaap Buijs.)

Rüter's initial report, probably edited by Buijs later to be more politically correct, stated that during a visit to the LO, Van Hall and Buijs were welcomed with fried eggs, a rarity in Amsterdam during the Hunger Winter. Van Hall ranted against such "favoritism."[655]

Buijs's son remembers that a stack of smoked eel was stored at the family's home for the railway strikers. The Buijs family hardly had anything to eat themselves and the smell of freshly smoked eel made their mouths water. But not a single fish was left behind for their own use. The code of honor did not allow it. The minutes of the Kern, under the heading "Attitudes and Ways of Life of Underground Workers," stated disapprovingly:

> Citizens who are not part of the Resistance complain that our workers live far too lavishly. People in Amsterdam have said: "As long as you work for the Resistance, you have a gentleman's life: a lot of food, a lot of smoking, and enough money." (*Source:* Minutes of the Kern.)

Resistance members undoubtedly had the opportunity to put themselves in a favored position, But the Van Halls, like the Buijs family, did not take advantage of their intermediary position to obtain extra food and other necessities of life. Walraven's younger sister Vera lived on Zaandam's Westside from the first year of the war, because she was a social worker at the local perfume factory, Polak & Schwarz. In the harsh winter of 1944-1945 she and Tilly regularly went to Wormer, the area around Purmerend and the Beemsterpolder, to try to find food. When Walraven visited Tilly's parents, he noticed his in-laws had hunger edema. He provided a food package, but not through Resistance contacts.

Geert Mak reported the last time little 11-year-old Attie remembered seeing her father. She would never forget her father's visit and her mother's reaction, although she could not remember the exact date, just that it was a cold evening in that last winter of the Occupation:

> Walraven van Hall was emotionally burned out after months of hard work. He unexpectedly sailed into the kitchen one day, surprising his wife Tilly and their three children. He rarely came home during those months, because it had become so dangerous. He made the grueling journey from Amsterdam to Zaandam on a bicycle with wooden tires. He was exhausted. His wife tried to warm him up and gave him some food. Finally, she climbed resolutely onto a chair. From the back of the kitchen cupboard she took the last two sugar cubes, carefully saved for the most extreme emergency. She gave them both to him. (*Source:* Geert Mak, *A Small History of Amsterdam*, Amsterdam: Uitgeverij Atlas, paperback, 1997, 287.)

The risks of working underground were increasing. Despite his young children, however, Walraven did not think he could step out of the line of fire. Too many people and organizations had become dependent on his knowledge and commitment. Tilly agreed that her "oil man"[656] husband had to continue his activities to unite opposition to the Germans. Son Aad said: "Mother knew everything. She was fully aware of my father's illegal activities. They decided together that there was no turning back."[657]

Remmert Aten wrote that the last time he was with Van Hall was on a Sunday morning in Van Hall's Zaandam house along with near-neighbors Buijs, Sabel, and Pel:

When events occurred in the Zaandam area, Wally was kept fully informed of what happened. I often think of that last meeting, how he was the soul of that small company that led the Resistance in this region! When Inspector Pel and I met a fortnight later, Wally and Jaap Buijs had both been captured. (*Source:* Remmert Aten.)

On January 22, Walraven attended a meeting of the Rolls Royce courier service. The secretary wrote, in her weekly report that Walraven ("Mr. Van Tuyl") was specially invited, not as an "oil man," i.e, to settle disputes, but as a fuel man.

He had already found some coal, so 2,500 Resistance workers in Amsterdam each got twenty-six gallons.[658] Also, 75 tons were reserved for the agencies, so all could get what they needed. The company discussed downsizing the expanding courier service. Van Tuyl strongly opposed this. "We have to row a race with mostly untrained people. So the cook also has to row." Rolls Royce and Van Hall met every Monday morning to discuss the situation. Meanwhile, the Resistance courier service remained. (*Source:* Secretary's report, meeting of Rolls Royce.)

Tonny Eggink reported seeing Walraven one evening, a week before his arrest. Eggink said:

Walraven made me guess how much money he had spent that month. He told how many good friends of his had already fallen. He talked about going to Friesland. We talked about his family, about Zutphen, about the end [of the war] that was approaching. I said to him, "And then Wally?" "Then rest, rest. Will take a boat trip to South America, and then be a banker in Zaandam again." Humble Wally, I never saw you alive again. (*Source:* Tony Eggink, Walraven van Hall, 10 februari 1906–12 februari 1945, 90.)

Frans den Hollander was one of the last to speak to Van Hall. It was at his apartment at 513 Herengracht,[659] the day before he was arrested: "I had coffee with him. Two couriers were also present. He looked very bad, completely overworked. He said to me: 'You and Gijs are the only ones who know where I am. They can never find me.'"[660]

On January 12, 1945, the National Work Committee (LWC) issued a concise communiqué:

> In connection with the action against the declared compulsory labor service,[661] the joint resistance movements in the Netherlands have formed a National Work Committee. The Working Committee of the Kern has ceased to exist. This message is intended for all Resistance organizations, but may not be published. (*Source:* National Work Committee.)

The Kern was never intended as an umbrella Resistance body. It was a group to stimulate cooperation. It fulfilled its objective. This brainchild of Van Hall helped pave the way for the new institution that was preparing for liberation.

First Betrayal, January 12, 1945

Meanwhile, the Nazi wolfhounds were closing in on Walraven van Hall. On January 12, 1945, a meeting of the 1940-1945 Foundation was scheduled in Amsterdam. Arie van Namen was involved as an employee of the Resistance newspaper *Vrij Nederland*. He wrote about the meeting later. He remembered it was a cold, gloomy day, and it was snowing. The meeting was at 10 am. It was originally scheduled to be at his brother's house, but was rescheduled to the house of the NSF legal adviser, Van Arkel:

> We were a small group, six of us at the table[662]—the Zaandam lumber merchant Jaap Buijs, Bob Gillieron, Jan Smallenbroek, Teus van Vliet, Van Arkel, and I.[663] At precisely half past ten, Van Arkel

suddenly stood up with a frightened face and shouted: "Betrayal! Run!"[664] Then things happened fast. We had brought our bags and put our various news articles on the table. No names were on them, but the articles were still dangerous.[665] Smallenbroek and I were sitting next to the garden doors. We ran out first to the back of the garden, Smallenbroek leading the way. I was stunned to see a man at the fence, and another in the back. I ran to the left and was almost over the fence when they caught me. I looked back into the barrels of four revolvers—two men with a revolver in each hand. They ordered me to lie down on the ground immediately, Smallenbroek also. (**Source**: Arie van Namen, known in the Resistance as Dolf de Bruin.)

Jan Smallenbroek described the weapons in the hands of the SD agents as submachine guns: "We walked right into STEN guns.[666] We were thrown to the ground, searched, and handcuffed together."[667]

Jaap Buijs did not follow the others into the garden. "Everyone panicked and ran the same way. When I heard German voices behind the house, I realized that the house was surrounded, and quickly took some incriminating papers to safety behind a central heating system."[668] Van Namen described the next scene:

We were brought back inside. There was Buijs, who was a lot older than us.[669] He took care of the finances and was a friend of Walraven van Hall. The Van Halls were the financiers of the resistance and had under their control the 40 million guilders that the government had guaranteed in London. Van Arkel, Gillieron, and Van Vliet apparently escaped, so we were three. (*Source:* Van Namen.)

Van Namen's assumption that three escaped was partly correct. The moment the SD arrived, Van Arkel grabbed Teus van Vliet by his jacket and pulled him along. Bob Gillieron followed them. The trio managed to hide under the floor of a side room. The scene was described in *The Great Commandment:*

"Search the whole house!"[670] shouted Viebahn, leader of the German team. The chattering Van Arkel [Johan/Han van Lom][671] said: "If they hurt my wife, I'm going to go out," whereupon Bob, who seemed to have nerves of steel, said to Hugo:[672] "If he goes out, let's strangle him." From their hiding place they could crawl to the neighboring property. Van Arkel's wife, who was taking care of their child at the time of the raid, was in shock: "Suddenly there was a loud ringing, banging, roaring, guys everywhere. My guests ran in all directions. My heart stopped for a moment. This was a nightmare, it could not be real. All but three, including Han, were arrested. I was forced to stay in the front room with a gun to my chest." (*Source: The Great Commandment*, cited.)[673]

Neither the 1940-1945 Foundation board nor Van Arkel's wife knew that the trap was set because of betrayal in their own circle.

Who was Van Arkel? The NSF had needed an attorney to draft the charter of the 1940-1945 Foundation.[674] Van Arkel, the pseudonym of Johan van Lom, was an enthusiastic 26-year-old lawyer, already affiliated with the renowned Amsterdam law firm De Pont although not yet finished law school. *Parool* chief executive Wim van Norden was a member of the original 1940-1945 Foundation board and was close to Jan de Pont. Van Norden asked De Pont for the name of a lawyer from his firm to draft the charter. "De Pont told me that he had an assistant, a very good lawyer, who can help. So he had this young man come to his office. It was Van Lom—a nice, friendly young man with one of those Harris Tweed jackets with leather elbow patches."[675]

In the autumn of 1944, Johan ("Han") van Lom drew up the draft charter which created the foundation on October 13. The board did not know that the married Van Lom was in a relationship with a childhood friend of his wife, 24-year-old Tjodina ("Ini") Tijmstra. On the staff of the Government Employment Agency in The Hague, she went into hiding because of her Resistance activities. From September 1943 on, she stayed at South (*Zuider)* Amstellaan 44 with Johan and Cornelia ("Non") van Lom. When Non gave birth to a daughter ten months later, Ini moved out but lived nearby—and Ini's extramarital relationship with Han continued.

When Han van Lom joined the Resistance, he agreed to distribute three hundred copies of the *Parool* newspaper every day. But he outsourced that commitment to his girlfriend Ini. Sadly, at the end of November, Ini was arrested by the *Landwacht* (Dutch collaborators) while delivering newspapers. A search of her house revealed other Resistance documents. Non van Lom, who had not previously known about Ini's newspaper work, said: "Han was deeply affected by Ini's arrest, because he was the one who had persuaded her to deliver Resistance newspapers."[676]

Han was terrified that Ini Tijmstra might be sent to a concentration camp. At the end of December 1944, trying to get her released, he visited Amsterdam's SD local office to plead her case.[677] He walked into the welcoming arms of Detective Sergeant[678] Friedrich Viebahn. The SD knew of Van Lom's marital status, his affair with the *Parool* distributor, and his collaboration with Marianne Tellegen, alias Dr. Max. In Van Lom's own words:

> Viebahn detained me in conversation for several hours. He would not say when he would release me. He alluded to potential unpleasant consequences if my relationship with Ms. Tijmstra was known. I felt even more threatened when Viebahn called me by both my real name and my Resistance pseudonym, and then accused me of familiarity with Dr. Max. (*Source:* Van Lom, Confession Statement.)

Yes, it was blackmail. The Detective Sergeant asked Van Lom how his wife would react to hearing about her husband's infidelity with Ini. Viebahn promised to keep the secret, if the trainee lawyer would cooperate. He promised also to release Ini. Van Lom was anxious:

> That's when the 1940-1945 Foundation meetings came up. He point-blank informed me that if I told him the date and place of the next foundation meeting, I could see Ini and he could arrange her release." (*Source:* Van Lom, Confession Statement.)

Van Lom took the bait. He named January 12 as the next meeting date and his own home as the location. To divert suspicion of Van Lom him as a betrayer, Viebahn promised him a chance to hide during the planned SD ambush. Viebahn said: "The plan was that Van Lom would take Hugo[679] with him into the air raid shelter to have a credible witness who could confirm Van Lom's escape and who could later be the starting point for Van Lom to provide new contacts in the Resistance."[680] Arie van Namen confirmed the story:

> None of us knew any of that in the House of Detention, but it's true. He betrayed us, but with the emphatic promise that the Germans would not shoot us. Viebahn sought to enforce that promise: "You can't shoot them!" He said he involved [Willy] Lages and [Hanns Albin] Rauter.[681] Lages later confirmed the promise to me personally: [On my] "German honor! German faithfulness!"[682] (*Source:* Arie van Namen.)

Buijs, Van Namen, and Smallenbroek were imprisoned until the end of the war. They were indeed not executed, but since they knew nothing about the promises to Van Lom, they suffered long interrogations with death threats. The prisoners were told repeatedly they would be executed if they remained silent, as the Germans were impatient to learn more about the top of the Resistance. Smallenbroek testified:

> I set up a story for them, but (he laughs) they knew everything. Everything. I had stuffed my pocket diary between the car cushions and they found it. Every night when the cells opened up, I thought, now it's my turn." (*Source:* Jan Smallenbroek, *Woord gehouden. Veertig jaar Stichting 1940-1945.* "Word Kept: Forty Years—Foundation 1940-45.")

Buijs was several times put under heavy emotional pressure. His interrogators threatened to blow up his house and arrest his wife and children. The timber merchant wrote in his prison diary on January 19 that he was brought out of his cell again.

I was interrogated at length and impatiently by a certain Rühl.[683] However, I had had time to think about what I could say that would not provide him with any information out of the ordinary. Finally he became furious and snapped at me: "You are trying to protect your friends, but we will soon catch them, including your friend Van Hall. As soon as we know where they meet next, we will talk to them." (*Source:* Jaap Buijs, *Prison Diary.*)

More Betrayals, January 26–27, 1945

Despite lengthy interrogations, the three imprisoned men said nothing that could harm others. Van Lom, however, remained an easy mark. His girlfriend was released as promised, but Viebahn still threatened Han that he would tell Non about the extramarital relationship. As "hush money," Viebahn required Han to disclose another date and location for the 1940-1945 Foundation board meeting. Johan van Lom was trapped. Both his wife and his girlfriend had lost trust in him. Ini wrote in her diary that she was overjoyed at being released:

> But my heart was still stabbed with fear. It was too easy. Something wasn't right. In an evening with the Heyliger family I pressed Han until he told me: "I went to the SD this morning and said, here I am." He said he told the SD that he only gave legal advice to the Resistance. "You can arrest me, I said, but that won't help you. I may cooperate, but only if you promise the people arrested with me will not be shot." They agreed. Then he asked for my release. "I swore I wouldn't get involved with those guys, but now I have to do it. The lives of my friends depend on it." (*Source:* Ini Tijmstra, Diary.)

It was half the truth. LO[684] representative Teus van Vliet (alias Hugo) contacted Van Lom. On Friday, January 19, they met at the corner of Van Vliet's street, Zuider Amstellaan, and Maasstraat. The two of them organized a new meeting a week later at Jan Luykenstraat 28, inviting others from the

Resistance leadership. The young lawyer Van Lom betrayed the new meeting time and place to Friedrich Viebahn, who promised to arrest only one man, whom they wanted intensely, Van Vliet. Viebahn said he would invent the charge that Van Vliet stole a bicycle. That way, Viebahn could keep secret from the Resistance the role of his new informant, Van Lom, alias Van Arkel.[685]

Van Vliet was, as planned, arrested on the January 26 for "bicycle theft" in such a way that the other participants in the meeting did not notice.[686] Viebahn said later:

> After his arrest, Van Vliet was transferred to the Apollolaan, where I interrogated him. After being interrogated for about half an hour, he asked me to fetch his wallet and handed me a note from his wallet, which read: "Saturday 12:30, Land. W."[687] The text refers to a meeting of the Landelijk Working Committee, a day later. (*Source:* Viebahn, statement to postwar Special Court.)

Van Vliet handed the meeting address to the Germans: Leidsegracht ("Lg") 15, the office of civil-law notary Rijkens.[688] He was demoralized by how much accurate information his interrogators already had, especially regarding the leaders of the Resistance:

> Viebahn and Rühl appeared triumphantly in my cell and threw ID cards on the table with the self-satisfied remark: "We have been looking for them for a long time." The game of their questions and my dodges began again. They knew a lot about the Resistance leaders, especially about Van Tuyl. (*Source:* Van Vliet, testimony before the Special Court, May 1949.)

In Van Vliet's mind, his Resistance colleagues unquestionably knew he'd been arrested. So they would therefore call off the January 27 meeting. Van Vliet was weary after being interrogated for twelve hours straight:

At the end of the day, about seven o'clock, when everyone was leaving to go home, I finally explained that my note on the Leid-segracht was about a meeting of the National Work Committee. They knew I had a meeting at the Central Bureau in those days and was arrested just when I wanted to enter. The only reason I would have missed this important meeting was because I was detained. So I counted on everyone having being warned by my absence, and not showing up. I am still puzzled why the meeting was held. (*Source:* Teus van Vliet, testimony to Special Court, May 1949.)

Van Vliet was not wrong to expect the meeting would be cancelled. Weeda agreed with him that they would have canceled the meeting if they had known Hugo was arrested:

But I had to bring one and a half million guilders to Haarlem, so I did not go to that meeting. My courier went instead, to bring documents. Lambertus Neher also was absent; he was stuck in another meeting. (*Source:* Weeda.)

A few years after the war, Weeda's LO colleague Henk van Riessen said he warned Domestic Forces[689] employee Jan Goedkoop on January 26 that Van Vliet had not appeared that day in Jan Luykenstraat. Goedkoop was expected the next day on the Leidsegracht. Van Riessen said:

Goedkoop relayed my warning. It is a mystery why everyone still went to that meeting. When Van Vliet did not return as agreed, I and others immediately warned Goedkoop and Van Hall by telephone that Van Vliet had been arrested and that they should not hold a meeting the following Saturday. We agreed not to assume arrested Resistance workers would be silent. Also, that no one should be invited to a meeting that a prisoner under interrogation knew about. (*Source:* Henk van Riessen, official report from 1947.)

Johan and Cornelia ("Non") van Lom on their wedding day in front of their house at Zuider Amstellaan 44. (private collection)

Another LO representative, Douqué, also sounded an alarm:

> I warned Goedkoop personally and I also spoke to Van Hall by telephone, on Saturday morning. I was astonished to hear later they went to that meeting after all. That Friday I had evacuated the central office of the LO with Van Riessen. (*Source:* Heinrich Douqué.)

On January 27 around noon, the SD took over Leidsegracht 13-15 and waited for the arrival of their visitors. In the hours before Van Hall left for the Leidsegracht, he was staying in his safe house on the Herengracht,[690] a ten-minute walk away. Hanneke Eikema wrote that before they left the house, the group listened to Winston Churchill give a speech on the BBC:

> That morning, the cold was creeping through the walls, windows and doors of the stately old house on one of Amsterdam's canals. Five members of our group stayed in this big house: Van Tuyl, his assistant Brinkie,[691] a young sabotage group member named Wim, a courier

named Ankie, and me. [. . .] We carefully stowed away the radio in its cubbyhole. It was time to go to the morning meeting.[692] Van Tuyl left the house first. His last words before he left were: "Never let anyone know that you know Van Tuyl. The Germans have been looking for me for a long time. Goodbye, I'll see you later." And then he left, tired and hunched over, wrapped in a worn winter coat. I followed a few minutes later, my arms full of Brussels sprouts, some stale toast and a small bag of coal. (*Source:* Hanneke Eikema.)

On the way to the LWC meeting, Goedkoop bumped into a few colleagues, including Van Hall. At the corner of Kerkstraat and Leidsegracht, they briefly discussed the warnings they had received. Twice before, that week, they had heard Van Vliet had been arrested. They assumed it was another false alarm, and so decided to go ahead with the meeting.

During the next half hour, one after the other, Frits Nieuwenhuijsen (National Committee of Resistance/Grand Advisory Committee on Illegality), Pastor Henk de Jong (representing *Trouw*), Jan Goedkoop (Secretary to the Domestic Forces Commander), and Walraven van Hall all walked into the arms of SD agents. Finally, Hanneke Eikema came through the front door. She would be the only one of the dozens of the Zaandam region's couriers to fall into enemy hands. She said:

The moment I entered the house, two huge Germans with submachine guns jumped at me, yelling at me to drop everything I was carrying. The sprouts and coals bounced across the floor. One of the Germans slipped on a piece of coal and cursed. With the barrel of a gun in my back, they forced me to walk upstairs. When I entered the room on the second floor, I saw five men[693] lying on the floor with their faces to the floor and hands folded above their heads. Van Tuyl was one of them. The Germans offered me a chair and a cigarette. I accepted it, started smoking, and behaved as normally as I could. Not a word was said to the men on the floor or to me. The silence was so thick you could have cut it. It was as if we were waiting for torture or death. One of the men on the floor moaned softly. (*Source:* Hanneke Eikema.)

Eikema believed the moan came from Walraven van Hall. But Frits Nieuwenhuijsen's son has argued it was more likely to have come from his father, who was the same age and build,[694] and had two strong reasons to groan. First, he had already been warned about the betrayal. Before going to Leidsegracht 13-15, this NC[695] representative was on the Herengracht nearby visiting his friend Hoyte Sillevis Smitt, a liaison officer for the Resistance. Smitt warned Nieuwenhuijsen that the meeting had been betrayed to the SD. As soon has he heard the warning, Nieuwenhuisen rushed to the Leidsegracht to warn the others. But he was too late. Second, when he realized that the SD had already arrived, he attempted to turn around and flee. But as he was scrambling down the stairs, he was shot in the thigh, another good reason for a groan.

The SD scored a coup. Eikema reported: "After about ten minutes, German reinforcements arrived, and two heavily armed German officers took me outside. It was the last time I saw my boss, Van Tuyl, and some of the other members of the Friday-morning meeting."[696]

Henri ter Meulen, partner of Hope & Co., bankers, was working from that position as cashier general of the NSF. He said:

> Early on January 27, 1945, Wally called me to ask for another meeting. He knew I always ate alone in the evening at the American Hotel and suggested I come to him for a drink and dinner at 5:15. When I arrived at his apartment on the Herengracht, I found a note on the door saying someone would be back in fifteen minutes. When I returned, the note was still there. At six o'clock I called Wally's niece [Elizabeth, Lies] Boissevain, who advised me not to return. Then I heard from Gijs that Wally had been captured by the Germans. (*Source:* Henri ter Meulen, partner of Hope & Co., bankers, source.)

Gijs van Hall wrote:

Leidsegracht 13 and 15 (Amsterdam City Archives)

On January 27, I cycled home to Blaricum with food for my family from Natura.[697] In the afternoon, B. H. de Jongh, who will be remembered from my account of the railway strike, became very agitated by the announcement that Wally had been arrested that morning. He insisted that I should leave my home. He took me to his small summer house on the Loosdrecht lakes. The next day I went back to Amsterdam and found out what had happened—Wally, despite feeling ill, had gone to a meeting of the National Work Committee. (*Source:* Gijs van Hall, *Ervaringen van een Amsterdam-mer,* "Experiences of an Amsterdammer.")

Only one person missed the deadly dance, Henk van Randwijk. The *Vrij Nederland* leader said: "An inner voice had told me, 'Stay away for a while.' No, not an inner voice; it was a fortune teller who said I was in extra danger for two weeks. In any case, I came a little later than 1:30 on purpose, and saw my arrested colleagues being pushed into cars."[698]

Van Randwijk's fortune teller, who had a good reputation in Resistance circles, was consulted shortly before and was said to have warned of "intensified danger." When Van Randwijk saw his comrades being forced into a car, he turned his bike around and rode into the snowy city as nonchalantly as he could.

After Van Hall's arrest, the NSF deviated from its rule that after an arrest, documents and people of interest to the Germans should be moved. This time, everyone remained where they were, and everything stayed put. Peter Plantenga, one of the later NSF leaders, explained:

> When Wally was arrested, none of us moved. In the past, one arrest was commonly followed by another, but Wally's arrest was different. We knew, with absolute certainty, that the SD would get no new information. That assumption turned out to be correct. SD employee Emil Rühl expressed his disappointment after the war—"we did not learn much from the various interrogations." (*Source:* Peter Plantenga, quoted by Emil Rühl, Testimony to Postwar Tribunal.)

Despite Van Hall and other members of the NSF remaining silent before the SD interrogators, the wave of arrests did not end after January 27. Persistent interrogation of pastor De Jong led, two days later, to the SD raiding the Amsterdam printer of *Trouw*, located on the Lijnbaansgracht. The owner, Paul Bakker, and seven of his employees were arrested. Unfortunately, *Trouw* founder Wim Speelman arrived at the printing house while the SD was still searching the building. Speelman had forged identity papers, but Friedrich Viebahn recognized him. Speelman was handcuffed as well and taken away.

Three administrative employees of the printer Bakker were soon released. Paul Bakker himself and four other employees were shot on February 9 as Death Row candidates.[699] Cynically, this execution was held near Van Hall's Zaandam house, on the corner of the Prins Hendrikkade and the Burcht.[700]

Speelman did not escape the firing squad. On February 17, he too was shot dead near Halfweg, midway between Haarlem and Amsterdam.[701]

Suspicion grew within the leadership of the Amsterdam Resistance that an insider was the traitor. Their suspicion landed on Johan van Lom. His wife also had reason to wonder about him, and she wrote:

> One of the people I helped to escape was also caught, again after a meeting with Han. I thought I would go crazy. I couldn't bear it, and I said so. Han made a violent scene. He was devastated, but he just said, "I'm not a bastard. You don't understand." He promised me he would break with the SD. I asked Ini to go into hiding with him so she could take care of him, because he had become very weak. Ini and Han moved into a house on Prinseneiland. Han had me bring a note[702] every day, and I also brought Han a treat. One evening at midnight, long after I had gone to bed, he returned. He said: "I have to get out. Viebahn (the SD man he said he worked with) has discovered my new address." As he stood by the door to leave, he asked me: "Go to Viebahn, tell him a story, that I have disappeared and was probably eliminated by the Resistance." Early the next morning, Han and Ini went to The Hague by bicycle. (*Source:* Non van Lom, Notes.)

The Resistance Deals with the Informer

Han van Lom had a last meeting with his German tormentor, one and a half weeks after the arrest of Teus van Vliet. Viebahn described it later:

> Van Lom visited me again and asked if I was interested in arresting the senior leadership of the Domestic Forces. When I said yes, he told me he had spoken to De Vos van Steenwijk, who was active in the Domestic Forces, and, like Van Lom, worked at the De Pont law firm and also was a reserve officer. Van Lom said he had offered De Vos his services for the Domestic Forces, explaining he knew the top

leadership of the Domestic Forces in Amsterdam. He said that after he took the oath of allegiance, he would be accepted into their midst. (*Source:* Friedrich Viebahn, Testimony to postwar Special Court.)

After a short stay in The Hague, Van Lom returned to Amsterdam, where his wife met him for the last time, March 5, 1945. Non van Lom wrote:

That Monday morning, he was extremely nervous and wouldn't speak to anyone. Only when we were alone, and I was lying on the couch, did he come to me and put his head in my lap, saying nothing. I stroked his hair and asked: "Baby, what's wrong?" He replied in a choked voice, "I wish I had never started it." When the others came in, he sat down by the stove again and said nothing more. He was angry that his food wasn't cooked, that he could not find his shaving brush, and that his bicycle pump was missing. After two hours, he left without a goodbye. He never came back. (*Source:* Non van Lom, Notes.)

That afternoon, the courier Willy van den Donk made a fateful appointment with Van Lom at the Westermarkt. She wrote:

After an investigation was launched, we were almost sure he was the one who betrayed us. We decided that Van Lom must be detained and executed. I was to go to him and tell him that a meeting had been arranged and take him to the appointed place. Several members from the top leadership of the LO, the National Assault Gang, CID, and the 1940-1945 Foundation[703] were waiting for him. They had already decided he must be put out of the way, if he was found guilty. It was too risky to let him go, because he knew too much and was too well versed in the Resistance. He was one of us. (*Source:* Willy van den Donk, Postwar Report.)

In his ignorance, the young lawyer walked with her, closely followed by three people from the National Assault Gang.[704] She brought Van Lom to

Keizersgracht 401, the office of Jan de Pont. There two people interrogated him for two hours—Wim Sanders (a top man of the Central Intelligence Service) and Henk van Riessen (the chairman of the central bureau of the LO). Sanders asked Van Lom to tell him his life story, from the moment he started working at De Pont. Van Lom beat around the bush. Van den Donk wrote:

> Van Lom was shocked when he was then told what the meeting was about. He denied everything at first.[705] Sanders and Van Riessen consulted with each other and then Sanders returned alone. When he brought up Van Lom's love for the *Parool* courier and made the link to his traitor role, Van Lom broke.
>
> "Who told you that?" he asked.
>
> "You told me that yourself," said Sanders. "It follows logically from your story."
>
> In tears, Van Lom made a full confession. He said:
>
> "Sir, I have betrayed everything. What do you do with a traitor?"
>
> Sanders replied:
>
> "You will figure that out yourself, but at least we don't use German methods. You may now dictate your own statement."
>
> Van Lom was very anxious about what awaited him. He asked questions about this, to which the answer was that he should look at the result of his betrayal, and then perhaps he could come to his own conclusion. (*Source:* Willy van den Donk.)

Wim van Norden wrote:

> Sanders said: "It became very unsavory—an annoying, dramatic session, because there were several of us and Van Lom was alone. But we couldn't let him walk. He had to die." When Van Riessen asked him about the reasons for his actions, Van Lom said: "I have no character, sir." Van Lom's confession was recorded, and he signed the typed report. He also left his fingerprints along with his signature. Sanders departed and Van Lom told his story again, in more detail,

to several LKP members. A report was also made of this, which all those present signed. Subsequently, the death row inmate was served a cup of tea with a cyanide tablet. However, the poison tablet did not dissolve sufficiently. Instead, the group decided to shoot Van Lom. Outside, an LKP member carried out the sentence. (*Source:* Wim van Norden, interview with Erik Schaap.)

Only after Liberation did Wim Sanders inform Van Lom's desperate wife of the execution. She wrote later: "The morning after this confession, he was shot dead on the edge of the Keizersgracht. A month later his body was found with a bullet in the back of the head and he was buried as an unknown in a mass grave at the Northern Cemetery.[706] My love for him is infinite and I believe in him."[707]

Prison

The arrest of Walraven van Hall was an immense loss for the Resistance. The shrunken group's remaining leaders, who kept the NSF afloat after the betrayal, almost immediately brought in Peter Plantenga. An employee of the Incasso-Bank, he had been active in Resistance work since 1940 and starting in 1943 carried out liaison work for the National Support Fund. During the railway strike, he cycled back and forth between Amsterdam and South-Holland[708] or Utrecht every week, transporting large sums of money to the regional leaders there. He then returned with any securities and mail for the Incasso-Bank. His bank credentials provided him with a cover. After the war, Plantenga was appointed director of the NSF, which then became a foundation. He gradually phased out the fund. Because of the secrecy the NSF maintained during the war years, Plantenga had never known the origin of the millions of guilders he transported. He said: "I never knew how the financing worked, and, honestly, I never wanted to know. I dealt only with the distribution. That's why, during the war, I never understood the reason for requiring receipts."[709]

On January 27, 1933, the SD[710] took Walraven van Hall to the Detention Center on Weteringschans in Amsterdam on January 27. They tried in vain to

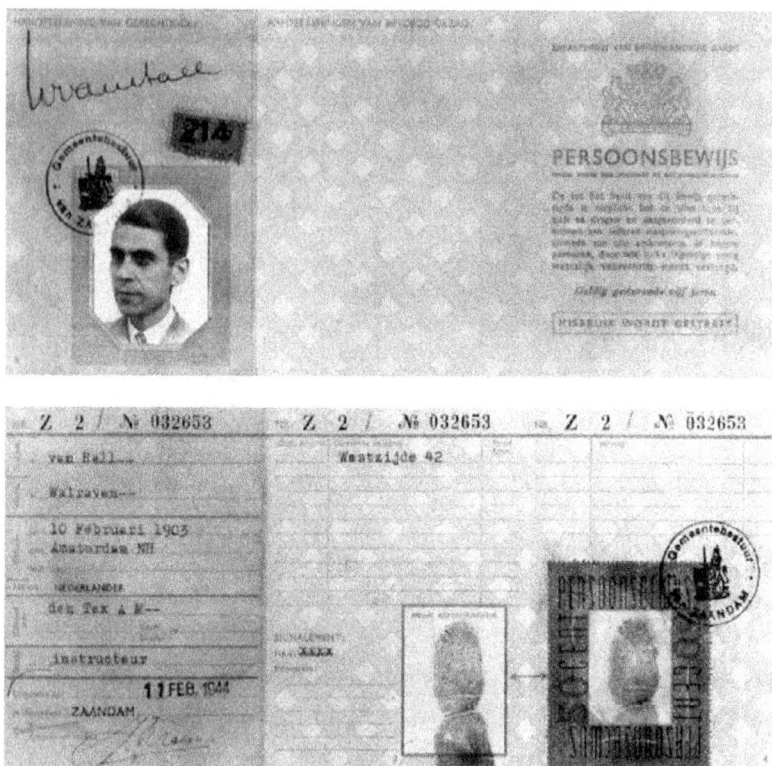

*In 1944, the Identity Card Center produced a forged identity card
Walraven van Hall. Both his profession and date of birth have
been adjusted accordingly. (Van Hall Foundation)*

get him to talk. His brother Gijs wrote: "Initially there was still hope. The SD
did not yet know that they had captured the long-sought 'Van Tuyl,' in the
person of Van Hall."[711]

At the time of his arrest, Walraven did have a forged ID in his pocket, but
that was in his own name and therefore did not lead to one of his alter egos.
That ignorance lasted at least until February 6. Van Hall was still referred to
under his pseudonym on an organization chart about the Dutch Resistance
illegality that the SD drew up that day.[712] The overview was drawn up by Teus
van Vliet. Gijs van Hall wrote:

Van Vliet survived the war, partly because he made a diagram for the Germans in which he described the entire Resistance, including the names of the various organizations and the pseudonyms of the leaders as far as they were known to him, and that was most of them. Soon afterwards, the Germans discovered that they had Van Vliet's brother in their hands, so another prisoner betrayed his identity. That sealed Walraven's fate. (*Source:* Gijs van Hall, *Testimony.*)

Remmert Aten said: "There was nothing we could do. We were all ready, but the leadership gave no sign for us to act. The chance of rescue must have been low. That we failed, and nothing could avert Walraven's fate, was terrible."[713] Gijs van Hall wrote later:

> Looking back . . . maybe we could have gotten him free if we had contacted Seyss-Inquart as representatives of the Resistance. Those contacts were still possible then. But a police officer from Zaandam, with whom we had contacts, told us, and in hindsight that was right: "They don't know who he is." Then we thought, if that's the case, it's better to leave him as unknown than to draw special attention to him. Later, they found out who he was. [714](*Source:* Gijs van Hall, *Zaanstreek in years of occupation.*)

Cell Neighbors

After a week, Walraven ended up in a cell next to his friend Jaap Buijs. Fate? Buijs wrote in his diary:

> February 2. Suddenly my cell door opened and to my great dismay Wally entered my cell between two German guards. I don't know if this was intentional or a mistake. Then I heard the cell next to me open and he was locked in there. A moment later he started tapping, but as I had never had any contact with another prisoner, I couldn't

understand it. He then put his mouth to the crack of his window, called me and told me that he was arrested January 27th. He had first spent time in a light cell across the street and had now been transferred. Walraven asked: "How the hell is it that you are in such a filthy cell?" I told him I hadn't confessed and that was probably the punishment. He then explained to me how the tapping worked and we then talked to each other until late at night, much to the dismay of our fellow inmates. I was so tired then, from the effort, that I slept soundly for the first time. (*Source:* Jaap Buijs, Diary.)

Prison conditions were appalling. The cells were darkened. Heating, water and soap were not provided. Hardly any food was available, and receiving mail or visitors was certainly not an option. Buijs noted: "My treatment got worse and worse. Little food, rotten potatoes, no fat, and no heating. Two very thin blankets and a straw bag almost without straw on the stone floor. Plus no light."[715]

Occasionally something could be heard from another cell, such as the voice of Reverend Henk de Jong, one of those arrested on January 27. At nightfall he sang: "I will pay you, O God, my thanksgiving. Praise you in my evening song." Buijs wrote:

February 3. I was taken out of my cell and then saw Wally standing outside his cell. We were placed next each other. We showed no sign of knowing each other. Apparently they didn't know that he had been in the cell with me. By tapping on the wall we had contact with each other, and therefore, as our case did not seem so gloomy, good and pleasant conversations with each other. He had started to imagine that his wife and children would also have been arrested and luckily I managed to reassure him that this was not so. Later, however, his case became more and more serious. On February 8, the thugs knew they had Van Tuyl in their hands and that's when his case became hopeless. How much we talked to each other in those days and what a battle this dear fellow fought to say goodbye to his family. (*Source:* Jaap Buijs, Walraven van Hall. February 10, 1906–February 12, 1945.)

In January 1945, the Germans arrested several leaders of the Dutch resistance, including Walraven van Hall. On February 6, the Sicherheitsdienst succeeded in making an overview of the illegality. It shows that the SD manages to control the NSF leader ("Van Tuijl: festgenommen"). (collection author)

Courier Weeda, alias Brinkie, wrote:

> When we had to flee from Zaandam and took up residence some-where in Amsterdam, we sat together every evening and always first talked about Westside 42. Often he would say: "Brinkie, that's my only fear, that I have to leave my family behind if something hap-pens." Indeed this was his only fear, for otherwise he feared nothing and no one. (*Source:* Weeda.)

Tilly and the children went into hiding immediately after Walraven's arrest. The two eldest, Attie and Aad, were housed at different addresses in Zaandam. Tilly and 4-year-old Mary-Ann moved in with Amsterdam's Goed-koop family. The house on the Westside was stripped of valuables by friends. These belongings were loaded onto a barge via the back garden, transported across the Zaan river and stored elsewhere. When after some time it became clear that the Germans were leaving the family members alone, they and their possessions returned to the Westside.

Trouw employee Jan Smallenbroek, who was already transferred to the Weteringschans prison on January 12, caught one more glimpse of Walraven from his cell. "Through a hatch we got black coffee. When that hatch opened, I saw someone I knew very well, Van Hall. There was no way to get in touch with him."[716] But Arie van Namen succeeded in making contact. He said four years after the war:

> On Saturday, January 27, I was informed by knocking signals that Hugo was sitting next to me in a cell at the Weteringschans prison in Amsterdam. I was very shocked by this, because I was afraid that if Hugo were interrogated, my lies would become known to the SD. [. . .] On January 27, 1945, I noticed simultaneously that Walraven van Hall was locked in a cell on the other side of mine. He expressed his opinion that his arrest must have been the result of a note in Hugo's pocketbook that had been found on Hugo by the SD. At Van Hall's request, I asked Hugo about this by knocking signals. He did not give a positive answer. (*Source:* Arie van Namen.)

Jaap Buijs, who ended up in the same cell as Van Namen a short time later, does something similar.

> Van Hall then told me that he thought that the Defendant had said something, but that he, Van Hall, did not understand it. Van Hall used the word betrayal. On February 8, 1945, he informed me that Hugo (Van Vliet) or Goedkoop had betrayed the case, because the Germans knew everything, literally everything. (*Source:* Jaap Buijs, Diary.)

In his notes, the Zaandam timber merchant Buijs described in detail the last days he spent with his friend, separated by a stone wall.

February 7 and 8. Bitterly cold. Food miserable and far too little. However, many good conversations with Wally, who was especially gloomy on the 8th and needed a lot of support, because they knew everything about him, including that he was Van Tuyl. We both tried to guess who could have said all this. How miserable it is when you can only comfort a buddy by that cold tapping. You would love to shake his hand and let him feel your sympathy. (It later turned out that Hugo had made a drawing of the Resistance organization, and handed it in on February 6, betraying everything. The bastard!)

February 9. Interrogated again. They now also seem to know everything about me. They just didn't know the NSF connection. Still, I was now convinced that I wouldn't make it through either. I discussed this with Wally, who then told me that there was a chance of that. There seemed to be some agreement that would prevent this from happening. It was crazy, but there was some comfort in knowing that not only was Wally going through that misery, but you were living under the same pressure yourself. (The possibility was this: Lom had said he was willing to betray us, provided we weren't shot. Viebahn and Rühl wanted to keep that promise. Lages didn't, when it turned out who we were.)

February 10. Wally's birthday. This day was deeply moving, as his case was getting worse and worse and he was now firmly convinced that he would not get through. Interrogated again in the afternoon. Rühl said he now wanted me to come free and tell him how the NSF worked. Hugo had said everything and denying it didn't matter. As proof, he said Van Hall was head of the NSF and I was his deputy. Someone gave them key information about the NSF. (In Scheveningen[717] I asked Hugo if this was true. He vehemently denied it. Later, however, it turned out to be absolutely true.)

February 11. Interrogated again. Have confessed that I was chairman of the Kern and Natura, but vehemently denied that I knew anything about the NSF. This in order not to be forced to say something about Wally. Didn't mention any names. Rühl, however, neatly listed all the participants in the Kern Meeting, of which he had a list (Hugo!!). (*Source:* Jaap Buijs, 1949.)

Now we come to another note—small, barely two inches by four inches.[718] "Mrs. VAN HALL, ZAANDAM" was written in robust, businesslike pencil letters in the top right corner. The further text of the sheet described on both sides was all the more personal. Walraven penned his four-line farewell message to his wife on one side, and reserved the back of the piece of paper for another four lines, mostly for his children.

My dear, I'm so sorry I couldn't spare you this. You've had it hard enough already. The accusations are very serious. The first days will be difficult and cause misery to you. Be brave dear, find peace in children. They have also held up well these years. Oh dearest, what a good time we had together these 13 years. I know, thank God, you are surrounded by loving family and friends. It has cost me a lot of struggle, but I am willing to accept the worst. Attie will take her turn in a few years. Aad manages himself, but school has to improve. The little Pug will become one of a kind. Love to all parents and friends. Take courage dearest. Your Wally. (*Source:* Walraven van Hall.)

The sheet was full. Walraven gently pushed it into the slit of a pair of underpants, laundry that would probably go back to Zaandam. It was only after his death that his last written words, hidden between other pieces of clothing, reached Tilly van Hall.[719]

Execution, February 12

Since 1950, sculptures carved in French limestone have been installed on Jan Gijzenkade in Haarlem. The maker, Theodoor van Reijn, created a kneeling man and woman laying a wreath together. On the pedestal is the biblical text:

"And now faith, hope and love abide these three, but the greatest of these is love."[720]

The image is reminiscent of the drama that took place 25 meters away, on the other side of the road. That drama began for Walraven van Hall on February 10, 1945, his 39th birthday. That Saturday, a group of former RVV[721] members, who had developed into a robbery gang in the previous weeks, committed an armed robbery of a bicycle dealer. They drove through North Haarlem with their loot. Members of the German military police[722] searched their car as part of a routine check. In order to get away, one of the occupants fired at the Germans with a submachine gun. A non-commissioned officer fell mortally wounded, and a soldier and a civilian were injured. The same evening, the Haarlem police informed the Amsterdam SD about the event.

SiPo[723] had replaced the abolished courts as of July 1944. They therefore retaliated, as usual, by staging multiple executions. On the order of SD local branch[724] leader Willy Lages, his subordinate Friedrich Viermann[725] called *SiPo* commander Karl Schöngarth. He ordered the execution of eight prisoners. Viermann, in 1949, testified: "I then gave Dr. Schöngarth eight names of the so-called *Todeskandidaten,* those who were at the top of the list of those sentenced to death." From the diary of Jaap Buijs:

> February 12. One of the worst days of my life. Wally was taken out of his cell twice in a row. The second time he said he had to hand in hat and coat and that was the end. He asked me to listen further and stated certain wishes for supervision of his children, and so on. I told him that if I made it through, I would try as much as I could to take away the little worries for his family every day and continue to do what I could. He said he didn't even want to ask me. But because he knew me, it came naturally to him. He was picked up again at half past four and when he came back he said that he would be shot with others in the evening. He asked me to tell Til that his last thoughts would be with her and the children. After that, he said that he had a terrible struggle being separated from his sweetheart, and then said goodbye. I was totally devastated. How expensive is freedom. When

I heard the stern order to get out of his cell, I was at a loss. (*Source:* Jaap Buijs, Diary.)

What Buijs did not write down was that he asked one of the officers[726] whether he could take Walraven's place for the execution. The officer refused to consider the offer.

The site of the execution was on the quay on the south side of the Jan Gijzen Canal,[727] north of Haarlem. Ingeborg de Wit witnessed it, at age 17. She wrote to the widow of Reverend Henk de Jong, one of the eight victims.

> On the day of the firing squad, my brother and I were on our way to collect dead branches for my mother to burn. The day before, we had witnessed the shooting of a German officer crossing the bridge[728] on bicycle. We flew home, afraid to tell our mother about it. The next day, around the same time, near the same bridge, your husband was murdered. We were forced by German soldiers on the quay next to the canal to stand with other people. Then a German armored truck arrived with SS men and soldiers. They pushed out eight people, who were wearing almost nothing. (*Source:* Ingeborg de Wit, letter to Mrs. Henk de Jong.)

Nine-year-old Rob Hahn also had to watch that Monday. In 2002 he said:

> They were clubbed out of the truck with the butts of guns. They were lined up across the street from where the monument to the victims is today, so that the Germans' line of fire went over the canal. We were forced to watch, at five o'clock in the afternoon. The leader of the execution squad ordered his train-guard unit[729] to fire. (*Source:* Rob Hahn.)

Shortly before the fatal shots, Walraven shouted out, keeping the promise to Jaap Buijs that he made in his cell: "Thinking of you, Tilly." Bystanders heard him clearly. Seconds later, he fell, mortally wounded.

Ingeborg de Wit said later:

> I remember the explosion of the guns of the German soldiers. We were defeated, scared, and filled with hatred. We were forced to walk past the victims. I didn't want to look. (*Source:* Ingeborg de Wit.)

When Rob Hahn returned later to the site of the execution, he saw the eight bodies lying in the ditches next to Rijksstraatweg:[730]

> I don't know how long they had been lying there. The Amsterdam undertaker (and loyal SS and NSB member) Johannes Bleekemolen and garage owner Pierre van der Lee picked up the victims in the early evening and brought them by truck to the Kennemerduin area. There Bleekemolen removed their shoes and rings. He took the shoes home to serve as fuel for his stove. He gave the rings to the Sicherheitspolizei. The bodies were buried in the dune sand near the Zeeweg.[731] Five days later, Bleekemolen sent the funeral bill, 195 guilders per person, to the municipality of Haarlem. (*Source:* Rob Hahn.)

Grief Spreads

Little by little, word of Van Hall's death spread throughout the Netherlands and the river of tears began to flow. Jan Rot wrote that he arrived at Leidsegracht 48 on February 13:

> Mrs. Koppenaal, even paler than usual, asked me: "Do you hear about Mr. Van Tuyl?"
> "No ma'am, what is it?"
> "They killed him yesterday in Haarlem . . ."
> "The bastards!"[732]
> I ran away quickly. I didn't want to show my tears.
> (*Source:* Jan Rot.)

Walraven's courier, Laurens Weeda. said: "I am a military man, hardened in the tropics and in our fight against those thugs. But when the champion fell on February 12, I cried like a child."[733]

Gijs van Hall wrote:

> We heard it the day after he was shot. I went at once by bike to Zaandam, to Tilly, Walraven's wife. She was coming my way, and we met. Daughter Attie remembered hearing her mother cry in the kitchen. But her mother didn't explain why, at the time. After Wally's death, the children lost not only a father, but in a sense their mother too, because for months she was unable to do much of anything. (*Source:* Gijs van Hall, *Diaries.*)

On February 16, the leaders of the Domestic Forces, the armed Resistance groups now reporting to Prince Bernhard, met in Amsterdam. The note-taker wrote:

> Knecht [Carel Overhoff] announced that Van Tuyl was executed, which cut to everyone's heart. Knecht himself would not have been in this place without Van Tuyl, he recalled. He spent time remembering Van Tuyl, how he did everything in the interest of all of us and of the country. Those present observed a moment of silence. (*Source:* Domestic Forces, Minutes of meeting, February 16, 1945.)

A few days after the massacre, the German commander noted the death of the eight victims:

> *As a retaliatory measure[734] for the cowardly murder attempt on two members of the occupying power on February 11, 1945, the following people were shot publicly on February 13, 1945:*
>
> *1. Van Hall, Walraven, born 10.2.03 in Amsterdam, resided at Westzijde 42 in Zaandam. [. . .] I ask that the possessions of the above-named persons be collected from Weteringschans prison by March 1, 1945. Otherwise they will be disposed of. . . .*

Execution site Walraven van Hall, May 1945. (North Holland Archives)

The reported execution date and Van Hall's date of birth were incorrect. His reported birth date is on fake identification that aged him to escape the Work Assignment.[735]

Gijs's wife Emma expressed her feelings about Walraven in a letter she sent a week later:

> One of the greatest men of the Resistance has passed away. The insiders realize that he was a determined, convinced, and honest man, who radiated energy, genuine goodness, and great amiability. The shock of his terrible death, which he always faced, struck many hearts deeply. Old and young people of all kinds, in all circles, loved him. Yes, like many others, he fell for the fatherland. But he had also hoped to live to see the resurrection of his homeland, and participate in its reconstruction. (*Source:* Emma van Hall, Letter.)

Jaap Buijs wrote in his diary in those days:

February 12 to 18. Totally broken. I couldn't sleep or eat, and then that terrible cold. My birthday (February 17) made me worry what was happening at home, since I had heard nothing. I thought about Wally's wife, how he and she loved each other so much. Then I grieved how she would feel, when I could say nothing that might comfort her.

February 19 and 20. I had a wonderful experience. I fell asleep for a moment and awoke with a jolt to find my cell dimly lit. I got up and approached the wall, and ran into it; the cell was smaller than it seemed. I read on the wall: "Above all, take courage," written in light pencil. It was an epiphany. The next day, I looked carefully and found it was indeed written faintly on the wall. (*Source:* Jaap Buijs, Diary.)

Postwar Reburial, Memorials

As a member of a postwar purification committee, Jan Rot had to try traitors. That happened in the Weteringschans prison. In a corner cell he found, scratched amidst many other names, the signature W. VAN HALL. "I still remember the letters, slightly sloping upwards,"[736] Rot said later of the handwriting of his murdered friend. "The letters were scratched into the wall tightly and firmly. Poor Van Tuyl? No, strong Walraven van Hall!"[737]

On June 4, 1945, Van Hall was found in a shallow burial pit in the dunes near the Overveen Artillery Street.[738] He lay there with the other seven murdered on the Jan Gijzenkade. Undertaker Bleekemolen added one more body, that of Resistance worker Henk Hoekstra. He was from Blaricum, a brother-in-law of Remmert Aten, who was killed in a raid on his house on February 11. Walraven van Hall was one of the 422 murdered persons, almost all members of the Resistance, whom the Germans had buried in the Kennemer dunes near Bloemendaal.

The first task was identifying the victims. Former Resistance fighter and surgeon Hendrik Wamsteker of Haarlem took charge of this. Most of the dead had been robbed of their shoes and other belongings, some even of their clothing. Identification was mostly based on clothing remnants and marks such as tufts of hair and objects found, Difficult cases required looking at dental work. Dentists from all over the Netherlands assisted in this sad task. Searchers used lists kept by the Germans, and there were also the bills and the testimony of the Nazis' prison undertaker, Bleekemolen. At the beginning of July, Van Hall's wife had to identify her husband on the basis of the clothing they had found.

Next, the first memorials were created. Very soon eight memorial stones were put in place, some hidden in dune pans, others near the cycle path on the Seaway.[739] Then sandstone monuments were carved onsite by father and son. The son, Toon Lavertu, said: "Around us were still the pits where the executions had taken place. It was full of machine gun shells. The ground still cried out, "Murder!"[740] Four decades later, the eight memorial stones—damaged by wind, rain, heat, and freezing—were replaced by red granite ones.

Once his body was identified, the remains of Walraven van Hall were moved and re-interred at the nearby *Erebegraafplaats* (Cemetery of Heroes) in Overveen, where he today lies in section 35, near his mother Nel's relatives— Jan Karel, Gideon, and Louis Boissevain.

The Zaandam daily *The Typhoon* ran an *In Memoriam* on its front page after Liberation. Starting with four lines describing Walraven van Hall's Resistance activities, the newspaper ended with a farewell from Jaap Buijs:

> On February 12, 1945, Walraven van Hall from Zaandam fell before the firing squad of German executioners, after having fought with unequalled energy and great personal courage in the Dutch Resistance. Van Hall was one of those who suffered and fought for the fatherland. So many of these heroes gave their lives. He was one of the greatest. [. . .]
>
> Van Hall was a noble man. We all loved him so very much. Again and again he inspired new courage in us Resistance workers. When things went wrong, he always led us with his great confidence and his inexhaustible optimism! (*Source:* Jaap Buijs, *De Typhoon*, May 15, 1945.)

In another article in *The Typhoon* that day, Buijs, "one of the oldest and most prominent Dutch resistance fighters," added:

Half of everything of mine belongs to my best friend Van Hall. It is hard for me that I cannot share it with him now. He above all should have lived through these days of liberation, for which he gave his life. His death greatly diminishes my ability to enjoy the liberation—only with Van Hall here would I be ready to celebrate. (*Source:* Jaap Buijs, *The Typhoon.*)

Survivors

Shortly after the liberation, Tilly told her children that "Uncle Jaap" was back home. They visited him at his residence. Attie said: "He was lying on a bed in the conservatory, very thin, and burst into tears when he saw us."[741]

Buijs never fully recovered from his friend's death. Until the end, however, as he promised in prison, he supported Tilly and the children. Similar help came from Gijs van Hall, who was also marked by grief and regret. He became the guardian of Aad, Mary-Ann, and Attie.

How did the remnants of the National Working Committee, whose members were captured on January 27, 1945, experience Liberation?

Jaap Buijs, as mentioned, survived the war as a result of Lages's "German Honor."[742] He was released from his cell in the "Orange Hotel," the Scheveningen prison, on the evening of May 7, 1945. A day later he and other survivors had their first free discussion of the Foundation 1940-1945.

Hanneke Eikema spent three months in prison on Amsterdam's Havenstraat. She was unsuccessfully interrogated about her ties to the Resistance. Soon after the war, Eikema emigrated to Sweden. She married a member of a noble family and had a son whom she named after Walraven. She eventually moved to the United States, to Montana, where she died in 2012.

Jan Goedkoop left prison a free man after the German surrender and resumed his work with the Domestic Forces. However, it emerged that while in prison during the Occupation he gave up the names of two Resistance workers who were still at large. He also gave Viebahn a drawing of the telephone network used by the Domestic Forces. In December 1945, Goedkoop was sentenced to three years in prison for treason and a ban on contact with the former Resistance.

Teus van Vliet also had to answer to the Special Court in Amsterdam. On May 10, 1949, he was charged with two counts: First, that he told Friedrich Viebahn where, on January 27, 1945, the meeting of the National Work Committee[743] would be. Second, that he drew up for the Germans an organizational chart of the Dutch Resistance. He got off lightly. He was sentenced to a fine of 500 guilders, for the second offense only.[744] The court also forbade him for two years from working at any organization that emerged from the Resistance and forbade him from making any public statements about his Resistance activities.

On May 7, 1945, several managers from the National Support Fund from the western Netherlands met at the Amsterdam Industrial Club. Despite the liberation, the habitual fear of betrayal remained deeply embedded among the Resistance leaders.

Only one month later, on June 8, during a national NSF meeting in the Deventer Hotel restaurant, *The Emperor's Crown*,[745] did the district heads and other leaders get to know one another under their real names. They decided to set up the National Support Fund Foundation, with this objective:

> To continue, insofar as necessary, the support provided in the years 1940 up to and including 1945 by the National Support Fund, Seamen's Fund, and Landlubber[746] Funds, and the liquidation and settlement of the obligations entered into on the basis of this support, which the Foundation has been paying or has handed on to other organizations. (*Source:* National Support Fund Foundation charter.)

NSF Spending, 106.3 Million Guilders

The meticulously detailed accounts kept by the Van Hall brothers enabled reconstruction of what happened to the millions the NSF acquired.

PURPOSE	NSF SPENDING, MILLIONS DUTCH GUILDERS (1945)
During Occupation	83.8
Postwar—NIOD, Cemetery of Heroes, National Monument	22.5
TOTAL	106.3

During the Occupation, the NSF spent 83.8 million Dutch guilders[747] on Resistance organizations, people in hiding, and the railway strikers. The NSF had 22.5 million guilders left at the time of liberation. After the war, NSF money paid for the construction of the Eerebegraafplaats in Overveen, where Van Hall and 371 other victims found in the Kennemerduin area were reburied. Other donations included co-financing the National Monument on Dam Square in the capital and the National Institute for War Documentation (NIOD). The NSF was disbanded in 1953.

The total of 106.3 million guilders would have equaled $59.5 million in 1945 dollars at the immediate prewar (1938) exchange rate of 56 cents per guilder. (The Nazis declared the guilder worthless at the beginning of the Occupation but the Queen said she would accept guilders after the war.) That would be $1,009 million in 2024 dollars.[748]

Honors for Walraven

By Royal Decree of May 7, 1946, Walraven van Hall was awarded the Resistance Cross 1940-1945. He is one of only 94 Resistance fighters so honored.[749] A year later, Tilly received a certificate from the Ministry of War, crediting her husband as someone who "worked voluntarily for the intelligence service under very dangerous and difficult circumstances during the German occupation of the Netherlands."[750]

Van Hall's work in the Resistance was also appreciated overseas. On April 8, 1953, U.S. President Dwight Eisenhower bestowed on him the Medal of Freedom (with gold palm), the highest American civilian decoration. Israel gave him a Yad Vashem ("Righteous among Nations") award in September 1979 for his assistance to Jews.

Tilly and her children continued to live on Zaandam's Westside 42 until November 3, 1952, when they moved to Amsterdam. Twelve years later, Zaandam merchant Jan de Vries took over their patrician house from the intermediate owner Anna Maria Honig. He then demolished "the residence with the six houses,"[751] replacing it with an opulent shop building, the Zaanlandse Schoenhande.[752] The tangible memory of an extraordinary resistance fighter was gone.

Van Hall was forgotten for a while, although in the early postwar years it seemed unlikely that that would happen—in 1945 and 1946 Tilly received countless letters of condolence and other expressions of support. Senders included Queen Wilhelmina and the postwar Prime Ministers Schermerhorn and Drees. Drees described Walraven as "one of the most central and inspiring figures in the underground struggle."[753] Schermerhorn went a step further, calling him the "completely central and leading figure of the Resistance."[754] In 1946, the memorial book, *The Zaan Region,*[755] was dedicated *in sad and happy days* to "the great inspirer of the Resistance."[756]

Van Hall was one of six Zaandam resistance fighters commemorated on May 5, 1947 with a street named after them in the expansion of Zaandam. In the hall of the Amsterdam stock exchange, a plaque recalls his acts of resistance. Loe de Jong has honored him many times in his *magnum opus.* In 1987, he said in his Erasmus Lectures at Harvard: "No one contributed more than Van Hall to keeping the complex, sometimes stiff, gears of the Dutch Resistance running."[757]

But the general public had forgotten about Van Hall until the 1990s, when Geert Mak praised him in his best-selling book on Amsterdam's history.[758] Twenty years after the liberation, former Resistance member Remmert Aten reminisced about the oil man in *The Typhoon:*

I have a great admiration for Van Hall and his wife. He had a huge ability to organize us and get us resources whenever we needed them. If I had to name ten key people from the national Resistance, Van Hall would be one, and he would be near the top. He has not been honored nearly enough—neither by Zaandam nor by his country. (*Source:* Remmert Aten, *The Typhoon.*)

This book is another tribute, to help keep his memory alive.

The grave of Walraven van Hall at the Erebegraafplaats in Overveen.
Next to him is the grave of HR de Jong, who was also executed
in Haarlem on February 12, 1945. (collection author)

The current war memorial at the Jan Gijzenbrug in Haarlem. (Anton van Daal)

28 *Lèse majesté*. Disrespect for the sovereign. This was a major offense, treasonous, punishable by death.

29 **Fourteen coaches.** The family had sixteen children by two wives, so just one sibling was missing. See Michael C. Van Hall, *Three Centuries*, 52.

30 **Beautiful legacy.** The religious will is dated Utrecht, December 20, 1843. "Suze left her mark on the Reveil and the Separation (*Afscheiding*). . . . In 1954, an article appeared in the Dutch newspaper *Trouw* about Suze with the title "Women from the Reveil. . . . Among her friends was . . . Mrs. Boissevain De Clercq, who is also a figure of note." M. C. Van Hall, *Three Centuries*, previously cited, 56-57.

31 **She pleaded.** A more complete version of the 1843 religious will appears in Michael C. van Hall's translation of the book by his father Maurits Cornelis van Hall (1901-1963), *Drie Eeuwen* (Amsterdam: W. Ten Have, 1961); the translation is titled: *Three Centuries: The Chronicle of a Dutch Family* (Indianapolis: Xlibris, 2018), 56-57.

32 **Mennonite Van Schermbeek aunt.** The Van Hall book, *Three Centuries*, does not elaborate on this foster parent (Michael van Hall, 65). Puzzling.

33 **Maurits Cornelis van Hall.** The grandfather of Walraven van Hall was the curator of a school in Elburg. His opposition to religious extremism is apparent from his letters and visits to the school. He raged against the "exaggerated religious views in the Veluwe." Schaap, *Walraven*, 2014 edition, **Note 2**, 17.

34 **Palace of People's Industry.** *Het Paleis voor Volksvlijt.* M. C. Van Hall, *Three Centuries*, 82 (referenced there incorrectly as Paleis van Volksvlijgt). It was modeled on the Crystal Palace in London.

35 **Mak.** He cites a stage critic's description of the interruption in the *Algemeen Handelsblad* (edited for decades by Walraven van Hall great-uncle Charles Boissevain, who died two years earlier), February 2, 1929.

36 A genius, but crazy. All three children of Walraven and Tilly van Hall recalled this comment in the 2010s.

37 **Banque de Paris et des Pays-Bas.** Later Banque Paribas, since 2000 BNP Paribas. It has a building on Seventh Avenue in New York City.

38 **NV,** *Naamloze Vennootschap,* means "nameless venture," indicating that the owners are shareholders in a public company and are anonymous. It indicates a public corporation. The company was engaged in harvesting peat as a fuel. The area is rural (a nearby place is humorously called Siberië). The nearest municipality is Hoogeveen.

39 **Member of Parliament.** Maurits van Hall received a dagger and a state sword from the government. When the Nazis in June 1940 ordered all weapons to be handed in, his daughter-in-law Petronella [mother of Walraven and Gijs] instructed the gardener to bury the sword in the garden. After the war, the weapon was never found. Schaap, 2014 edition, Note 3, 17.

40 **Johan Rudolph Thorbecke.** A Dutch liberal statesman of the 19th century (1798-1872), he was best known for heading the commission that revised the Dutch Constitution in 1848, under Willem II, after liberal democratic revolutions in 1848. He also became Prime Minister three times under Willem III.

41 **House of Newtown.** *Huis De Neufville*, a possible reference to Neufvilles, a Walloon town in Belgium.

42 **Canal Belt.** The developers of the *Grachtengordel* residences tried to make each house equal to the next. But affluent homeowners like the Van Halls combined two or more houses, either next to each other or sharing back yards, or both. The Canal Museum has many good stories about the evolution of the houses on the canals.

43 Grandson. The grandson was Maurits Cornelis van Hall. The house is now the headquarters of the Hollandsche Society van Levensverzekeringen.

44 *Bouffantes*. This French word means shawls in Dutch. It is not used with this meaning in English.

45 Veluwe. Large rural area east of Utrecht.

46 **Sulfur.** Sulfur has long been known to be an effective anti-bacterial agent. https://www.ncbi.nlm.nih.gov/pmc/ articles/PMC7081397/.

47 **Jenny.** Female donkey.

48 *Smerige.* The Dutch word means, literally, "filthy, grubby, dirty."

49 **Hester Boissevain van Hall.** I knew her as "Tante Hessie," sister of my grandmother Olga Boissevain van Stockum. Hessie lived in Hattem, where I visited her first in 1947 and finally in 1959. Hessie's father (and my great-grandfather) Charles was editor-publisher of Amsterdam's leading newspaper, the *Algemeen Handelsblad*.

50 **Three Centuries.** Maurits Cornelis van Hall, Drie eeuwen: De kroniek van een Nederlandse familie. Amsterdam, 1961, 67-71. Translated into English as *Three Centuries: The Chronicle of a Dutch Family*, published by XLibris, 2016, revised 2018, 71-81.

51 *Pâté de Foie Gras.* This menu item would have been a nod to the origins of the Boissevains in the French Dordogne, home of the goose-stuffing farmers who today still create the pâté. Animal rights advocates today criticize the delicacy because of the forced feeding of the geese.

52 **The South Seas.** This archaic term is broader than Oceania and includes the Dutch East Indies, which the Dutch called "India." It was producing easy money for Dutch traders—from Javanese coffee, for example.

53 **Doctorate of Jurisprudence.** Unlike the U.S. system today where a lawyer's first degree is a J.D. (doctorate), the Dutch doctorate of jurisprudence is a further legal degree requiring research and a dissertation.

54 **Commissaris.** Translated as a commissioner or supervisory director. In the United States, a supervisor is usually a full-time staff member. No one on Wall Street today would hold so many directorships.

55 **Hattem.** An ancient Hanseatic League town, it is just three miles from Zwolle. The conservative nature of the small town in the 1920s is described vividly in Van Hall, *Three Centuries* (English edition, 1999, 87-88).

56 **Veluwezoom.** The oldest national park in the Netherlands, protected since 1931, it is especially gorgeous in late August and September.

57 **Rabbit Mountain.** *De Konijnberg.* One of the two Van Hall homes in Hattem. As mentioned already, Adriaan's brother Jan and Nel's cousin Hester lived in *Astra* in Hattem and then the *Kolkhuis*.

58 Kolkhuis. The final Hattem home of Jan and Heste//r van Hall, where Tante Hessie received her guests when the Marlin family visited in 1947 and I visited in 1959.

59 **Tucked into a comfortable crib.** *Een gespreid bedje,* "a spread-out cot."

60 **Walrave.** Walrave is a common given name among Boissevains. It is French, like the original Boissevains. For example, Gideon Walrave "Gi" Boissevain (1897-1985) was the son of Charles Daniël Walrave Boissevain and Willemina de Vos. Walraven is a less common name in the Netherlands. (Thanks to IEB for comment.)

61 **Beurs van Berlage**. https://stamps.org/Portals/0/ArticlesDistinction/Netherlands-Amsterdam-Stock-2017.pdf.

62 **Hendrik Berlage.** https://www.britannica.com/biography/Hendrik-Petrus-Berlage.

63 **Walraven's grandfather.** Michael C. Van Hall, *Three Centuries* (English edition, 2016), 65-86, 128-129. See End Note 1 above.

64 **The Bank for Small Loans.** *De Bank van Lening* was in a good position to know about indigents. People could borrow against almost any kind of collateral—*beleende panden* ("mortgaged property") meant pawned personal property, left as collateral for small loans. A municipal bank, it prefigured today's micro-lenders. (Thanks to MLB)

65 **Oh father! No more.** *Ach! Vader, Nier meer!* This poster slogan became a song, *Ach vaderlief, toe drink niet meer.* ("Oh dear father, please don't drink any more.") Wags changed *Ach!* to *Acht* to suggest eight more drinks.

66 **Impoverishment.** This idea wasn't just from Karl Marx. Frenchman Turgot in 1766 argued workers were impoverished by factories (Marx's *Verelendungstheorie)*. Classical economists said

competition would force workers' wages down to a subsistence level—Adam Smith credited the power of entrepreneurs; David Ricardo and Thomas Robert Malthus attributing it to population dynamics; and, from them, Ferdinand Lassalle formulated the Iron Law of Wages. Edward Bernstein called this "impoverishment theory." Paul M. Sweezy said this was no prediction; it was a law.

67 **Jordaan.** A radicalized working-class neighborhood on the east side of Amsterdam during the 1930s, it was gentrified after World War II and is now one of many tourist destinations in the city.

68 **Richard and Henriette Roland Holst.** In 1926-34, Richard Roland Holst headed the Rijksakademie van Beeldende Kunsten, where my mother Hilda van Stockum studied in 1928-30. Roland Holst gained fame from the catalog for an 1892 Van Gogh exhibition in Amsterdam—he put a Van Gogh wilted sunflower on the cover. Roland Holst married Henriette van der Schalk in 1896. She was a poet, nominated for the Nobel Prize in Literature, and an active Communist. Roland Holst died in 1938. During World War II she was in the Resistance, editing two Communist magazines—*De Vonk* ("The Spark") and *De Vlam* ("The Flame").

69 **Collateral.** Evert Agema, the father, most likely pawned household items to the Bank for Small Loans, *De Bank van Lening*, which, as mentioned before, is a municipally sponsored pawn shop. (Thanks to MLB.)

70 **The Green Amsterdammer.** *De Groene Amsterdammer.* Founded in the 19th century, this weekly magazine is still published and is internationally oriented. The name is not from environmental concern but from the green ink the magazine originally used to stand out. It was not published during the Occupation, but after World War II the famed war historian Louis de Jong wrote for it regularly. http://historisch.groene.nl/.

71 **Girls in the workshops.** Dubbed *Atelier meisjes*, literally, "studio girls," they were actually working in rooms with rows of tables where the girls cut and sewed fashionable clothing. The girls were paid little. Sweatshops in the 1910s and 1920s are remembered in London, Paris, and New York City, but they also existed in many smaller cities.

72 **Suzie van Hall van Tienhoven.** Adriaan's sister Suzie was the mother of Sonja, who married Bob Boissevain. They sheltered four Jews, for which all eight of Sonja's family earned a Yad Vashem award. Suzie should not be confused with Adriaan and Suzie's niece Suze, a dancer who married Cornelis Jan (Cees) Kelk and joined the Dutch Resistance with her older brother Frits van Hall, a sculptor. Suze became Willem van der Veen's partner.

73 **Keizersgracht 327.** The house was later occupied by Charles Ernst Henri Boissevain and his eleven children. It was the subject of several paintings by well-known artists.

74 **Nicolaas Witsen.** He was appointed mayor of Amsterdam thirteen times between 1682 and 1706.

75 **Walrave Boissevain.** Brother of Walraven's wife Nel Boissevain van Hall, and the person after whom Walraven was named.

76 **Cheerful laugh.** Nel Boissevain van Hall, letter.

77 **Foreign spas.** The Boissevains favored the *Bircher-Benner Clinic*, Keltenstrasse 9, Zürich (I was there for a week in 1963). Dr. Bircher was a vegetarian and believed in the superior nutritional value of a raw-food diet. He invented *Birchermüsli* ("muesli"), with a base of overnight-soaked oats, grated apples, and condensed milk.

78 **Dr. René de Monchy.** Salomon Jan René de Monchy was born on April 7, 1893 in Rotterdam. He married Nel's daughter and namesake, Petronella Gerarda van Hall, in Amsterdam in 1921. (He was 28; she was 23.) https://www.openarch.nl/nha:d90417f3-412e-4c89-821e-00c65d62984b/en. See North Holland Archives in Haarlem (Netherlands), Civil registration marriages, archive 358.6, inventory number 2503, 21-07-1921, *Huwelijksakten van de gemeente Amsterdam*, 1921, record number Reg. 3F fol. 21v. His father, Salomon Jean René de Monchy, was 30 in 1893 when René was born. His mother, Antoinette s'Jacob [*sic*], was 29. René and Petronella had a son Charles in 1924.

Petronella died in 1939; René lived another thirty years, to 76.

79 **Nel Boissevain van Hall.** In Dutch form, Nel van Hall-Boissevain—the husband's surname is first, separated by a hyphen. This book uses the Anglo-American style, which has no hyphen and shows the husband's name last.

80 **Dr. Salamon de Monchy.** Salamon, René de Monchy's uncle, was from a French family in Picardy. He was appointed Mayor of Arnhem and then Mayor of The Hague from 1934 to 1940. He presided over the marriage of Prince Bernhard and Princess (later Queen) Juliana. At 60, in 1940, he was sent to Buchenwald, but survived. Dr. de Monchy (1880-1961) returned to the Hague to be Mayor until 1947. https://www.parlement. com/id/vg09lm0bc8xl/s_j_r_de_monchy and https://resources.huygens.knaw.nl/bwn1880-2000/lemmata/bwn3/monchy (both in Dutch). (Thanks to MLB).

81 **Gymnasium.** The Dutch *gymnasium* was a high school with extra years to prepare students for universities, which at that time expected their incoming applicants to know Latin and Greek.

82 **Christiaan Gunning.** His father was briefly married to Elisabeth Boissevain, eldest sister of Walraven's mother Nel Boissevain. The sisters were daughters of banker Jan Boissevain. Schaap, 2014, **Note 4**, 23.

83 **Brugman.** The Dutch expression *praten als Brugman* means to talk eloquently and convincingly. According to the *Delft Student Almanac* the debating society was founded in 1868. https://bit.ly/3wK4v7M. (MLB, IB.)

84 **"The Bellows."** *De Blaasbalg.* Published by G. J. van Heuven Goedhart, later editor-in-chief of the *Parool*, "The Bellows" appeared five times in 1939, with a circulation of one million copies, to "warn our people against anti-Semitism, national socialism, and fascism in all their forms and to proclaim the value of democratic freedom." Schaap, 2014, **Note 5**, 23.

85 **Nazism, an Overview.** https://www. britannica.com/summary/Nazism.

86 **Russian Revolution.** The first revolution was in February 24-28 (old style), 1917 or March 8-12 (new style). It overthrew Tsar Nicholas II and killed his family. It was succeeded by the Provisional Government, which was overthrown by the Bolsheviks in October (November, new style) 1917, establishing the Soviet Communist government era. https://www.britannica.com/topic/February-Revolution.

87 **Zandvoort.** This seaside town ("Sand Fort") was a popular resort on the North Sea, west of Amsterdam. Bob Boissevain and other members of the Boissevain family owned homes there until the invasion, after which the Occupation evicted residents and fortified the beach against a British attack from the sea or air.

88 **HBS program.** HBS stood for the *Hogere Burgerschool* ("Higher Civic School"), a controversial Dutch secondary-school type prevalent in 1863-1974. It reached a U.S. community-college level with a five or sometimes a six-year high-school program— equivalent to a prestige *gymnasium*, without the Latin required for university entrance. Starting in 1968, it was replaced by the *Voorbereidend wetenschappelijk onderwijs* or *VWO*, a "preparatory scientific education," allowing for university placement in scientific subjects.

89 **Walraven's Sailboat.** A photo shows the boat had one mast. Walraven's younger brother Beppo notes this *sloep* ("sloop") was rigged unusually with two *fokkezeilen* (headsails, i.e., sails attached to the forestay, not to the mast). The boat is called a *jol* (usually "yawl," but this means a two-masted boat; in Walraven's case it meant a "jolly-boat"), named the *Hollebolletje.* It was rigged like a cutter, i.e., a single-masted boat with two or more sails. (Thanks to MLB and IB.) For sailboat types, see http://www. jordanyachts.com/3745e.

90 **The Spaarne.** This partially canalized river, named after a local reed, connects the North Sea Canal with the Ringvaart. It is separated by a lock from Haarlem.

91 **Not crystal clear.** Beppo's complaint will be echoed by Nico van Heek, as we shall see.

92 **The NV Royal Holland Lloyd.** The *Koninklijke Hollandsche Lloyd* was created in 1899 for the freight trade between Amsterdam and South America. Shipping cattle ceased

in 1903 when Britain prohibited import of live cattle. In 1906 the company began taking passengers between Amsterdam and Buenos Aires. From 1917 to 1919 it made calls at New York. Passenger service ended after 1935. https://www.theshipslist.com/ships/lines/khlloyd.shtml.

93 **Vuur.** *"Fire."* This was not just a mechanical problem. No technical anchor-related terms appear in the Dutch: *de lier, hondenkoppeling, kettingwieltrommel, palstang, kluispijp* —the winch, dog clutch, sprocket drum, ratchet bar, vault pipe. Walraven is describing sparks and flames from the anchor chain rubbing rapidly against the side of the ship. The word *vuur* implies so much friction it was more than *De vonken spatten er vanaf* ("Sparks flew off"). It was worse: *Het vuur spat er vanaf* ("The flames lick off"). The ship could have burned up. (Thanks to MLB.) (IB recommends review by Charles *Twello* Boissevain, the historian.)

94 **Sloop deck.** From the context, this was under the "galleon bow" where the helm would be located. These are steamships, using terms carried on from the 19th-century sailing ships.

95 **The Royal Industrieele Groote Club.** The Royal Industrial Grand Club is still a private club with many reciprocal clubs in the United States, such as the Army-Navy Club in Washington, D.C.

96 **Remington.** In May 1901, the Remington Company left Ilion, New York and moved its entire operation to 43-45 First Street, Utica, New York. Philo Remington sought and received financial support from Weston Mott and from Willoughby & Owen, carriage makers who wanted to invest in the future of ground transportation. The Utica-manufactured horseless carriage weighed about 900 lb and seated either two or four passengers. It was eventually sold by investor Charles Stewart Mott to General Motors. https://www.remingtonsociety.org/remington-automobiles/.

97 **100 guilders.** In 1927 this was worth $40, so $1 was then worth 2.5 guilders. The $40 then is worth $680 in 2024 dollars—a good price for a car. Exchange rate for guilders to dollars: *Federal Reserve Bulletin*, January 29, 1929, 35. (CPI of 17x from first page of BLS.gov.) https://fraser.stlouisfed.org/files/docs/publications/FRB/pages/1925-1929/28191_1925-1929.pdf.

98 **Diligence and ability.** Royal Holland Lloyd.

99 **A sadness for Wally.** Beppo van Hall.

100 **83 Washington Place.** This is just west of Washington Square, in the New York University area, Greenwich Village. Built in 1900, the 5-story apartment building has 12 units.

101 **The Stock Market Crash.** The Crash of Black Monday on October 28, 1929 was followed by economic decline and global financial panics until March 5, 1933, when panics were ended by the inauguration of Franklin Roosevelt and quick and strong action by his Treasury Secretary, railcar and locomotive czar William H. Woodin. However, his rescue was too late to prevent Hitler's Nazi Party gaining power in Germany based on economic discontent. https://www.bundestag.de/en/parliament/history/parliamentarism/third_reich/third_reich-200358.

102 **Shipping company.** Was this Boissevain & Co.? If so, Robert Boissevain would probably have been the contact. Maybe the Netherland Club files at the New York Public Library or the Millay Collection at the Library of Congress will have something on this. Eugen died in 1949, the year before his wife Edna St. Vincent Millay. His and her papers went to his wife's sister, who donated some records and sold some to the Library of Congress.

103 **Job at a Bank.** This might have been at a brokerage firm, which were until 1933 considered part of the banking business. Again, the Netherland Club archive or the Millay Collection might shed light on this. Eugen would have been in touch with the Van Halls when they visited. Boxes of his letters are in the Millay Collection.

104 **The Netherland Club of New York.** Formed in 1903, it was in 1903-1912 in 3 Gramercy Park West and in 1912-1939 at 3 and 4 Gramercy Park West. Both houses were built in 1846 and were once lived in by James Harper, Sr., Mayor of New York and founder in 1817 with his brothers of Harper and Brothers. http://daytoninmanhattan.blogspot.

com/2013/12/nos-3-and-4-gramercy-park-west.html. The Club moved in 1939 to The Holland House at 10 Rockefeller Plaza, also home to the Dutch Consulate General. During World War II, the Club was visited by Princess Juliana and Queen Wilhelmina. Its Archives are at the New York Public Library.

105 **Naturalized U.S. Citizen.** Walraven's maternal cousins Robert and Eugen Boissevain and Olga Boissevain van Stockum also became U.S. citizens. (Their brother Jan Boissevain may have also, but he retired with his wife Charlotte to the Cap d'Antibes on the French Côte d'Azur. I visited her in 1959, after he had died.)

106 **Dutch East Indies.** Eugen, Robert, and Jan Boissevain, three cousins of Walraven, were the owners of Boissevain & Co, which in the late 1910s and 1920s was heavily engaged in the coffee trade in Java. The business was severely affected by the Crash of 1929.

107 **Mother sympathized.** Nel Boissevain van Hall to her son Walraven, October 1930.

108 **Father transferred the funds.** From this and other stories, Schaap does not provide much evidence that either Adriaan or his son Walraven excelled at stock-or-bond-picking, or at startup investing.

109 **Shrouded in silence.** This is the fate of most early-stage investments in startups.

110 **Mindless and irritating herd.** Dutch: *. . . maar is het leven op den duur niets voor een Europeaan die gewend is om met mensen om te gaan en niet met een willoze en vervelende kudde zoals in NY.* Literal English: "But my life during this time was nothing for a European used to engaging with people and not with an unwilling and annoying herd as in New York."

111 **Office life in New York was interesting.** Why was the office so interesting? Possibly because of the scope of the 1929 disaster. The United States had been growing rapidly in the 1920s and was now a catastrophe in the last years of Hoover's presidency. Tragic, but interesting.

112 **Visa rule.** This rule is still widely in effect. https://innagram.com/visa/do-i-have-to-go-back-to-my-home-country-to-renew-my-visa.html.

113 **The Salland Region.** This is in the center of the Dutch province of Overijssel, between the Kop van Overijssel to the west and Twente to the east. To the east of the whole province is Germany. To the south, Gelderland. To the west, the Veluwe region of Gelderland and Flevoland. To the north, Friesland and Drenthe.

114 **Nel Boissevain van Hall.** In Dutch style, Nel van Hall-Boissevain.

115 **The Great Depression.** The Federal Reserve dates the U.S. Great Depression from the market crash in 1929 to U.S. entry into World War II in 1941. https://www.federalreservehistory.org/essays/great-depression. Economists date national recessions primarily by the period of a decline in gross product, which was in free fall during 1929-33 and was turned around somewhat by Roosevelt's policies. But unemployment lingered through the 1930s. Former Fed Chairman Ben Bernanke said "We [the Fed] did it . . . But we won't do it again." [See link above.] The Dutch economy suffered longer than other countries, because the Dutch government clung to the Gold Standard. High poverty and unemployment led to social unrest in working-class Amsterdam neighborhoods and, in Germany, to the rise of Hitler. E.H. Kossmann, *The Low Countries 1780-1940* (1978).

116 **Küchenmeister's.** This paragraph was not in Schaap, 2014, 29, but was added in a 2018 update.

117 **Gold standard.** Under the gold standard, the Dutch guilder was pegged at 2.5 to the dollar. The Dutch government kept up this peg until 1936, when predatory monopoly moves from Nazi Germany made it impossible for the Dutch to stay on the gold standard; 25,000 guilders would have been $10,000 in 1931, or $187,000 in 2023 dollars.

118 **No longer had an office in Amsterdam.** Walraven van Hall, letter dated February 11, 1932.

119 **Apprentice.** He was a *volontair,* which looks like a "volunteer," but is rather a trainee or an apprentice. The U.S. equivalent would be an intern. The Dutch today would say *stagiair.* (Thanks, MLB and IB.)

120 **Concealed firearms.** Schukking, *Memoirs* (2014 edition).

121 **Empty.** Walraven van Hall, letter to Tilly, date.

122 **Nel Boissevain van Hall.** In Dutch style, Nel van Hall-Boissevain.

123 **Sailboat.** This small boat was possibly a "slutter," with one mast, like a sloop with two foresails, similar to the rigging on a cutter.

124 **Hollebolletje.** "Hollow ball." Probably a pun on the family name, *Hallemannetje* (a van Hall fellow).

125 **Pretended:** Nico van Heek.

126 **Monkey died.** Tonny Eggink, 2014.

127 **Upper middle class.** These words are in English in Schaap, 2014, 30.

128 **The bottle is finished, Ma'am.** This story is retold by Jurriaan Walraven Kamps, great-grandson of Walraven and Tilly van Hall in the pages for Walraven on the Cemetery of Heroes website. http://www.eerebegraafplaats.nl/WalravenvanHall/WallyvanHall.html.

129 **Family party:** Probably a Boissevain party. His mother was from this family and Tilly's Den Tex family was intermarried with them. Hester, twin sister of Charles Boissevain the *Handelsblad* editor, married a Den Tex.

130 **Childhood friend of Tilly:** Victoria Coleman, letter to the children of Tilly and Walraven van Hall, 1989, after Tilly had died. Coleman dated the party as in December 1930, but Walraven was then still in the United States. Perhaps it was a few months later, when Walraven had just returned to the Netherlands. According to Van Hall's daughter Attie, sparks flew around Easter 1931, when the two met in Hattem. Schaap, 2014, **Note 6**, pp. 32-33.

131 **Hattem.** A rural town not far from Zwolle where two Van Hall brothers settled after marrying two Boissevain cousins.

132 **Kolk.** A kolk is a pond. There was one at the Kolkhuis, the home of Jan and Hester van Hall. I visited her with my family in 1947 and 1959 and probably at least once more in between as a child. I remember the location well, with Tante Hessie wearing the square of cloth on her head to signify she was an old lady.

133 **Patrician.** The Dutch use the word "patrician" to mean well-established and well-off, but not part of the nobility. In English it means aristocrat, but in the democratic Netherlands, royalty and aristocracy mean people with titles, while a patrician is someone untitled but with an aspiration for an aristocratic life style and genealogy.

134 **Nobility.** In the Netherlands, people keep track. Patricians are listed in the annual "Little Blue Book" (*Het Blauwe boekje*). The nobility are listed in their own book, the "Little Red Book" (*Het Rode Boekje*). Both are published in the Hague and include the *wapen* (the coat of arms) of each family.

135 **Royal Dutch Steamship Company.** Dutch initials KNSM. https://www.ggarchives.com/OceanTravel/SteamshipLines/RoyalNetherlands-KNSM.html#google_vignette.

136 **Hester Boissevain den Tex.** Hester and Charles *Handelsblad* Boissevain were twins. So they were both Walraven's mother Nel's first cousins. Walraven was therefore related to Hester via both his mother and his wife.

137 **Baby carrier.** In British English, a carrycot.

138 **It was revolutionary.** Letter from Dea to Attie, 1966.

139 **German election.** The March 1933 election was the last genuine one in Germany until after World War II. Hitler named himself Führer and from then on the outcome of elections was never left to the voters or to chance.

140 **He voted liberal.** Walraven's father showed his son how to behave in the financial workplace. His more progressive mother Nel showed him how to behave at home. Both skills made him a leader during the Resistance.

141 **Bah!** My grandmother Olga Boissevain, Nel's cousin, also used "Bah!" a lot, as did my mother.

142 **Pentislaan.** Near the home of the Van Hall couple. Schaap, 2014, **Note 7**, 33.

143 **The Dutch Nazi Party.** The NSB was the *Nationaal-Socialistische Beweging in Nederland.* These home-grown Nazis were led by Anton

Mussert until September 1944, when Mussert and panicked NSB friends fled to Germany.

144 **Grandmother Van Hall**. "To be clear, Grandma [Van Hall] was not Jewish, but unlike typical Dutch people had dark eyes and dark hair." Schaap, 2014, **Note 8**, p. 33.

145 **25,000 Guilders**. Approximately $800,000 in 2024 U.S. dollars. https://www.calculateme.com/precious-metals/gold/weight/13-grams.

146 **Beautiful Garden**. Attie van Hall, interview with author Erik Schaap.

147 **Beurs**. From the French Bourse, the stock exchange. (The French word is from the Latin *bursa*, purse. Beurs also means wallet in Dutch.) The Beursplein is the square outside the Amsterdam stock exchange. (IB.)

148 **Air Defense Service**. Dutch initials LBD.

149 **The Air Defense Service**. (The Service's initials in Dutch: LBD) supervised, among other things, compliance with blackout rules. From the beginning of the war, every civilian was required to screen all windows at night with heavy curtains or strips of blackout paper, to make it difficult for bombers to locate civilian targets. Where bombs fell, the LBDs supervised salvage and rescue operations. Schaap, 2014, **Note 9**, 36.

150 **Invaded**. Hitler never declared war on the Netherlands. He did not even offer a pretext for invasion.

151 **Mary Dawson Strawbridge** (1906-1994) attended Germantown Friends (Class of 1924) and then Mademoiselle Lacarrère's school in Paris. In 1927, Mary married William Penn Shipley Jr. They had two children; one, Marianne Nancy, died in 2021. https://bit.ly/3RRwkVU. Her mother **Anna Hacker Strawbridge** (1880-1981) attended Germantown Friends School and married Francis R. Strawbridge in 1902. She was President of the National Society of Colonial Dames and lived to be 101. **Source**: The Shipley-Strawbridge Family Papers Collection, Bryn Mawr College, Bryn Mawr, Pennsylvania. bit.ly/48OZj3i.

152 **Air Defense Service**. Called LBD, for the Dutch *Lucht-Beschermings-Dienst*. "Air Protection Service." They watched for planes.

153 **Joris in 't Veld**. He served as Mayor of Zaandam from January 1, 1937 until March 4, 1941 when he was removed as Mayor by the German Occupation. After the Occupation, In 't Veld was reinstated as Mayor.

154 **It's no mistake**. The Dutch *Het is mis* means "It's wrong," or here "Something is wrong." The context clearly is: It is no mistake.

155 **Paratroopers**. Thousands of German paratroopers were dropped near The Hague. But the Luftwaffe lost one hundred planes to Dutch anti-aircraft fire. The paratroopers failed to capture the Queen. Hitler and Göring, furious, asked for immediate surrender or they would bomb Rotterdam. The Queen surrendered but the news arrived too late and downtown Rotterdam was reduced to rubble.

156 **State Artillery Devices Company**. *Artillerie Inrichting*. See *Historische feiten, weetjes en verhalen op, rond en over de Artillerie Inrichtingen. Artillerie Inrichtingen Hembrug* (in Dutch). "Photos of Hembrug Factory." zaans-industrieel-erfgoed.nl (in Dutch). *Het Staatsbedrijf der Artillerie Inrichtingen* (pdf). grebbeberg.nl (in Dutch).

157 **General Henri Gerard Winkelman**. Born 1876, died 1952, he was a career officer in 1896-1934. Recalled from retirement to serve as commander-in-chief of the army and navy in 1939, he directed the Dutch defense until the invasion (May 10-15, 1940). After the Queen and Cabinet fled to England on May 13, he was left in charge, with orders to fight as long as it made sense. After Rotterdam was bombed, he ended civilian losses by surrendering on May 15, 1940. He became a prisoner of war on July 2, 1940. Source: *Encyclopedia Britannica*.

158 **State Artillery Devices Company**. It restarted production more than a month after the invasion, June 20, 1941.

159 **Black swans**. Schaap's Dutch reads "white ravens," itself an uncommon expression in Dutch. However, the meaning is clear. They were *rarae aves*, rare birds—in English, black swans. (MLB.)

160 **The Geuzen**. Literally "Beggars," the Geuzen were Dutch resisters during the country's Spanish occupation (1568-1609). The largely Calvinist Dutch guerrilla troops

and privateers initiated the Dutch revolt against Catholic Spain. The derisive term was used against the lesser nobility who in 1566 petitioned Margaret of Parma, governor-general of the Netherlands, for relief from persecution of Protestants. The nobles won concessions and adopted the "Geuzen" label. In 1567, Margaret's successor, the Duke of Alba, was less tolerant. Many Protestant dissidents fled abroad, returning to fight. By 1573, the Geuzen had reconquered the maritime provinces of Holland and Zeeland.

161 **The "Phony War."** This label did not apply to Jews. They were immediately tracked down and stripped of their civil service jobs and then their assets. The efficient Dutch administration was unfortunately used to serve German administrators of the Holocaust. https://jcpa.org/article/wartime-and-postwar-dutch-attitudes-toward-the-jews-myth-and-truth/.

162 **Squire.** Translation of "Jonkheer," which refers to the untitled aristocracy, such as younger sons of the nobility.

163 **Dutch Republicans.** They favored elected government, without any role for the monarchy.

164 **Non-Aggression Pact.** The Ribbentrop-Molotov Agreement between the two unlikely bedfellows was signed in August 1939 and was broken by Hitler less than two years later. Hitler did not want to fight on two fronts too soon.

165 **Correct Attitude.** *Politics and Culture,* CPN's monthly magazine, June 1940.

166 **Communists.** A year later, the Communists became aggressively hostile to the Nazi Occupation once the Germans invaded the Soviet Union (June 22, 1941). Within the Dutch Resistance, relations between the Communists and the religious leaders were often tense.

167 **Action against Jews.** Note how quickly the Occupation moved against Jews in the Air Defense Service (LBD), while they were seeking to ingratiate themselves with the rest of the Dutch population.

168 **Dutch Nazis.** A recent synoptic review looks at the 1940 upending of Amsterdam's deserved centuries-old reputation for tolerance.

It notes the February (1941) Strike, over deportation of Jews by Seyss-Inquart, was unique in Europe. Barry Davis, "Diaspora," *Jerusalem Post,* July 7, 2022. https://www.jpost.com/diaspora/article-711454.

169 **NSNAP.** Stands for *Nationaal Socialistische Nederlandse Arbeiders Partij.* The National Socialist Dutch Workers Party, one of the two smaller Nazi parties, was founded by Ernst Herman van Rappard.

170 **De Bijenkorf.** This high-end department store is today operating in Amsterdam and six other Dutch cities.

171 **Plotske.** Salomon Plotske and his immediate family were killed by the Occupation in 1942. A monument to them is at their home, Zuider Amstelaan 97. https://www.joodsmonument.nl/en/page/153709/salomon-plotske.

172 **Silo thinking.** Pre-war Dutch welfare was based on religious "pillars"—Roman Catholic, Protestant denominations, smaller religious groups. (The more common term in English is "silo," from the separate storage silos for oils and grains on U.S. farms.) It meant unproductive religious rivalry and easy identification of Jews.

173 **Polarized parliamentary democracy.** Dutch Union was to be the center.

174 **Escape valve.** Gijs van Hall.

175 **Suburban.** In Laren-Blaricum, two upscale towns in the Gooi, east of Amsterdam. Gijs lived in Laren.

176 **It cannot openly declare itself.** Gijs van Hall.

177 *Zaankanters.* Literally, Zaan trotters.

178 **Five hundred statements of support.** *De Zaanlander,* July 31, 1940.

179 **Dinkelberg Complaint.** Mayor Jan Kalff van Krommenie, letter to Hans Linthorst Homan, July 31, 1940.

180 **Carrying Nazi News.** "March 24, 1942. In the Kerch Peninsula of The Ukraine, weak attacks by the enemy [Soviets]; in the Donetsk area, stronger attacks. The enemy were repelled." Within a year, the Soviets defeated

the Germans at Stalingrad, the bloodiest battle ever, 2.2 million casualties.

181 **Vigilance.** In Dutch, *De Waakzaamheid.*

182 **Tusenius.** K. H. Tusenius was an early supporter of the Dutch Nazis. He joined Arnold Meijer's small Nazi National Front party. His 1936 article on the Dutch Nazi movement is *De kansen van het Nationaal Socialisme in Nederland: groei en neergang der N.S.B.*, "The opportunities of National Socialism in the Netherlands." He regrets that the early growth of the N.S.B. from 1931 was followed by "decline." Tusenius is cited in a 487-page Ph.D. dissertation by Joshua Robert Sander, "The Greater Germanic Reich: Education, Nazification, and the Creation of a New Dutch Identity in the Nazi-Occupied Netherlands." University of Tennessee at Knoxville, 2018, 15. https://trace.tennessee.edu/cgi/viewcontent.cgi?article=6440&context=utk_graddiss.

183 **Dutch Union Membership.** Few Dutch Union member lists survived the war. Its meteoric rise meant the party never properly administered memberships. So people now report conflicting numbers. Schaap, 2014, **Note 10,** 41.

184 **Smaller Dutch Nazi parties.** The NSNAP had 15,000 members. Arnold Meijer's National Front had 10,000.

185 **Wrong place.** Linthorst Homan, *De Unie,* "The Union."

186 **SDAP.** The A is for Arbeider, Dutch for worker. Social Democratic Workers Party. The SDAP was a patriotic Dutch holdover from the pre-war parties, whereas the NSNAP was in support of the Nazi Occupation.

187 **Coming from their blood.** Meinoud Rost van Tonningen, NSB leader and Commissioner, SDAP, from his speech. The Dutch reads: . . . *maar dat de stem van het bloed is.*

188 **The Castle.** *Burcht* in Dutch.

189 **Demise.** *Ondergang* is the Dutch. It means ruin, decline. It is fair to say that the Dutch Union declined.

190 **Secure something more important.** Jacques Presser, *Ondergang* (book in Dutch). In other words, the unachievable best is the enemy of the achievable good. Compromise is hard when the negotiators are so far apart.

191 **Half-Jews.** People with one Jewish parent. The Nazis raged against Aryan-Jewish marriages but for the most part they did not deport Jewish spouses (1) if the couple had children, (2) if the Jewish spouse filled an important job. This subject was one of the main topics of the notorious Wannsee Conference in January 1942, which formally launched the "Final Solution to the Jewish Question."

192 **"Native" Jews.** Editorial, *Members' Magazine,* Dutch Union, October 12, 1940.

193 **Branch.** The Dutch word is often translated as "department," but the VPCs were regional and in English would therefore be called branches.

194 **Provisional local committee.** Abbreviated VPC, for *Voorlopig Plaatselijk Comité* (Provisional Local Committee).

195 **Dinkelberg would have to step down.** A. A. Aberson, letter to Dinkelberg, at NIOD archive.

196 **Founding Date of VPC Zaandam.** Because so few records were preserved about the Union, the founding date of the Zaandam branch is misstated. The book *Verzet aan de Zaan* ("Resistance on the Zaan") gives the date as July 23, 1940, a day before the Dutch Union was created nationwide. J.J. 't Hoen dates it in *De Zaanstreek* as August 1940. Both dates are incorrect, according to NIOD documents. Schaap, 2014, **Note 11,** 43.

197 **The SDAP.** This pre-war socialist workers' party opposed Kapital, Kirk, König (king), Kazerne (military barracks), and Kroeg (saloons). It refused to join the Nazi NSNAP. In 1939, moderate SDAP members joined a coalition led by a Protestant, De Geer. Two joined the Dutch government-in-exile, Albeda and Jan van de Tempel. In 1944, Jaap Burger joined them. The SDAP was banned in 1940 and many members joined the Resistance.

198 **Immense Popular Movement.** *Regional Chronicle of North Holland,* February 1941.

199 **It's May again.** *Regional Chronicle,* May 1941.

200 *Het Wilhelmus.* This Dutch National Anthem begins: "William of Nassau, of Dutch blood am I / Faithful to the fatherland, Rooted here till I die. https://www.youtube.com/watch?v=gwBrR_G70RE.

201 **Wormerveer.** North of Zaandam, on the Zaan river.

202 **Diverse.** Literally, "transversal," meaning "intersecting."

203 **The Green Police.** The *Grüne Polizei* were so called because of their uniforms. They were the Dutch police assigned to routine tasks relating to public order, as opposed to Nazi political and investigative roles.

204 **Police Found Nothing.** The Dutch original uses the Latin *Resultat nihil.* Result, nothing.

205 **Damage will be compensated.** *Uniekrant* (Dutch Union News), August 1940.

206 **Secretary Aberson.** Letter to Jaap Buijs.

207 **Nazi "WinterAid."** This was intended to provide aid to "needy Dutch people." But given the Nazi origin of this appeal, many Dutch people—with the motto "Not a button from my fly, / For the WinterAid guy"—refused to participate in the appeals for this charitable, but also propagandistic, institution. Schaap, 2014, **Note 12,** 45.

208 **Make himself useful.** Tonny Eggink, *Walraven van Hall. 10 februari 1906-12 februari 1945.*

209 **People wanted by the Nazis.** Not just Jewish people (who had a "J" stamped on their ID cards), but people who were wanted for work in Germany, or Resistance workers.

210 **Union House employee.** From a letter to the Union by regional secretary Aberson.

211 **The Reichskommissariat.** This was headed by Austrian Reichskommissar Arthur Seyss-Inquart.

212 **The NSNAP.** The National Socialist Dutch Workers Party (in Dutch, *Nationaal-Socialistische Nederlandsche Arbeiderspartij*) was a minor Dutch Nazi party founded in 1931 and led by Ernst Herman van Rappard. It had few members, like the National Front.

213 **Suppression.** *Gelijkschakeling.* Literally, "equalization," a meaningless euphemism.

214 **Amsterdam Stock Exchange.** In Dutch, *Beurs,* as in the French Bourse, from the Latin *bursa,* purse.

215 **Association of Commission Houses.** *Vereniging van Commissiehuizen.* Stock brokers were traditionally paid by a commission, a percentage of the value of the stocks exchanged. A *Vereniging* is an association.

216 **Stock trader.** The trader is unidentified. A Kraut ("cabbage") is slang English for a German. The comparable Dutch slang was *moffen,* from *Muffe,* an old term for German speakers in the Dutch northeast, before Germany existed.

217 **Dutch Nazis.** Members of the NSB, the main Dutch Nazi Party, or two smaller pro-Nazi parties.

218 **Jews.** Specifically, Jewish stockbroker colleagues. This same question might have been asked before government in exile asked the railway workers to go on strike in September 1944. The Dutch suffered more than the Germans.

219 **Fines.** Amsterdam had to pay 15 million guilders in "compensation," Hilversum 2.5 million guilders, and Zaandam 0.5 million guilders. Schaap, 2014, **Note 13,** 49.

220 **Fundraising.** At first, funds were raised primarily as donations from individuals. That raised enough money.

221 **Cousin.** Van Hall's cousin Frits van Hall worked also with his sister Suzie, Schaap, 2014, **Note 14,** 49.

222 **Cash Association.** *Kas-Vereeniging.* This specialized bank was formed in 1865, hence the archaic spelling of Vereniging. https://pm20.zbw.eu/folder/co/0140xx/014030/about.en.html.

223 **Arnold Jan d'Ailly.** Leader of one of two Dutch banks that did not help the National Support Fund in 1940-44, in 1944 d'Ailly turned round and helped Gijs and Walraven obtain substantial sums for the Resistance from the bank through "additions to reserves." D'Ailly was Mayor of Amsterdam in 1946-56. Gijs van Hall was Mayor in 1957-67.

224 **Commissioner.** *Beauftragter* was the German word. Occupation officials all had German titles. The American equivalent would be a Governor of the Federal Reserve Board in Washington, DC.

225 **The Dutch State Bank.** *De Nederlandsche Bank,* the Dutch central bank. Although founded in 1814, its roots go further back, to 1609, with the creation of the Amsterdam Exchange Bank, which operated like a central bank. https://www.cambridge.org/core/books/abs/sveriges-riksbank-and-the-history-of-central-banking/four-hundred-years-of-central-banking-in-the-netherlands-16092016/FFE0331A290CF44FE65C33F04B6B0E40.

226 **Association of Stockbrokers.** *Vereniging van de Effectenhandel,* abbreviated *VvdE,* not to be confused with the Association of Brokerage Firms, which was formed after the war was over.

227 **Mr. Van Hall.** Walraven's father.

228 **Carel F. Overhoff.** Overhoff later assisted Walraven and Gijs in their underground financing network in the last year of the war. But his reputation as a Resistance hero took a hit after the war, when an inquiry found that, while he was chairman of the Association of Stockbrokers (VvdE), he sold stolen Jewish securities. In 1948 he was convicted of writing checks to himself, as early as 1929, from the account of his Amsterdam employer, Kerkhoven & Co. He had to resign as chairman of the VvdE, lost his Military Order of William award for his Resistance activities, and was sentenced to prison for 2-1/2 years. Schaap, 2014, **Note 15,** 51.

229 **Withdraw Support.** The Occupation claimed the British would forbid the shipping companies from paying to their wives and other dependents the salaries and pensions owed to their officers and sailors.

230 **Max Steenberghe.** He was the Minister of Commerce, Industry and Shipping and was a member of the RKSP, the Roman Catholic State Party. The prewar political parties were based in part on religion.

231 **Radio Orange.** Two weeks later, on May 1, 1941 the Ministry of Agriculture and Fisheries was added to Steenberghe's portfolio in the Queen's cabinet in London.

232 **Boiler boy.** These were often underage apprentice youths, unlikely to be married or have any dependents.

233 **Seamen's Fund.** The Dutch name was *Zeemanspot*—combining *Zeemans* (Seamen's) with the word *Pot* (Jar). *Pot* is a metaphor for a place to put money, namely the place for a seaman's family to get money and for donors to give it. Since the Middle Ages, ship owners and sailors started funds to help widows of drowned seamen, or buy the freedom of captured sailors. "Seamen's Pot" preserves the rich allusions, but "Seamen's Fund" is clearer.

234 **Johann van Marle.** He was the son-in-law of Hilda Boissevain de Booy. He was married to Olga de Booy, named after her aunt Olga Boissevain van Stockum.

235 **Van Marle.** His wife Olga was a cousin of Walraven's mother, Nel Boissevain van Hall.

236 **I didn't get very far.** Source: Abraham Filippo, letter to Gijs van Hall.

237 **Feenstra.** The "friendly relative" was Mr. Feenstra from Schiedam. Schaap, 2014, **Note 16,** 53.

238 **I contacted Mr. W. Van Hall.** Filippo, 1945 report.

239 **Machinists' Union.** In Dutch, the *Machinistenbond.*

240 **W. Van Hall would work with us.** Andries Teunissen, early Seamen's Fund worker.

241 **Hollandia factories.** Filippo, letter to Gijs van Hall.

242 **Rotterdam's Attitudes:** Teunissen. Rotterdam's Seamen's Fund leaders presumably expected Amsterdam leadership to look after their own sailors.

243 **Van Meerveld.** Also spelled sometimes Van Meerveldt. Schaap, 2014, **Note 17,** 53.

244 **I will not now abandon colleagues.** Van Heek.

245 **50,000 guilders.** Van Heek.

246 **Ton.** A "ton" of guilders meant 100,000 of them. Since 1839, a guilder was required to

weigh exactly 10 grams. So 100,000 guilders weigh exactly 1,000,000 grams, or 1,000 kilograms = a ton. The short U.S. ton is 2,000 pounds, the long or British imperial ton is 2,240 pounds, and the metric ton is exactly 2,200 pounds).

247 **Vos de Mooij.** De Mooij does not appear in the index to Schaap, 2014..

248 **Resistance, 45,000 people.** Loe de Jong, *History of the Second World War* (in Dutch), 1975.

249 **Birthday Fund.** Initially, money was paid out on birthdays, hence the nickname Birthday Fund. Schaap, 2014, **Note 18**, 55.

250 **Brandsma.** Pseudonym of U. W. H. Stheeman. Schaap, 2014, **Note 19**, 55.

251 **Jan Bottema.** Lieutenant Bottema paid for his Resistance work with his life. He was shot in Wormerveer on December 17, 1944 as reprisal for an attack by the Zaan resistance. Schaap, 2014, **Note 20**, 55.

252 **Praeses.** Spelled sometimes Preses, the word is taken from a ancient Rome, when it meant a governor. It is used primarily still in student government.

253 **A group of people.** They were a representatives of Professor Heringa (Nieuwenhuijsen), Van den Bosch, Van Hall, Van Hövell tot Westerflier, Mesritz, and Valkenburg.

254 **Wally's mother-in-law.** Van Veloen said Van Hall's mother (Nel), but meant Van Hall's mother-in-law [+Abramina Adriana Engelberts den Tex]. Tilly den Tex's mother lived at 10 Leidsegracht, a canal that connects the main residential canals. Schaap, 2014, **Note 21**, 55. [+Tilly's paternal grandmother was Charles *Handelsblad* Boissevain's twin sister Hester. Wally's mother, Nel Boissevain, was Hester's niece. https://www.findagrave.com/memorial/193138005/anna-mathilde-van_hall.]

255 **Professor Heringa.** Van Velsen, letter to Tilly van Hall.

256 **Lambertus Neher.** This NC foreman soon realized that this goal was too ambitious, after which the NC specialized in the exchange of information and the production of Resistance pamphlets. Neher always worked closely with the NSF and befriended Walraven van Hall. Schaap, 2014, **Note 22**, 55.

257 **Van Velsen.** Not in Schaap, 2014, Index (*Namenregister*) or Bibliography (*Bronnen*).

258 **SDAP.** The prewar Social Democratic Workers' Party. "Workers" in Dutch are *Arbeiders*. The Dutch word is spelled with a d. (The German word for work is *Arbeit* with a t, as in the infamous *Arbeit Macht Frei*, "Work Makes (You) Free," the ghoulishly misleading motto that greeted prisoners at Auschwitz— site of the largest mass murder in world history. Rudolf Höss brought the motto from Dachau, the previous camp he oversaw. Prisoners said: "Work makes you free, / Via Crematorium Number Three." Source: PBS, https://www.pbs.org/auschwitz/40-45/beginnings/. Also https://bit.ly/3RV74ha.) The Dutch *arbeider* is an employee earning a "wage" rather than a "salary"—"blue collar" in English. (Thanks to IEB.)

259 **Zaanstreek.** Zaan region.

260 **Van Tuyl.** This was the pseudonym that Walraven van Hall used most frequently during the Occupation.

261 **Jan Rot.** In Schaap, 2014, Index (*Namenregister*) but not the Bibliography (*Bronnen*).

262 **SiPo.** This is the abbreviation of *Sicherheitspolizei*, the Nazi "security police" in 1936-39, which combined the political police (Gestapo) and criminal investigators (Kriminalpolizei), under SS Group Leader (*Gruppenführer*) Reinhard Heydrich. In 1939, SiPo was merged with the Reich Security Main Office (RSHA), but the prewar names continued to be used. Rudolf Höss said: "Only the SS were capable of protecting the Nazi State from internal danger. All other organizations lacked the necessary toughness." **Source**: PBS, see note above on SDAP.

263 **Squeaking gate.** That might have been purposefully undone maintenance, announcing visitors.

264 **Johannes Hermanus Scheps.** *Scheps Inventariseert* ("Scheps Inventories"), Apeldoorn, 1973. Article on Walraven van Hall. Book cited in Schaap, 2014, 177, *Bronnen*

(Bibliography). Walraven was not known to be very religious, so the religious theme might have been to look for less religious divisiveness after the war.

265 **Labor Party (**Dutch: *Partij van de Arbeid,* **PvdA).** It was formed in 1946 with prewar Social Democrats (**SDAP**) as a significant core. The economic-and-social-liberal People's Party for Freedom and Democracy (Dutch: *Volkspartij voor Vrijheid en Democratie,* **VVD**) was founded in 1948 from the prewar Freedom Party. The Catholic People's Party (Dutch: *Katholieke Volkspartij,* **KVP**) continued from before the war, and is, after merging with other Christian-oriented smaller parties, still known as CDA (Christen Democratisch Appel).

266 **Dutch People's Movement.** Walraven's ideas were tried after his death, when the Dutch People's Movement (the *Nederlandse Volksbeweging,* **NVB***),* was created on May 12, 1945. After initial enthusiasm by politicians and much of the population, the NVB succumbed to partisan differences. Some of its initiators switched to the Labor Party, the **PvdA**, founded in 1946. Walraven saw that little remained of the Social Democrats (**SDAP**), while the **VVD** and **KVP** continued on. Not for decades would a "depillarized," more humanist, society take shape.

267 **Knecht.** Pseudonym of Carel Overhoff, Commander of the Interior Forces in Amsterdam—Erik Schaap. Van Tuyl was of course the pseudonym for Walraven van Hall.

268 **Ration Card Depot.** It was in the "Fopma building" in Amsterdam. This is the only reference to it in Schaap, 2014. Fopma is a surname for about 500 Dutch people.

269 **Heinrich Douqué.** He was a leader of the National Organization for Help to People in Hiding (LO). During the later Occupation, an estimated 315,000 people were hiding, of whom 28,000 were Jewish. www.annefrank.org.

270 **Beursplein.** Employee of the Seaman's Fund (*Zeemanspot*). The *Beursplein* is the square outside the stock exchange (the *Beurs*).

271 **We did not support the NSB women.** Filippo.

272 **Wally and I wondered.** Gijs van Hall.

273 **About $50 million 2024 dollars.** Converting to 2024 dollars is a challenge. The Nazis declared Dutch guilders of no value but the Queen said on Radio Orange that the government would honor guilders after the war. A prewar guilder was worth 56 U.S. cents and that is still the ratio for the Antilles Dutch guilder. If we use that exchange then 5.2 million guilders was about $50 million in current dollars (the 2024 dollar is worth 1/17th of the 1944 dollar; see www.bls.gov). The guilder went out of use in the Netherlands in 2002 after it adopted the euro.

274 **British Government.** The British assurance is not documented. A CIA report on the Dutch Resistance says the Dutch queen sent money, but there is no evidence any reached Van Hall. She did eventually announce over Radio Orange that she would repay loans after the war. https://www.oorlogsbronnen.nl/thema/De%20Zeemanspot.

275 **Disconto Institute for Seamen.** *Disconto Instituut Zeelieden,* also known as the DIZ. https://www.oorlogsbronnen.nl/thema/De%20Zeemanspot.

276 **Loan Receipts.** In later years, numbered currency denominations (guilders and rijksdaalder notes) were used. Schaap, 2014, **Note 23,** 59.

277 **Sniffer-dogs.** Gijs van Hall.

278 **Wally.** As noted previously, Walraven's nickname, used by family and friends.

279 **Minimum Loan Amount.** Smaller loans are likely to increase the number of transactions and therefore the likelihood of detection. The larger the minimum loan amount, the fewer the number of transactions.

280 **National Support Fund.** As we shall see, the Seaman's Fund later expanded to include support for many Resistance activities and was renamed the National Support Fund (*National Steunfonds,* or NSF).

281 **My brother knows nothing.** Gijs van Hall.

282 **Left the Ruhr area.** Until October 1941, it was official Nazi policy to encourage emigration from Germany. But emigrants had to get a visa to another country and there were restrictions on what emigrants could take

with them and increasing demands on what they had to leave behind. https://encyclopedia.ushmm.org/content/en/article/german-jewish-refugees-1933-1939. The "Final Solution" was to send remaining Jews to the death camps.

283 *Judenrein.* Literally: "Jew Clean" or "Jew Free." This was the Nazi Occupation order to *exclude* Jews. They also created Jewish ghettoes to *enclose* them. Both controls were used by the police, under orders of the racist SS.

284 **Theo Olof.** He had a distinguished musical career. His obituary is here: https://www.gramophone.co.uk/classical music news/article/obituary-theo-olof-violinist.

285 **Marriage of convenience.** Jews married to gentiles were usually left alone, especially if there were children.

286 **Are you not a Jew?** To be clear, the question was an accusation and a threat. (Thanks to IEB.)

287 **Formally introduced.** An infamous conference at Wannsee, near Berlin, in January 1942 presented the plan to senior SS and civil service representatives. The "Final Solution" called for extermination of all Jews in Europe.

288 **Final Solution.** The German policy, *Endlösung,* is usually translated as a vague "Final Solution." But the full phrase, *Endlösung der Judenfrage,* is not vague. The Nazis meant to purge almost all Jews, genocide. In a speech to the Reichstag on January 30, 1939, Hitler was very clear: "[If] international finance Jewry inside and outside Europe should succeed in plunging the nations once more into a world war, the result will be not the Bolshevization of the earth and thereby the victory of Jewry, but the annihilation of the Jewish race in Europe." Source: Jeffrey Herf. *The Jewish Enemy: Nazi Propaganda during the World War II and the Holocaust.* Harvard University Press, 2006, 52.

289 **Gerrit Jan van der Veen.** His devoted girlfriend was Suzie van Hall. Van der Veen led the forgery operation.

290 **As you wish.** His point was that he would not be following them, and they could go into hiding.

291 **Westerbork.** The Dutch government set up the camp in 1939 for Jewish refugees from Nazi Germany. After the German

invasion, Westerbork was shifted into reverse, serving as a transit camp where Jewish and other inmates performed forced labor before being shipped east to other concentration or death or death camps.

292 **Extermination machine.** Killing of Jewish people in Europe had been proceeding in somewhat randomly until a conference in the Berlin suburb of Wannsee on January 20, 1942, where the plan for the *Endlösung,* the "Final Solution," was presented to Nazi Germany's second- and third-tier SS and civil service officers. Photos of the 15 who attended are here: https://www.jewishvirtuallibrary.org/wannsee-conference-attendees. The plan was that most Jews in German-occupied Europe would be deported to camps in occupied Poland and murdered. The organizers expressed pleasure at the lack of pushback at Wannsee. The conference was called by the director of the Reich Security Main Office SS-*Obergruppenführer* Reinhard Heydrich, to ensure cooperation of the various government departments. Christopher R. Browning, *The Origins of the Final Solution: The Evolution of Nazi Jewish Policy,* September 1939-March 1942. With contributions by Jürgen Matthäus. Published by the University of Nebraska Press, Lincoln, and by Yad Vashem, Jerusalem. eBook (PDF), April 2004, 978-0-8032-0392-1 $40.00.

293 **Freiberg.** This was an adjunct to the Flossenbürg concentration camp. https://www.britannica.com/place/Flossenburg-concentration-camp-Germany. This was near the Czech border.

294 **Child was gassed.** Tilly den Tex van Hall.

295 **Transported to Auschwitz.** Tilly den Tex van Hall.

296 **Ton.** A "ton" is Dutch slang for 100,000 guilders. A metric ton is what the guilders would weigh, or once would.

297 **Converting large notes.** This is an example of how the Van Halls turned a bad situation into an opportunity.

298 **Full cooperation.** Gijs van Hall, postwar statement.

299 **Lost their income.** Working from home was not yet a thing.

300 **Landlubbers Fund.** The *Landrottenfonds* was created as a counterpart to the Seamen's Fund (*Zeemanspot*). The combined fund, along with other special funds, including one for Jews, became the National Support Fund (*Nationaal Steunfonds*) or NSF.

301 **The first loan.** Postwar report on NSF activities, probably Gijs van Hall in 1948. (P. Sanders wrote in 1960.)

302 **The Gooi.** This area included such upscale suburban communities as Bussum and Naarden (which shared a train station), Blaricum, and Hilversum. Charles Boissevain's home, "Drafna," was in Naarden.

303 **Landlubbers Fund.** G. Bergsma was the Fund's chief cashier. Schaap, 2014, **Note 24**, 65.

304 **We were exclusively supporting sailors' families.** Filippo collaborator.

305 **Chamber for the Arts.** The *Cultuurkamer*, literally "Culture Chamber," controlled payments to artists.

306 **Aryan Statement.** To join the Chamber for the Arts, artists had to swear they were Aryans.

307 **Black art.** Underground sales of art created by artists who are not members of the Chamber for the Arts.

308 **Forging Identification Cards.** https://jck.nl/en/exhibition/identity-cards-and-forgeries. When the Germans introduced identity cards (*Persoonsbewijzen*) to identify Jews, van der Veen, Arondeus, the printer Frans Duwaer, and others including Suzie and Frits van Hall produced some 80,000 false identity papers.

309 **Jan *Canada* Boissevain.** This Jan was known in the family as "Jan *Canada*" because he was born in Canada when his father was serving there as a Dutch diplomat. Princess Juliana moved to Canada with her family during the war (a park in Ottawa was named for her) and Canadians were active in liberating the Netherlands in May 1945.

310 **CS-6.** The group was named after their home address, Corellistraat 6. Jan Karel was known as Janka. Gideon was known as Gi. Neither survived the war—both were shot at the Waalsdorpervlakte, an open area in the dunes where 250-280 members of the

Resistance were killed by firing squads. It now has a monument to the Resistance..

311 **Escape route.** The story was told in a book by Resistance member Betty Goudsmit-Oudkerk.

312 **Royal descendant.** Princess Margriet was born to Princess Juliana in Ottawa, Canada, in 1943. She was named after the marguerite daisy, which was worn as a protest during World War II.

313 **Aad van Hall.** In Schaap, 2014, Index but not Bibliography.

314 **Gerrit Huig,** postwar memoir. He is in the Schaap, 2014, Index but not the Bibliography.

315 **Tuchthuis.** Penitentiary, literally: a house of discipline. This was run by the Dutch criminal justice system, not by the SS, so he was not taken away to a concentration camp.

316 ***Zaandamse Artillerie Inrichtingen.*** Before the Occupation, they supplied artillery equipment to the Dutch military.

317 **Trotyl.** Abbreviation of *trinitrotoluene*.

318 **Intended for Sabotage.** Douwe Soepboer, in Schaap, 2014, Index but not the Bibliography.

319 **PTT.** The Dutch Post, Telephone, and Telegraph.

320 **Enforcing the rules.** In Dutch, Walfraven was now a *regelneef,* a controller, enforcer, a "rule cousin." The word has a positive connotation, someone who is an organizer, manager, takes charge. (Thanks to IEB.)

321 **Liquidate.** By 1943 the Resistance was ready to eliminate collaborators, with elements of a trial. The Dutch word *geliquideerd* is still used for mob underworld killings, usually meaning executing with a gun.

322 **'s-Hertogenbosch.** Next town north of Eindhoven. Its name is a contraction of the Old Dutch *des Hertogen bosch*, "the forest of the duke," i.e., Henry I of Brabant. It is widely known as Den Bosch.

323 **Louis van Bunge.** A journalist and Resistance worker in Den Bosch. Schaap, 2014, **Note 25**, 69. [+The Index shows this as the only mention of Van Bunge in Schaap's book.]

324 **Weeda.** He survived the Occupation, along with Gijs van Hall, Jaap Buijs, and other friends of Walraven. https://meitotmei. nl/de-uitgestelde-bevrijdingsdag-van-een-zaandamse-domineesdochter/.

325 **Downed English pilots.** Such a pilot is featured in my mother Hilda van Stockum's book, *The Winged Watchman* (Farrar Straus, 1962), still in print (by Bethlehem Books) and selling steadily every year. Her brother Willem was an RAF pilot and was shot down in France, where he is buried in an honorary grave with his crew and another RAF plane crew. The French honor them every June.

326 **The tasks he performed. Source:** Weeda, postwar report.

327 **Westside 42.** The Dutch spelling of Walraven van Hall's Zaandam address is Westzijde.

328 **Landlubber Fund.** Some sources mention the National Support Fund and the Landlubber Fund interchangeably. Schaap, 2014, **Note 26**, 71.

329 **Mrs. Van Hall helped us.** Weeda, postwar report, referring to Tilly.

330 **Aad van Hall.** He is in Schaap, 2014, Index but not the Bibliography.

331 **Donations.** Initially, relatively small donations were the main source of funds. Donations amounted to approximately six million guilders during the entire war. As the Landlubber/NSF spending rose, donations became less important. Large loans became the main source of revenue. Schaap, 2014, **Note 27**, 71.

332 **Aad van Hall** (1936-2021). His nickname was also used for an uncle. In the Schaap, 2014, Index, but not the Bibliography.

333 **The Dutch State Bank.** *De Nederlandsche Bank.* The central bank.

334 **Leonardus Trip.** He was replaced as head of the Dutch State Bank, *De Nederlandsche Bank,* by Dutch Nazi Party thug Meinoud Rost van Tonningen.

335 **Gerbrandy.** From September 1940, Pieter Sjoerds Gerbrandy was chairman of the Council of Ministers of the Dutch government in exile. [He can be identified in photos by his large mustache.] Schaap, 2014, **Note 28**, 71.

336 *Responsible Citizens.* These words are in italicized English in the original Dutch.

337 **Weird things.** Wally was being sarcastic about breaches of security. *Wonderlijk* does not mean wonderful, but rather weird. (Thanks to IEB.)

338 **Espionage Support by the NSF.** By May 1945, the Landlubber Fund and the NSF paid out more than 965,000 guilders to various espionage groups. Schaap, 2014, **Note 29**, 71.

339 *Englandspiel.* The British MI6 Special Operations Executive lost 54 agents sent in pairs to coordinate the Dutch Resistance with Allied plans. Amazingly, the Germans captured and killed almost every one, which helped ensure Operation Market Garden's failure, prolonged the Dutch Occupation by eight months, and created the horrific "Hunger Winter." It was a "textbook illustration, the world over, of how not to conduct clandestine work." See Roger Beam and Jo Wolters, *Englandspiel: The England Game—SOE's Worst Wartime Disaster* (Yeovil, UK: Haynes Publishing Group, 2009). This was the worst British intelligence disaster of World War II, possibly of British history, possibly of world history. Here is a short, riveting film about it: https://www.youtube.com/watch?v=cBodD838uDI.

340 **LO.** *Landelijke Organisatie voor Hulp aan Onderduikers,* the National Organization for Helping People in Hiding.

341 **Van Tuyl.** As noted previously, this was a Resistance pseudonym of Walraven van Hall.

342 **They knew we were not fraudsters.** Gijs van Hall.

343 **India, Indonesia.** The Dutch used the word "Indië" to mean the Dutch East Indies, a Dutch colony from 1796 until its occupation by the Japanese from 1941 to 1945. The word is sometimes translated in English as "India," but to be clear in this book it is translated as "Dutch India." After Japan's defeat and withdrawal in 1945, Sukarno quickly declared Indonesia's independence. Queen Juliana withdrew from Indonesia in 1949. (Thanks to IEB.)

344 **Approached the banks myself.** Gijs van Hall, postwar report.

345 **Tons.** Reminder: The weight of 100,000 guilders is a metric ton.

346 **Emergency rations.** Gijs van Hall.

347 **Eligibility for Support.** The nine categories were: (a) next of kin of non-convicted executed persons, (b) families of hostages, (c) families of prisoners awaiting trial, (d) next of kin of convicted and executed persons, (e) families of convicted prisoners, (f) civil servants dismissed because of a "patriotic" attitude, (g) families of soldiers in hiding, (h) families of other people in hiding, and (i) Jews. Schaap, 2014, **Note 30**, 73.

348 **Religion.** If the religion was Jewish, the recipient was referred to the J Fund, which of course required even more secrecy than the prior funds.

349 **Few people were willing to take such big risks.** In her 2013 biography (Père Marie-Benoît and Jewish Rescue, Bloomington: Indiana University Press) writer Susan Zuccotti suggests that childhood and family experience with religious discrimination makes someone more likely that someone would help a persecuted minority. She traces Père Marie-Benoît's empathy for Jews to his own childhood in a French region where Catholics were persecuted. An ancestor of Père Marie-Benoît was executed in the late 18th century for sheltering a priest who refused to swear allegiance to France. A priest uncle was exiled from France after his abbey was seized by the French army in 1880. Père Marie-Benoît had to go to Belgium to prepare for the priesthood because anticlerical laws forbade members of religious orders from teaching in France. Dr. Zuccotti believes that her biographee's childhood "sense of belonging to a persecuted minority within a hostile state" encouraged him to rescue Jews. https://primolevicenter.org/events/pere-marie-benoit-and-jewish-rescue-how-a-french-priest-together-with-jewish-friends-saved-thousands-during-the-holocaust/.

350 **Every Fortnight.** Jaap Buijs.

351 **Prakken.** Coincidentally, ABJ Prakken's son—like his father active in the Resistance—in 1961 became a Zaandam police commissioner, where Jaap Buijs and Walraven van Hall lived. Schaap, 2014, **Note 31**, 75.

352 **The Kern.** The Kern was a collaboration of underground groups. Schaap, 2014, **Note 32**, 75. [+Kern (like the English "kernel") means "central," literally "nucleus." So The Kern was meant to be a central committee with representatives from different underground groups. (Thanks to IEB.)]

353 **NSF Fraud.** There was one case of fraud at the NSF during the war, out of a total of more than 84 million guilders paid out in benefits. A Tilburg NSB member learned the NSF system and issued his own "bonds" in the name of the Dutch government, extorting 500,000 guilders from people who wanted to support the Resistance. The fraud was found, the victims were compensated after the war, and the perpetrator was arrested. Schaap, 2014, **Note 33**, 75.

354 **NSF Deaths.** Among those killed were NSF leaders Walraven van Hall and Iman J. van den Bosch and nine of the 23 branch heads. (But the NSF system was not revealed.) Schaap, 2014, **Note 34**, 76.

355 **It is a duty.** Rijk Keij, Leiden head. Van Hall was severe about the area's reluctance to obtain and keep receipts.

356 **Buijs, Weeda, van Hall.** Their Resistance pseudonyms were Ruys, Van den Brink or just Brinkie, and, of course, Van Tuyl.

357 **NSF, National Support Fund.** *Nationaal Steunfonds* in Dutch. This translation minimizes acronyms the reader has to learn. But the NSF, introduced in the previous chapter, remains—the Bank of the Resistance.

358 **National Assault Squad.** In Dutch, *Landelijke Knokploeg* (**LKP**). With 750 members in August 1944, they conducted sabotage and assassinations, and stole ration cards for the LO. Three men—Leendert Valstar ("Bertus"), Jacques van der Horst ("Louis") and Hilbert van Dijk ("Arie")—organized the LKP in 1943. It peaked at 2,277 members in September 1944, when everyone believed the Dutch war was ending. The LKP suffered 514 deaths. Only one LKP

leader survived the war—Liepke Scheepstra. **Source:** verzetsmuseum.org.

359 The National Organization for Helping People in Hiding. In Dutch, *Landelijke Organisatie voor Hulp aan Onderduikers, LO.* Created in 1942 by Helena Kuipers-Rietberg and Frits Slomp, it provided social services. It was the most successful resistance group in Europe. Helena was betrayed and died in the Ravensbrück camp, the largest camp for women and second only in size to Auschwitz. Of 12,000-14,000 LO workers, 1,104 were killed or died in Nazi camps. See verzetsmuseum.org and https://encyclopedia. ushmm.org/content/en/article/ravensbrueck.

360 Personal Identity Center. In Dutch, *PersoonsBewijzenCentrale, PBC. Bewijs* means "evidence," "identity." Created by Gerrit van der Veen, the PBC forged the hard-to-fake Dutch ID card, the *PersoonsBewijs (PB),* created by Jacob Lentz (1894-1963), an idiot-savant at the Dutch Ministry of the Interior who combined a photo, fingerprints, and a number. He was thus a big ally to the genocidal SS, hunting for Jews in hiding. Luckily, Jewish artist Alice Cohn, among others, forged the ID cards well. https://jck.nl/en/exhibition/ identity-cards-and-forgeries.

361 Work Assignment Program. The Germans used this name, *Arbeitseinsatz,* "Work Mission," as a euphemism for forced labor. They conscripted Dutch men 18-45 for work in their factories, short-handed because of casualties and needs of the *Wehrmacht.* The Occupation used Z cards to select Dutch workers to deport.

362 Spiritual starting points. Prewar Dutch welfare was organized by religion. This interfered with Resistance cohesiveness. Catholics, Protestants of different denominations, Jews, Communists, humanists disagreed .

363 Van Tuyl. Reminder: This was the pseudonym for Walraven van Hall.

364 Binder. Dutch *samenbinder.* Someone who binds together something or people. Schaap, 2014, 78.

365 Bromet. Ben Bromet's office was now a Resistance shelter.

366 General-Plenipotentiary Representative for the Work Assignment. *Generalbevollmächtiger für den Arbeitseinsatz.*

367 Z cards. Z cards enabled the *Zurückstellungsverfahren,* "deferral procedure," which allowed businesses to exempt their essential workers from deployment to Germany for the *Arbeitsensatz.* Schaap, 2014, **Note 35,** 79.

368 Hugo of the LO. Pseudonym of Teus van Vliet. Schaap, 2014, **Note 36,** 79.

369 Z-card Success. Gerard Everstijn. Fake cards were used by workers to claim exemption from deportation.

370 First Meeting. Keij speaks here of October 1942 and elsewhere of February 1943. Everstijn uses the latter date. The *Leidsch Jaarboek* (1946) cites January 1943. Schaap, 2014, **Note 37,** 79.

371 End their personal contact. In other words, end channeling funds to people in hiding through them.

372 SiPo. The Nazi *SicherheitsPolizei,* Security Police, was created by Heinrich Himmler in 1936, merging the Criminal Police (*Kripo*) with the Political Police (*GeStaPo*). It was closely aligned with the SD (*Sicherheitsdienst*), the intelligence agency of the SS, which controlled everything and was ideologically sworn to hunting and killing Jews. https:// encyclopedia.ushmm.org/content/en/article/ the-security-police-sipo.

373 CS-6. An alternative derivation of the name of the group is "Center for Sabotage, Group 6," but there is no evidence of any other group but number 6.

374 Gang of Thugs. Letter by Jan *Canada* Boissevain to his father.

375 Jan "Canada" Boissevain. He was born in Montreal, Canada. His father, Charles Daniel Walrave Boissevain, was a Dutch diplomat and served as Dutch Consul-General in Montreal before World War I. To distinguish him from the many other Jans in the family, his nickname became Jan *Canada* Boissevain.

376 Jan and Mies Boissevain. Both Jan *Canada* Boissevain and his wife Adrienne Minette (Mies) van Lennep Boissevain were active in the Resistance. Before the war, she worked on behalf of feminist organizations like the Society for Women's Interests and Equal Citizenship (*Vereeniging voor Vrouwenbelangen en Gelijk Staatsburgerschap*). During the Occupation, the family housed and protected Jewish refugees from Nazi Germany. The house where the family moved at the end of 1939 gradually became a center of Resistance activities. Fugitives were hidden there, false identities were prepared, and explosives and weapons were stored. Her two oldest sons, Jan Karel "Janka" Boissevain and Gideon Willem "Gi" Boissevain, were members of the Resistance group CS-6. Both parents were arrested by the Nazis and sent to concentration camps, where Jan died of illness and their two eldest sons were executed. Mies and a third son Frans, and two daughters, survived the war. After the war, Mies promoted a national liberation skirt (*nationale feestrok*), and some of these quilted skirts are in Dutch museums.

377 **CS-6.** What is known was in 2022-2023 assembled for an exhibition at the *Verzetsmuseum* in Amsterdam.

378 **Barber's intervention.** A good scene in the Dutch movie *Bankier van Het Verzets* ("Resistance Banker") is based on this story.

379 **Overduin.** She was surely related to Leendert Overduin, a pastor in Enschede. On September 13, 1941, *SiPo* rounded up 105 Jewish men from towns in Twente and deported them to Mauthausen. Three people asked Overduin if he would shelter them and he took them in. He could not take more, so Group Overduin was formed. It had fifty members and saved at least one thousand Jews from the camps. A 2021 YouTube documentary was made about it. After the war, Pastor Overduin helped the new fugitives—children of parents involved with the Dutch Nazi Party.

380 **Professor C.** was Professor Jan Coops (Resistance pseudonym "Oom Jan"). The mathematics and physics building of the Free University, where he worked, housed a Resistance group that had formed around him. The professor of chemistry used his knowledge of chemistry to help forge identity cards. Schaap, 2014, **Note 38**, 81.

381 **Could not exchange.** The Occupation invalidated 1,000-guilder and 500-guilder notes except for owners who could prove their legitimate ownership.

382 **The other board members.** Besides Krouwer, the members were H.E. Steenbrugge and S. de Vries (who took charge of Amsterdam), R. Aten (North and South Holland, with the exception of the Gooi) and L. Roorda (the Gooi and initially the rest of the Netherlands; later F. van Hoorn took care of the north and east of the country). Schaap, 2014, **Note 39**, 81.

383 **Aten knew nothing.** Remmert Aten, postwar memoir.

384 **Bob van Amerongen.** Bob van Amerongen lived to be 90, dying in 2014, one week after his son unveiled, on Liberation Day (May 5), a plaque at Keizersgracht 695 in memory of the Jewish Resistance, *Vrije Groepen Amsterdam* (VGA). The group was twenty percent Jewish, disproving the cliché of Jews not resisting their fate. Van Amerongen hid his Jewish father Jules and other Jews. The plaque for Bob honored his Resistance work. Bob grew up on the chic Wilhelminalaan in Alkmaar. His parents were teachers at the Murmellius Gymnasium. His gentile mother Henriëtte taught Dutch, his father Jules taught English. Bob was a good student and had a privileged childhood until the German invasion, after which the Van Amerongens experienced murderous Nazi racism. Jules was fired from his teaching job in late November 1940, along with all Jewish civil servants. Bob left school in protest at teachers' inadequate protest at the dismissal of their Jewish colleagues. In mid-1942, after the Wannsee directives (the "Final Solution"), Jews were deported to extermination camps. The following winter, Jules went into hiding. Many Jewish relatives appealed to Bob for help. In September 1943 he noted his sorrow at Dutch acceptance of the Occupation: Sometimes I have the urge to write on the streets and walls that *it is war, and that we are involved in it with all our smaller and larger interests. They don't know—they don't want to know.* In early 1943, Bob van Amerongen (then nineteen), together with schoolmate Jan Hemelrijk (twenty-five), founded the PP group, after the "Porgel"

and the "Porulan" fantasy animals in the clandestine rhyme *De Blauwbilgorgel* by Cees Buddingh. Van Amerongen helped find hiding places and arranged for money, ration cards, and supplies. In late 1944, the pair founded *Vrije Groepen Amsterdam* (VGA), an association of forty Amsterdam groups hiding Jews. Van Amerongen was partly responsible for large food transports on ships from Friesland. After liberation he stayed at Weesperzijde 34, where the forgery department of the PP group and VGA were located. He became a teacher of classical languages at the Stedelijk Gymnasium in Haarlem and rector in 1965-74. Van Amerongen died in Bergen. **Source:** Loes Gompes, *De Groene Amsterdammer*, May 27, 2014. https://www.groene.nl/artikel/bob-van-amerongen.

385 **Nervous.** Walraven wasn't nervous enough—he was shot in 1945. Van Amerongen lived to be 90, dying in 2014.

386 **Landwatcher.** In Dutch, the *Landwacht* recruits collaborating *Landwachters*. A villain in *The Winged Watchman* (Bethlehem Books, 1995), is a Dutch landwatcher-traitor, age 18, who threatens his own parents.

387 **Nothing came of it.** Disguising oneself in a battle has risks, as Patroclus sadly found in Troy.

388 **LO.** *De Landelijke Organisatie voor Hulp aan Onderduikers.* The National Organization to Help Underdivers (People in Hiding).

389 **Personal Identity Center.** The PersoonsBewijzenCentrale (PBC).

390 **Banknotes.** The 1000-guilder and 500-guilder notes the Occupation had invalidated.

391 **Mad Tuesday.** *Dolle Dinstag* in Dutch. It was on September 5, 1944, when the Allies appeared to have liberated Breda in the occupied Netherlands. Dutch people, elated, celebrated in the streets. Leaders and members of the Dutch Nazi Party fled to Germany. Both sides mistakenly thought that German surrender was only weeks away.

392 **After Liberation.** For a short period after the war, the NSF continued to provide aid to Jews. But by that time responsibility for individuals was shifting to the postwar government and to personal connections.

393 **Churchill's comment.** Winston Churchill said about the Dutch government in exile: "The only man among them was the Queen."

394 **Heard nothing.** That was not an accident. As noted elsewhere, Walraven feared the Dutch government in exile was leaky with information and it was therefore dangerous to communicate with them.

395 **"Total amount. . . . may not exceed 200,000 guilders."** Queen's Government in Exile.

396 **Bank robberies.** A possible reference to some successful robberies, or the failed one in Almelo, or just to desperate talk in Amsterdam.

397 **Dispose of.** The Queen guaranteed the Dutch Treasury would repay loans after the war. But the Queen offered no help to Walraven and his brother Gijs on obtaining the money in the meantime. Meinoud Rost van Tonningen, head of the Dutch State Bank, had attacked Anton Mussert's form of Nazism, calling him insufficiently anti-Semitic.

398 *Engelandvaarder.* Schaap (2014, 86) calls Homan an *Engelandvaarder*—an "England-sailor" or "England-paddler" because the long trip, via a series of European countries, was comparable to that of a privateer sailing to the Cape of Good Hope, whom the Dutch called a *Capvaarder.* Some made the trip successfully. (MLB)

399 **The Dutch Trading Company.** In Dutch, the *Nederlandsche Handel-Maatschappij*, which was a bank. It eventually merged with the Twente Bank to become ABN.

400 **Microfilm.** Schaap in the Dutch calls it a microphoto or micrograph. (Schaap, 2014, 86.) In 2023 we might call it a microfiche, but this is a more recent, postwar word. The first university microfiche was used at Harvard in 1938, and the Harvard University Library used this format to preserve old newspapers. The project was called the Foreign Newspaper Microfilm Project. https://bit.ly/3Ypfkrh.

401 **Hotel Die Port Van Cleve.** The 122-room hotel is open in 2023, north of the Magna Plaza shopping center, and west of the Royal

Palace on the Dam Square. It is on the site of the first Heineken brewery, opened 1864.

402 **The Kern.** As noted earlier, this was to be the "core" or "nucleus" (English "kernel") of the Resistance, as the NSF was its principal financing source.

403 **NC.** The high-level National Committee (*National Comité*) was intended to be what the NSF and Kern became. It was middle-of-the-road politically. Lambertus Neher was the connection between the NSF and NC.

404 **LO.** Reminder: *Landelijke Organisatie voor Hulp aan Onderduikers*, the National Organization for Helping Underdivers (People in Hiding), was described early in this chapter. The first contact was with Hendrik Dienske.

405 **We have a job for you.** Buis, Parliamentary Committee of Inquiry, 1952.

406 **Ten National Organizations.** They were the National Support Fund (NSF), the care group of the newspaper *Trouw*, the National Committee of Resistance (NC), the Council of Resistance (RVV), the Identity Card Center (PBC), the National Organization for Aid to People in Hiding (LO), Natura, the National Knokploegen (LKP), Ordedienst (OD) and the Food Wartime Commission (VOC). Schaap, 2014, **Note 40,** 89.

407 **Hundreds of thousands.** American readers of a draft of this translation, who mostly think of the Anne Frank story as describing the Netherlands in World War II, are astonished at the total number of people hiding (*onderduikers*) in the small, flat Netherlands.

408 **Eliminations.** Assassinations of known collaborators with the Occupation.

409 **NC.** National Committee of Resistance, previously mentioned. Originally formed to lead the Resistance, an OSS analyst described it as "right-center," one of four central Resistance groups. It had few members, but they were influential. OSS, Research and Analysis, *Current Intelligence Study*, No. 6, R&A 3016S. https://www.cia.gov/readingroom/docs/DOC_0000709432.pdf.

410 **Hiding places.** *Hoekjes* (Schaap, 2014, 89). *Schuilhoeken.* Hiding places for *onderduikers*,

targets of Nazi police searches seeking to go underground.

411 **Foundation 1940-1945.** In Dutch, *Stichting 1940-1945.*

412 **A great man:** Adolf Johann Cord Rüter, *Riding and Striking: The Dutch Railways in Wartime* ('s-Gravenhage: Martin Nijhoff, 1960; in Dutch). The late Leiden University professor questions the Queen's strike call against the Dutch Railways (the *Nederlandsche Spoorwegen, NS*), holding it partly responsible for the *Hongerwinter* (Hunger Winter). He has also written about the railway strike of 1903.

413 **The Ration-Card (TD) Group.** Named after the *Tweede Distributie* (Second Distribution) of the *Stamkaart* (Main Card), the rationing system introduced by the Germans, the TD sought to help get food to *onderduikers*, people in hiding, especially Jews. Schaap, 2014, **Note 41,** 89.

414 **Much larger LO.** As previously mentioned, the LO was the largest single resistance group in Europe.

415 **NSF.** Only in Zeeland and the western part of the Veluwe was the NSF unable to build an organization. Schaap, 2014, **Note 42,** 89.

416 **NSF Staff.** After the liberation, 1,862 names of NSF employees were registered. Schaap, 2014, **Note 43,** 91.

417 **Top-down.** Schaap, 2014, uses the English words.

418 **Triumvirate.** Walraven van Hall, Van den Bosch and Voorwinde (later Gelderblom).

419 **Dordrecht.** Dordrecht district head Sytze Roelof Beinema was shot on August 11, 1944 in camp Vught. The Germans failed to wrest the names from other NSF employees. Schaap, 2014, **Note 44,** 91.

420 **It had disappeared.** Gijs van Hall.

421 **Turkish Pass.** This was a piece of paper torn in half and divided between two people. By putting the matching halves together during encounters, both know the other can be trusted. It was often used during World War II to prevent infiltration, often combined with a password or other identification. Schaap, 2014, **Note 45,** 91.

422 **Turkish Pass—Why Turkish?** Did the Turks ever use such a pass? Online searches for "Turkish Pass" or "Turkse Pas" in the United States and the Netherlands show no use of a pass of this kind other than as an ID for someone Turkish coming to the EU. The half-coins in James Clavell, Noble House (1981) https://bit.ly/3LkRPLB are fictional.

423 **Jonkheer Willem Arnold Eduard de Ranitz** married Helena Clara van der Garden on November 24, 1944 in Amsterdam. He was 38 years old. He is first-line nobility Jonkheer (equivalent to a British Baron).

424 **Everyone was cheering.** Anonymous stock broker.

425 **The quiet rest was imaginary.** Nico van Heek.

426 **Advised.** Translation of the word *stuurt*. The primary meaning of *sturen* is to "send" or "steer;" but "direct" makes most sense here. (MLB)

427 **Wally regained his strength.** Van Heek.

428 **Depraved attackers.** *Onverlaten* means reprobates or miscreants. Weeda's use of the term to describe likely *Sicherheitsdienst* agents suggests that no one found out who the attackers were. (MLB)

429 **Caught nothing.** *Bot vingen*. Means literally "caught bone." (No fish, just the fishbones.)

430 **The Gooi.** This area includes Hilversum and the upscale suburban towns of Blaricum, Naarden, and Bussum.

431 *Sicherheitsdienst* **(SD).** The SD was Hitler's Security Service, also serving the Nazi Party. It reported to the dreaded racist *Schutzstaffel* (**SS**), or "Protective Echelon." The SD was founded in 1925, fully embracing Nazism. The SD was the first SS intelligence agency, tasked with finding and killing Nazi "enemies." The agency employed a few hundred full-time investigators and thousands of informants. It was a "watchdog" over the SS and the Nazi Party, empowering SS leader Heinrich Himmler and, under him, SD head (from 1932) Reinhard Heydrich.

432 **The SD discovered.** The SD had a huge card-index of Nazi enemies—labor organizers,

socialists, Jewish leaders, journalists, and Communists. It tried to arrest them all and send them to Dachau, a new prison near Munich. In 1934, Heydrich became Chief of the *Sicherheitspolizei* (**SiPo**) and SD. In 1938, the SD was made the intelligence agency for the State and Nazi Party, supporting the Gestapo. On September 27, 1939, SiPo became a part of the Reich Security Main Office under Heydrich. The SD helped crush the Wehrmacht intelligence (*Abwehr*); engineered the Austrian *Anschluss;* managed "Case Green" (the Sudetenland invasion); and faked the Polish attack that precipitated World War II. Heydrich was assassinated in 1942. The postwar Nuremberg tribunal declared the SD and the SS to be criminal and in 1946, Heydrich's successor was hanged, convicted of crimes against humanity.

433 **Ravensbrück.** This was the largest concentration camp for women in Germany and the second-largest concentration camp after Auschwitz. https://www.jewishvirtuallibrary.org/history-and-overview-of-ravensbr-uuml-ck.

434 **The PBC.** The *PersoonsBewijzenCentrale*, the Personal Identity Center, the forgery center for ID cards.

435 **Van Tuyl did it.** Arie van Velsen.

436 **Resistance Bank.** The NSF, National Support Fund (*Nationaal Steunfonds*), was ramping up its spending through loans The remarkable story of the biggest source of money for the NSF is described in the next chapter.

437 **The Dutch Heath Society.** The *Nederlandsche Heidemaatschappij*. Founded in Arnhem on January 5, 1888, its goal was to reclaim wasteland, promote reforestation, and extend irrigation and ground improvement. From 1897 it developed freshwater fisheries. At first, the society provided mostly free advice, but to survive it prepared plans and budgets, carried out projects, and even took care of maintenance. It participated in *Staatsbosbeheer*, the first reclamation in Drenthe (Zeijerveld) in 1907. After 1930, it pursued many projects in Drenthe to reclaim heaths.

438 **Fokker.** The largest airplane factory in Europe, it ceased manufacture of aircraft in 1996.

439 **The Council of Resistance.** *Het Raad van Verzet (RVV).*

440 **Breda.** A fortified town in North Brabant, in the southwestern Netherlands with a long history of military importance. The Royal Dutch Military Academy is at the center.

441 **OD (Ordre Dienst).** The "Order Service" was at first in 1940 a social group of former cadets whose training was ended by the Germans after their invasion. The OD prepared for an authority vacuum after liberation of the Netherlands. It exchanged intelligence with the Dutch government in London. Meantime, they helped the Allies.

442 **SD** (*Sicherheitsdienst*) and **SiPo** (*SicherheitsPolizei*). They worked closely together. From 1934, SiPo included the *Geheime StaatsPolizei (Gestapo)*, which was formed in 1933 as a sister organization to SD, integrating SS members and controls. The Gestapo was the main executive agency of the political-police system. [To a lesser degree the **Criminal Police, the Kriminalpolizei or Kripo** participated. The Criminal Police were somewhat independent since their structure was longer-established. In 1936, the police were divided into the *Ordnungspolizei* (Orpo or Order Police) and the SiPo or Security Police. The Orpo consisted mainly of the *Schutzpolizei* (urban police), the Gendarmerie (rural police) and the *Gemeindepolizei* (municipal police). SiPo was Kripo + Gestapo.]

443 *Rendez-vous.* The French in in Schaap's original, 2014, 94.

444 **Jan Eikema.** Walraven and Tilly van Hall occasionally attended the sermons of Reverend Eikema, who regularly spoke in covert terms in the Westzijd (West Side) Church against the persecution of the Jews and other Nazi actions. Schaap, 2014, **Note 46**, 95.

445 **Thus escaped.** Johann van Marle.

446 **Goirle.** Near Tilburg, second in size to Eindhoven in North Brabant, in the southern part of the Netherlands.

447 **Source:** Ausems.

448 **July 1944.** At that point, D-Day had occurred and both the Dutch and their occupiers were expecting to be liberated before the end of the September. Alas, liberation did not occur for eight tragic months.

449 **Roermond.** In the southeastern Netherlands, Roermond is in Limburg Province, east of the Maas (Meuse) river. Chartered in 1232, it was a prosperous cloth-trade center in the 14th-15th centuries. Mostly Roman Catholic, seat of a bishopric since 1559, it was occupied by Spain, the Austrian Habsburg Empire, the French, and the Belgians. It suffered serious damage during the German Occupation in World War II. A Redemptorist shrine/chapel is nearby.

450 **Ambrosius.** Pseudonym for Jan Hendrikx.

451 **Pseudonyms.** Van Dijk is the pseudonym of Andreas Gelderblom. Van Tuyl is of course the pseudonym of Walraven van Hall. Van den Berg is the pseudonym for Iman van den Bosch.

452 **Compartmentalized.** This was a reference to the prewar political system of "pillars." The different religious groups (Catholics and Protestant denominations) had seats at the national political table. (It took a great effort of the Dutch, and several years, for pillar-thinking to be ended after liberation.)

453 **Polder letter.** A *polderbrief* is the equivalent of a Committee Report, with negative connotations of being the work of a team that is pulling in different directions. In a polder, neighbors must cooperate to keep out the water. Many people are on the same level, so there are many "seats at the table." A "polder letter" tries to please everyone. A good idea in theory, but it leads to delays, inaction, and odd compromises. (Thanks to IEB.)

454 *Not amused.* English words used in Schaap, 2014, 98. Homage to the honed British skill at being *not amused.*

455 **Secret ambition.** De Clercq uses English words here.

456 **Orange-minded.** Orange is for the monarchy (from Willem I of Orange). The OD was loyal to the Queen.

457 **Council of Resistance.** The RVV.

458 **Gray Past.** The title refers to decision making in the fog of war, when information was hard to get and understand. See https://www.vn.nl/niet-zewart-niet-wit-maar-grijs-de-oorlog-van-chris-van-der-heijden/.

459 **Domestic Forces.** *Binnenlandse Strijdkrachten* (BS). This is also translated sometimes as Internal Forces.

460 **Dolle Dinstag.** As previously noted, for one day both sides believed the Allies had liberated the Netherlands.

461 **Antwerp.** Also, Breda was incorrectly reported as having been captured. The flight of the Germans on *Dolle Dinstag* may have helped embolden the Allies to try to take Arnhem. That disaster was called "the bridge too far."

462 **Oilman.** Van Hall's clever nickname, *olieman* or the diminutive *oliemannetje*, referenced his three key functions in the Resistance—providing fuel, lubricating the machinery, and calming troubled (Resistance) waters. (MLB)

463 **Lucifer.** The first friction-matchbox was invented in 1826 by English chemist John Walker. They were manufactured in London by Samuel Jones under Lucifer (Latin for "light-carrier") and sold in the Netherlands.

464 **Matchbox Luci.** An abbreviation of Lucifer.

465 **Part of a discussion group.** Van Bijnen.

466 **Thijssen and Van Bijnen.** These leaders of the LKP and RVV were both arrested by the Germans in November 1944 and were subsequently executed. Schaap, 2014, **Note 47,** 103.

467 **Domestic Forces (BS, *Binnenlandse Strijdkrachten*).** When the Netherlands was finally liberated in May 1945, the Domestic Forces were said to have grown to 150,000 to 200,000 persons. Schaap, 2014, **Note 48,** 103.

468 **Asked him for advice.** The Domestic Forces in Amsterdam under Carel Overhoff were not an unqualified success. Feike de Boer, appointed the first post-war mayor of Amsterdam, sighed to Colonel Koot at the end of March or beginning of April 1945: "I would rather have one company of Canadians in the city than the entire army of Knecht." (Source:

Loe de Jong, The Netherlands in World War II). Schaap, 2014, **Note 49,** 103. [Knecht was the Resistance pseudonym of Carel Overhoff.]

469 **Betty-Jane:** The plane could have been named after a well-known broadcaster, Betty-Jane Rhodes, or a famed woman test pilot in Texas.

470 **Captain Merrill Olson.** His military flying record is here: https://historyhub.history.gov/military-records/f/military-records-forum/23544/seeking-missions-flown-by-capt-merrill-olson.

471 **SD.** *SicherheitsDienst*, the SS investigative and intelligence arm.

472 **Not the end of it.** Literally: "Not the end of the stocking." A vivid Dutch phrase. On St. Nicholas Day, stockings were filled. Getting the last sweet from a stocking might have been a challenge for a child.

473 **The Grüne Polizei.** The "Green" (from their uniforms) or "Order" police, usually tasked with traditional police functions, without the intense racist hatred of the ideologically selected and trained SD and Gestapo.

474 **Johann van Marle.** It helped that his wife was the daughter of Nel's cousin Hilda Boissevain de Booy, and so was a cousin of both Walraven and Tilly.

475 **Mad Tuesday.** *Dolle Dinstag*, September 5, 1944.

476 **SD, *SicherheitsDienst*.** Security service, the investigative arm of the SS. Equivalent to the FBI on racist steroids. I explain this more than once because SD is a frequently used abbreviation in this book. The SD is The Resistance Enemy.

477 **Herbert Oehlschlägel,** senior SD officer, was shot dead, October 23, 1944, by four National Assault Gang (LKP) members. Schaap, 2014, **Note 50,** 105. [It might explain why the SD, after that, pursued Resistance leaders so fiercely.]

478 **American girlfriend.** Mary Strawbridge. See end of Chapter 2.

479 **Lazy party.** This Zaandam area youth event takes place on the Saturday before *Pinksteren*, Pentecost Sunday, the "50th" day—actually seven weeks or 49th day—after

Easter Sunday. Schaap, 2014, **Note 51**, 107. [According to tradition, whoever sleeps latest on Lazy Saturday must get the *Luilakbols*, "lazy buns," and treat the family to them.]

480 **Lazy partying.** A guess at the meaning: Someone broke a window trying to play a prank. Dutch: *We dachten dat het van het lui-lakken was.* Literally: "We thought it was laziness."

481 **Seamen's Fund.** Dutch *ZeemansPot.* Sometimes translated into English as Seamen's Pot—less clear but with with some history behind it.

482 **Following us.** Literally: "A man was turning around us," with the implication that he was showing unwanted attention and was a suspicious character.

483 **Dikker and Thijs.** Wilhelm Fredrik Dikker started a top wine and food store in Amsterdam and was later joined by Hervi Thijs, who had served as an assistant in Paris to Auguste Escoffier. In 1921 Dikker and Thijs moved to Prinsengracht and Leidsegracht and became famed among connoisseurs for their lobsters, oysters, and caviar. https://www.dikkerandthijshotelamsterdam.com/hotel/history.

484 **Zeeland corner.** *Zeeuwsche Hoek.* There is a Hoek (corner) coffee shop in Amsterdam, but no Zeeusche Hoek.

485 **Waterlooplein.** The square, which was named after the Battle of Waterloo, was in the old Jewish quarter. It is the site of a market.

486 **Advise on.** *Bundelen.* Literally, "bundle."

487 **The Red Lion.** De Roode Leeuw. This hotel is just of Dam Square.

488 **The form.** The NSF used an accident claim form as a receipt.

489 **Rijnstraat and Jozef Israels quay.** According to Gijs van Hall it was "on the bridge of the Waalstraat and the Amstelkade," a little further on. Schaap, 2014, **Note 52**, 109.

490 **Critical moment.** Erik Schaap uses the French words *moment suprême*. In an effort to simplify a complicated story, I have reduced foreign-language phrases in this translation. The story told here is also told, more briefly,

in Michael C. Van Hall, *Three Centuries*, cited, 110.

491 **Nieuwezijds Voorburgwal.** Near Central Station.

492 **Ransom at the NSF.** In *The National Support Fund 1943-1945*, Gijs van Hall also wrote: "Requests for ransoms were never accepted, because they would involve such large amounts that our resources would soon be exhausted. Moreover, the danger of failure or even fraud was so great that for that reason alone we put these blackmail efforts at arm's length." Schaap, 2014, **Note 53**, 109.

493 **Hive.** Their home is described as a "hearth" for the Resistance, but "hive" conveys better the idea of the home being a base for a range of illegal activities subject to severe punishment, including summary execution.

494 **Op den Velde.** Their work is described elsewhere in this book. There will be an index in a future edition.

495 **SS.** SS agents included the SiPo and SD.

496 **Beautiful glow.** Speaker unidentified.

497 **Bright eyes.** Arie van Velsen, as quoted before.

498 **Eyes could twinkle.** Jan Rot.

499 **Irresistible.** Speaker is unidentified.

500 **He warned me.** Gerrit Huig.

501 **Fruit basket.** Vos de Mooij.

502 **Versteeg's children.** Literally: "Versteeg's children can go under the wool." This code informed railway workers that the strike was on. https://www.spoorwegmuseum.nl/en/ontdek/nu-in-het-museum/versteegs-children/.

503 **Allied paratroopers.** Mostly British and American, but also some Canadian and Polish.

504 **Arnhem.** The British and American paratroopers were to prepare the way for the British Second Army to cross the Maas (the French Meuse), the Waal, and the Rhine rivers. A total of 3,500 planes and gliders took 7,000 men and supplies (including light arms) to their targets. Henri A. van der Zee, *The Hunger Winter: Occupied Holland, 1944-1945* (Lincoln: University of Nebraska Press, 1998; first printed London: J. Norman & Hobhouse, 1982), 28.

505 **Dutch Railways.** *Nationaal Spoorweg* (abbreviated NS).

506 **A. den Doolaard.** This was the pen name of a well-known Dutch author. Den Doolaard wrote speeches for Gerbrandy. Van der Zee, 37. Cornelis Spoelstra, Jr., was his real name.

507 **Supreme Command.** SHAEF, the Supreme Headquarters Allied Expeditionary Force, under Gen. Eisenhower.

508 **Call for a strike.** This call "was the most important act of defiance to the Nazis that the Dutch were ever asked to make." Van der Zee, 29.

509 **A large portion.** More than 93 percent. Eventually, fewer than 2,000 of 30,000 Dutch Railways workers stayed on the job. The others, more than 28,000, obeyed the Queen. Another reason the railroad workers left their jobs—the trains and tracks were often strafed or bombed by the Allies and sabotaged by the Resistance. Van der Zee, 29-30.

510 **Surprise.** Dr. Hupkes was ready for the Dutch Railways employees to stop working when the Queen gave the signal, but he had to wait like everyone else for the message on Radio Orange. Van der Zee, 29-30.

511 **Two to three weeks.** Hupkes was not alone, as *Dolles Dinstag* made clear. On September 17, Gerbrandy told Louis de Jong of Radio Orange: "On Saturday we shall be in Amsterdam." Van der Zee, 30.

512 **Operation Market-Garden.** The ambitious plan was to drop thousands of paratroopers into the Occupied Netherlands and take Arnhem, allowing a rapid Allied advance north and an attack on the Ruhr Valley. But Allied intelligence was weak. German tank strength was underestimated. It was "the greatest military gamble of World War II," and it failed. Cornelius Ryan, *A Bridge Too Far* (New York: Popular Library, 1974), 158-159, 168.

513 **Failed to advance as swiftly as planned.** The Allies met unexpectedly strong German tank groups, for which the lightly armed paratroopers were totally unprepared. The American paratroopers leaving from Leicester had an inkling: "We will be going to Holland and we won't be picking tulips." Frank van

Lunteren, *The Battle of the Bridges* (Philadelphia and Oxford: Casemate, 2014), 33.

514 **German railway officials.** Schaap, 2014, uses the German here, *Bahn Bevollmächtigte.*

515 **Reich railway.** Schaap, 2014, uses the German *Reichsbahn.* The Reich Railway sent 5,000 men to run the railways in the eastern part of the Netherlands.

516 **Murderous months.** The months were deadly both because the Germans were killing witnesses to wartime crimes, but even more because food was at a famine level in population centers and concentration camps. The Hunger Winter of 1944-45 was not a good advertisement for governments in exile calling the shots.

517 **Associatie Cassa.** It merged in 1952 with KAS BANK, which then added "since 1806" to its logo.

518 **Dutch Railways.** *Nederlandse Spoorwegen* (NS). The Dutch Railways is the world's third-busiest railway system after Japan and Switzerland.

519 **Being unruly.** Schaap's Dutch is: *Wim Hupkes heeft vier jaar lang gepoogd de bezetter buitenshuis te houden door afwisselend toe te geven aan de Duitse eisen en de kont tegen de krib te gooien.* To "throw one's butt [ass] against the crib" is to be "unruly" like an angry baby.

520 **Dutch Nazis.** Schaap uses the initials of the NSB, i.e., Mussert's Dutch Nazi Party.

521 **Work Assignment.** *Arbeitseinsatz.* Schaap uses the German word for transport of Dutchmen to German factories. The word is a euphemism for forced labor. Hupkes protected his railway workers by describing them as essential and therefore not eligible for *Arbeitseinsatz.*

522 **Jews on their way to concentration camps.** In September 2005, the Dutch Railways apologized unexpectedly to the Jewish community for transporting Jews during the Occupation prior to the strike. In 2000, Prime Minister Wim Kok was the first to make some apologies for the postwar Dutch governments' treatment of Jews. In March 2005, Prime Minister Jan Peter Balkenende, at Yad Vashem in Jerusalem, said the deportation of Dutch Jewry was a "pitch-black" chapter in

Dutch history; in April 2005, he became the first prime minister to mention (but without an apology) Dutch wartime collaboration. Manfred Gerstenfeld, "Apologies for Holocaust Behavior and Refusal to Do So," *Jewish Political Studies Review* 18:3-4 (Autumn 2006), 31. https://www.jstor.org/stable/25834695.

523 **Labor Council.** *De Personeelraad* consisted of representatives of the trade unions. Schaap, 2014, **Note 54**, 117.

524 **Continue for months.** The Netherlands was fully liberated on May 5, 1945. That was eight months after *Dolle Dinstag*, when Queen Wilhelmina herself was so sure that liberation was at hand that she put out the Dutch flag.

525 **Postwar assessments.** These assessments were then believed to be imminent.

526 **People.** Communists.

527 **Strength through Joy.** Schaap uses the German, *Kraft durch Freude*. This was a Nazi Germany-operated leisure organization, part of the German Labour Front, Germany's labor organization during Hitler's dictatorship.

528 **Support.** With the implication "Carry water for." Literally translated, "pull the cart for."

529 **Railways.** On November 22, 1944, three days after the conversation between the NSF and the NS management, the *Generalkommissar für Finanz und Wirtschaft* (German for "Commissioner General for Finance and Economy") ordered that payments to the railways could only be made after he agreed. Schaap, 2014, **Note 55**, 117.

530 **A grand figure.** *Een grote persoonlijkheid.*

531 **Moolah.** Dutch: *Wat een poen!* In other words, Hupkes was fixated on the money.

532 **Labor Council.** This group, the Personeelraad, is literally translated as the Personnel Council or Staff Council, but in English "personnel" or "staff" does not convey what the Council is—a committee of labor union leaders.

533 **Issues with the Labor Council.** Van Hall to Hupkes, November 30, 1944. These concerns related to the Labor Council's reluctance to cooperate with workers with Communist leanings. (As will be seen in this chapter.)

534 **NC leader.** The NC was the Nationaal Comité, the National Committee of Resistance, a middle-of-the-road group politically. The referenced leader was Lambertus Neher.

535 **Wished for in Haarlem.** Koot to Gerrit Joustra, chairman of the Labor Council.

536 **Dutch Trading Company.** *Nederlandse Handel-Maatschappij.* This had become a bank.

537 **Storing receipts.** Koot, letter to Joustra.

538 **W. Brouwer.** This meeting was supposed to have taken place in the morning, but Brouwer did not show up. Van Hall left empty-handed but returned later in the day. Brouwer was unreliable but Van Hall looked past that.

539 **OD representative.** The OD was a group of prestigious people with a military background, preparing to keep order after liberation. The OD's representative (*vertegenwoordiger*, which can also mean agent) was Cees de Cock.

540 **Dissidents.** Communist railway workers were paradoxically anti-union, continually harassing union leaders.

541 **We will pay ourselves.** He was presumably thinking the war would be ending in a few weeks and their strike funds would be enough to get them through to liberation. Otherwise this statement would be hard to understand.

542 **Railway Office.** *Spoorkantoor.*

543 **We serve,** not **I deserve.** Dutch: *Wij dienen,* maar niet: *ik verdien.* The play on words can work as well in English as in Dutch. This statement by Van Hall explains what drove much of the Resistance in-fighting and how he calmed it.

544 **No one else's flag.** Literally, "no country for him to sail with." Geen land nee te bezeilen. Schaap, 2014, 120.

545 **Brouwer collapsed.** The scene reminded me of the brilliant portrayal of Al Capone by Robert De Niro in The Untouchables (1987). After a similar betrayal, Al Capone took matters into his own hands. (Adults only: https://www.youtube.com/watch?v=Xy3MtznDeqg.) The Brouwer scene ends differently, but the emotions are the same.

546 **Hupkes.** A sympathetic short biography of Hupkes explains that he was genuinely concerned that after liberation Communist groups would take over the Dutch government. Brouwer seemed a safer bet than his Communist opponents. https://resources. huygens.knaw.nl/bwn1880-2000/lemmata/bwn3/hupkes.

547 **In his own hands.** W. Brouwer wrote to G. Joustra in a letter dated November 24, 1944 that he wanted to take the payment of wages "in his own hands," because of "various difficulties." Schaap, 2014, **Note 56**, 121.

548 **Railway employees.** Gijs van Hall stated to the parliamentary committee of inquiry in 1950: "The cases that had to be supported [after September 1944] suddenly numbered in the tens of thousands. From the Dutch Railways alone there were already 50,000 to 60,000 people." Gijs had to be referring to the total of employees and their immediate families. Schaap, 2014, **Note 57**, 121. The committee's report was published as *Enquêtecommissie regeringsbeleid 1940-1945—Verslag houdende de uitkomsten van der onderzoek.* 's-Gravenhage, 1949-1956.

549 **60 percent.** 37.1 million guilders.

550 **Didn't budge.** Literally, "kept his leg stiff."

551 **Mileage money.** The idea was that drivers be paid a premium after x number of kilometers traveled. The fact that nary a meter, let alone a kilometer, was being driven did not interfere with their campaign.

552 **National Assault Gang.** This group is also called the LKP, based on the initials of the Dutch name, *Landelijke KnokPloeg.* A literal translation is "goon squad" or "brawl crew." Sometimes "Group" is used instead of "Gang."

553 **The Dutch State Bank.** *De Nederlandsche Bank,* the Dutch central bank.

554 **German Commissioner.** Reichskommissar.

555 **Did not survive the war.** Frank Drake, History Online, *History Magazine,* September 2022. https://historiek.net/verzetsvrienden-maakten-in-1944-miljoenen-guldens-buit/148087/.

556 **Dutch Nazis.** Original has: NSB members. The job of the favored local volunteer *Landwachters* (Landwatchers) was to provide exactly this kind of information to the police via Dutch collaborators.

557 **SD.** Reminder: The *SicherheitsDienst* (Security Service) was the intelligence arm of Reinhard Heydrich's *Reich Security Main Office.* The *SicherheitsPolizei (SiPo)* or Security Police combined the criminal police (*Kripo)* with the state police (*GeStaPo).* See https://encyclopedia.ushmm.org/content/en/article/the-security-police-sipo.

558 **Mad Tuesday.** *Dolle Dinsdag.* September 5, 1944.

559 **German railway.** Original has *Reichsbahn.* I have reduced use of German and Dutch words.

560 **German army.** Original has *Wehrmacht.*

561 **Letter to Seyss-Inquart.** Schaap, 2014, provides the language of Rost van Tonningen's groveling admission in its original German: *Die Prüfung der Frage, wie dieser Streik finanziert wird, wurde einstweilen zurückgestellt.*

562 **People in hiding.** These were often individuals being hidden, but sometimes they were a family or a parent and child.

563 **Households.** Seamen typically had a wife or widow at home with a child or children and likely at least one other adult relative staying with them.

564 **The Dutch State Bank.** *De Nederlandsche Bank,* the nation's central bank. In this translation, the Dutch State Bank is used instead of the Dutch or Netherlands Bank because it is clearer that it is the national central bank.

565 **Redundancy benefits.** *Wachtgelden* in Dutch. In the United States, this is called unemployment compensation.

566 **Mad Tuesday.** On Dolle Dinstag, September 5, 1944, everyone thought the Dutch were liberated.

567 **Fellow banker.** Henri ter Meulen.

568 **Plan to appeal.** This meeting was scheduled without either of them knowing about the imminent railway strike.

569 **Ten Amsterdam Banks.** The eight that said yes were: Amsterdamsche Bank, Associatie-Cassa, Incasso-Bank, Kas-Vereeniging, Nederlandsche Handel-Maatschappij, Nederlands-Indische Handelsbank, Pierson & Co. and Twente Bank. Schaap (2014), **Note 58**, 123. (The other two banks said no, immediately, highlighting the risks.)

570 **Netherlands Trading Company.** In Dutch, *Nederlandsche HandelMaatschappij*. Created by the great King William I (ruled 1815-1840) after Napoleon's Dutch occupation, it became a major bank in the Dutch Indies. By 1940 it was mainly a bank. After the Japanese occupation of the colony, the bank was merged into ABN.

571 **High finance.** The original words in the Dutch were *haute finance*. Schaap, 2014, 123. The meaning was: the biggest banks.

572 **Most remarkable meeting.** Overhoff. In effect the eight banks joined the Resistance for a month. For many, they did it because they expected an Allied victory soon. In fact the Occupation continued for another seven more months. Luckily, the banks' support was never discovered by the vengeful Nazis.

573 **Communications were broken.** After the Allies retook Eindhoven on September 17, 1944, the south of the Netherlands was liberated, but the north was still occupied by Nazi leaders and the German army.

574 **Stung.** Literally, "bitten on." The point is that Van Leeuwen was furious at the Nazis.

575 **Plastic-wrapped.** The original Dutch reads: *In cellofaan verpakte*, "Packed in cellophane." Invented in Switzerland and first manufactured in France, and then improved by the U.S. branch of DuPont, cellophane is trademarked in some countries and in others became a generic term, gradually replaced by "plastic-wrapped." Cellophane is now widely called just "plastic." When a hair dryer (invented in 1920) is applied to plastic wrap, it is called "shrink-wrapped."

576 **Following the rules was everything.** The Dutch State Bank is heir to the Bank of Amsterdam, which managed the Dutch guilder, a fiat coin and currency that dominated European trade during much of the seventeenth and eighteenth centuries. It had "reserve currency" status, but lost it during 1781–92, when easy-money policies rendered the Bank insolvent—its net worth if fully disclosed would have been negative—and meant the Bank lost of control over the value of its money. See Stephen Quinn and William Roberds, "Death of a Reserve Currency," *International Journal of Central Banking*, December 2016, 63-103. https://www.ijcb.org/journal/ijcb16q4a2.pdf.

577 **The Board.** "The Board of Confidential Men" was a group formed in August 1944 that was empowered to act temporarily as government authority after the liberation, until the government in exile could return. Schaap, 2014, **Note 59**, 127.

578 **Eighty million guilders.** Message from the Queen's government exile, London, February 13, 1945.

579 **Ivar Kreuger.** See Frank Partnoy, *The Match King: Ivar Kreuger, The Financial Genius Behind a Century of Wall Street Scandals*, Public Affairs Books, Hachette, 2009. Kreuger committed suicide in 1932.

580 **Treasury bills** are short-term debt certificates. Those issued by The Dutch State Bank were stamped by the Netherlands Court of Audit. With a face value of at least 100,000 guilders, each bill was discounted at purchase and was repaid to bearer after one year. Schaap, 2014, **Note 60**, 127.

581 **Treasury bill.** *Schatkistpromesse*. As in the United States, Treasury bills were like cash, payable to the bearer.

582 **Personal Identification Center.** It was widely known by its initials, PBC, for *Persoon Bewijs Central*e.

583 **Cliché.** This relief printing plate, also called a stereotype, is cast in a mold from the original metal plate, allowing multiple machines or print runs from one plate. To avoid mixing colors, a cliché was needed for each color.

584 **Warmoesstraat.** Literally, "Chard Street." One of the oldest streets in Amsterdam, in the 13th century it was probably originally

a vegetable market. It is still in 2023 a busy shopping area, *De Wallen.*

585 New-Side Front-Bastion Wall. *Nieuwezijds Voorburgwal.* In Amsterdam's *De Wallen* area, the side of the wall facing the oldest part of the city was the *Oudezijds (OZ) Voorburgwal.* The printer was on the new side (*Nieuwezijd*).

586 Spin & Sons. C. A. Spin & Son was a printer in 19th-century Amsterdam. This might be the son's company.

587 Government Postal Savings Bank. The *Rijkspostspaarbank.*

588 Largest bank heist in world history. The closest competitor was Saddam Hussein's removal of a billion dollars from the Iraq central bank in 2003. But since he was dictator, it was not so much a theft as an act of a tyrant. See https://www.worldfinance.com/banking/ saddam-hussein-tops-list-of-5-biggest-bank-heists.

589 Another to face. Schaap added this paragraph and the next three after the 2014 edition, which references in its *Namenregister* Van Randwijk only in Chapter 7 and Van Tongeren not at all.

590 Group 2000. It was the *only* Dutch Resistance group founded and headed by a woman. She received a Yad Vashem award after the war.

591 Making Group 2000 part. In a corporate setting this would be called an attempted hostile takeover.

592 Heavy footfalls. Reminiscent of a German potentate.

593 Stood by her side. Van Tongeren, several places.

594 Stammering thanks. Van Tongeren.

595 The Foundation 1940-1945. On October 13, 1944, it was called *Stichting 1940-1944.* But the war dragged on eight months longer. So the name was changed to *Stichting 1940-1945.* We use only the later name. Schaap, 2014, **Note 61,** 127.

596 Natura was an initiative of NSF, NC, LO and VOC that started in the early summer of 1944. It provided food, clothing, and shoes to people in hiding and illegal workers. Jaap Buijs became its chairman. Schaap, 2014, **Note 62,** 129.

597 Cooperation was confirmed. The following were present: Walraven van Hall (NSF); L. Neher (National Committee of Resistance); T. van Vliet, H. Douqué, and H. van Riessen (National Organization for Aid to People in Hiding, LO) and E.E. Menten, the government commissioner nominated by the Resistance. Schaap, 2014, **Note 63,** 129.

598 Central Financing Foundation. *Stichting Centrale Financiering (SCF).*

599 Van den Bosch. Gelderblom probably did not know, when the SCF foundation deed was drawn up, that Van den Bosch had been shot a month earlier. Schaap, 2014, **Note 64.**

600 *Trouble-shooter.* The English words are used in the Dutch text.

601 Broken the cranes. Photos here: https:// www.alamy.com/devastation-amsterdamse-port-vernielde-crane-date-may-1945-location-amsterdam-noord-holland-keywords-ports-second-world-war-image341630065.html.

602 Your niece. Louise (Lies) Boissevain. Louise Maria Antonia Boissevain. Born October 20, 1924 in Amsterdam. Died November 1, 2006 at 82 in Glastonbury, Hartford County, Connecticut. Wife of Addick Adrianus Land. She is called Elizabeth, which may be her Resistance pseudonym.

603 My point of view. *Sta in mijn hemd.* The Dutch means, literally, "stand in my shirt."

604 Parkweg. Most other sources say Parklaan, also located in Groningen. Schaap, 2014, **Note 64,** 131.

605 Death row inmates. *Todeskandidaten,* German, literally "death candidates," hostages to be killed if the Resistance carried off some sabotage or assassination.

606 Civilian cars. The cost of gasoline was something few could pay for, anyway.

607 State Postal Savings Bank. *Rijkspostspaarbank.*

608 *Nacht und Nebel.* The "Night and Fog" directive from Hitler on December 7, 1941 targeted political activists and resistance "helpers" in territories occupied by Nazi Germany during World War II. They were to be imprisoned, murdered, or otherwise made to disappear, while the family and news media were to remain uncertain as to their fate.

609 *Tante Betje.* Aunt Betty.

610 **Government Postal Savings Bank.** *Rijkspostspaarbank,*

611 **Kas-Vereeniging.** This is the bank that merged in 1952 with Associatie Cassa to form KAS BANK.

612 **Main Group Industry.** *Hoofdgroep Industrie,* a division of the Dutch Ministry of Economic Affairs.

613 **Artillery Installations.** *Artillerie Inrichtinge,* based in Zaandam. He was ready to resist when the Dutch surrendered in May 1940, as discussed at the beginning of Chapter 3.

614 **Five Major Banks.** These were the Amsterdamsche Bank, the Incasso-Bank, the Dutch Trading Company (*Nederlandsche Handel-Maatschappij*), the Twentsche Bank and the Kas-Vereeniging. Schaap, 2014, **Note 66,** 135.

615 **C. J. van der Lee.** This was a Resistance pseudonym. Schaap, 2014, **Note 67,** 137.

616 **Don't wipe your feet.** Van der Lee.

617 **"Used" notes.** Deliberately aged notes.

618 **Misappropriating.** In other words, stealing.

619 **Dutch Trading Company.** *Nederlandsche Handel-Maatschappij.* Although it was originally only a trading company, it became a bank.

620 **Hand in.** Once identified as Jewish, the Nazis demanded a list of their valuables. (This was also the procedure in France. I have seen this in the archives of the Mayenne.) They were then required to bring in all these valuables on a certain day. These valuables were not returned. They fueled the Holocaust.

621 **Specialists.** Original Dutch reads "corner men," traders who specialize in certain securities.

622 **Bowed to Mammon.** Gerard Aalders, *Roof: The Misappropriation of Jewish Property During World War II.*

623 **Association of Securities Brokers.** *Vereniging voor de Effectenhandel.*

624 **Utrecht Mortgage Bank.** *Utrechtsche Hypotheekbank.*

625 **Aryanization Permit.** *Arisierungsgenehmigung.* The permit certified that Jewish ownership of the shares had ended and the company was therefore allowed to be traded.

626 **Caretaker manager.** A *Verwalter.*

627 **Palace for Industry.** *Paleis voor Volksvlijt,* Amsterdam.

628 **A Belgian Lippmann Rosenthal.** Letter from Adriaan van Hall. In other words, a Belgian broker that was a branch of Lippman Rosenthal or was a correspondent.

629 **$1,006 million.** See summary table in the next chapter.

630 **Guilders.** The original reads "euros," but there were no euros in 1944-45 and elsewhere guilders are used.

631 **Confessional.** Religion-based. *Trouw* during the war represented the Protestant denominations and was the most conservative of the major underground newspapers.

632 **Kultuurkamer.** The Artists' Fund or *Kunstenaarssteun* was founded in 1942 to assist artists not affiliated with the Kultuurkamer. Its Treasurer, Roel van Heusden, could have made good use of the NSF money, but Walraven van Hall wanted to stick to the NSF accounting system, which separately maintained code numbers linked to the names of supported artists. The *Kunstenaarssteun* preferred its own system and refused to adopt Van Hall's receipts method until February 1944, because of concern about risks to the artists, often well known. Schaap, 2014, **Note 68,** 139.

633 **Wasn't about to go skate on thin ice.** Literally: "go over ice overnight" (i.e., in the dark).

634 **Changed direction.** Original reads "tacked," which is what a sailor must do repeatedly to sail toward the wind.

635 **Van Hall was my great friend.** Cosquino de Bussy, to the parliamentary committee of inquiry in 1948.

636 **Domestic Forces.** Also known as the Interior Forces and BS, this was the name for the three armed Resistance groups united under Prince Bernhard.

637 **Assault Gang teams.** *KP* teams=*KnokPloeg,* "brawl crew." The national organization was the *LKP=Landelijke Knokploeg,* "National Brawl Crew." This was one of the three Resistance groups that was armed.

638 **Departure time.** Laurens Weeda, in Gijs van Hall, *The National Support Fund,* in an undated letter from him, spoke of 4 a.m. as the departure time, because, according to him, that was when the curfew ended. Schaap, 2014, **Note 69,** 141.

639 **Lies Boissevain:** Nickname of Elizabeth (apparently her Resistance pseudonym; her given name was Louise, hence Lies, pronounced Lease) Boissevain. A later YouTube interview with her, in Dutch, is here: https://www.youtube.com/watch?v=oo-wjsPFAx8. She is mentioned on two pages of Schaap, 2014: 140-141.

640 **Doldrums.** *Dode punt,* "dead center." A sailor's nightmare is the windless "dead center" of the calm doldrums at the equator.

641 **Van Tuyl.** As noted before, this was the primary Resistance name of Walraven van Hall

642 **Bottle sleeves.** These were meant to protect bottles against breakage or insulate the bottles to keep the contents cold or warm. During the Occupation, they were worn as clothing.

643 **Leidsegracht.** The cross-canal segment where the headquarters of the NSF was located, at number 25. Walraven was arrested at the double house at Leidseghracht 13-15. The canal houses were originally all the same size but over time owners combined two houses or a part of another house. See photo at Schaap, 2014, 155.

644 **Turn for the worse.** Dutch: *Achteruitgang* (decline). Schaap, 2014, 144.

645 **Vigor.** Schaap's Dutch has: *Activiteit.*

646 **Forced labor.** *Arbeidsinzet,* used here, is the Dutch for the German Arbeitseinsatz, which is best translated as forced labor or slave labor. The Occupation required all men of working age—provided they were not declared indispensable by their Dutch employers—to go to Germany to work as forced laborers.

647 **Placard from the Resistance.** Marie Boissevain.

648 **Robert Pel.** During the war, police detective R. R. Pel was head of the Zaandam area branch of the Personal Identification Center. The industrialist A.W. Sabel also worked in that region. He was an inspector of the National Committee of Resistance and district commander of the Domestic Forces (BS). Schaap, 2014, **Note 72,** 145.

649 **Call for recruits.** The name of this new Occupation call was *Liese-Aktion,* after German Nazi Hermann Liese, who was sent to the Netherlands to collect more Dutchmen for German factories, a reintroduction of the *Arbeitseinsatz (*German name*),* the Work Assignment, i.e., forced labor. But this time Liese was not supported by enough German troops to carry out *razzias.*

650 **Appeal for noncooperation.** The Resistance called for companies and people to refuse the call for workers.

651 **ID cards.** PersoonsBewijs in Dutch. Ausweise in German.

652 **Board of Confidential Officers.** The group of Dutch elders tasked with starting the transition to restoration of the Queen's government.

653 **Snow slide.** Mary-Ann van Hall, interview with Erik Schaapo.

654 **RIOD.** The Royal Institution for War Documentation. (the O is for Oorlog, "War.") This is where Loe de Jong did his research. The name was later changed from Royal to National (Nationaal), so it became NIOD.

655 **Favoritism.** Adolf Rüter, first report to RIOD (NIOD).

656 **Oil man.** Walraven was called *die olieman* (the oil man) because he poured oil on troubled waters. But he also brought oil in the form

of funds to pay for food and heat, when they could be purchased.

657 **No turning back.** Aad van Hall, interview with Erik Schaap.

658 **Twenty-six gallons.** Equal to one hundred liters, or one hectoliter.

659 **513 Herengracht.** Den Hollander misremembered it as 555 Herengracht. Schaap, 2014, **Note 71,** 147.

660 **They can never find me.** Frans den Hollander.

661 **Compulsory labor service.** The *Liese-Aktion,* as discussed early in this chapter, was a repeat of the Work Assignment that was previously enforced by *razzias.* The second round was much less successful in generating Dutch workers.

662 **Six of us.** Legal adviser Marianne Tellegen and National Committee member Arie van Velsen had transportation problems.

663 **Jaap Buijs** represented Natura and the NSF, B. Gillieron the Communist newspaper De Waarheid, Jan Smallenbroek the Protestant Christian newspaper Trouw ("Faithful"), T. van Vliet the National Organization for Help to People in Hiding (LO) and A. van Namen the left-wing paper Vrij Nederland ("Free Netherlands"). Van Arkel, pseudonym of J. van Lom, was hired as legal adviser. Schaap, 2014, **Note 74,** 147.

664 **"Betrayal! Run!"** In Dutch: Verraad, vlucht!

665 **Articles.** They were designing the next issue of Vrij Nederland and other Resistance papers.

666 **STEN guns.** STEN guns were the Allied submachine guns, produced in Enfield, England, named after two gun designers (S and T), with -EN for Enfield. https://www.youtube.com/watch?v=KDn-jVRdO_8. More likely, these were 32-round, faster-shooting *Wehrmacht* MP-40s. https://www.youtube.com/watch?v=VftlMpk5Y38.

667 **We were thrown to the ground.** Jan Smallenbroek, *Woord Gehouden:Veertig Jaar—Stichting 1940-1945* ("Word Kept: Forty Years—Foundation 1940-45").

668 **Source:** Jaap Buijs, *Woord Gehouden:Veertig Jaar—Stichting 1940-1945.* ("Word Kept: Forty Years—Foundation 1940-45").

669 **Jaap Buijs.** He was 56 years old at the time of the arrest. Schaap, 2014, **Note 75,** 149.

670 **Search the whole house.** Das ganze Haus soll untersucht werden. Another Schaap edition (not 2014) reads: Das ganze Haus soll untersucht sein. Same meaning in English.

671 **Van Arkel.** Resistance pseudonym for Johan (Han) van Lom.

672 **Hugo.** Resistance pseudonym for Teus van Vliet.

673 **The Great Commandment.** The multi-authored reference book, in Dutch, is titled Het Grote Gebod: Gedenkboek van het Verzet in LO en LKP, Kampen, 1989.

674 **1940-1945 Foundation.** It was first called the 1940-1944 Foundation (*Stichting*). The Allies were expected to liberate the entire Netherlands by the end of September 1944, but the *Bridge Too Far* failure meant the Occupation continued for eight months more. To avoid confusion, the name in this book is the 1940-1945 Foundation.

675 **It was Van Lom.** Wim van Norden, interview with Erik Schaap..

676 **Han was deeply affected.** Cornelia (Non) van Lom, Han's wife.

677 **Local office.** The SD Außenstelle, the branch or field office. Since the Night of the Long Knives in 1934, the SS replaced the SA as Hitler's favored means of personal control of Germany. The SS had 250,000 members in 1939, composed of the military *Waffen-SS* and the Allgemeine-SS. The latter controlled the police forces—the Sicherheitspolizei (Sipo), Kriminalpolizei (Kripo), and the legacy Gestapo—and also the intelligence unit, the Sicherheitsdienst (SD). https://www.historyhit.com/what-was-the-difference-between-the-nazi-sa-and-ss/.

678 **Detective Sergeant Friedrich Viebahn.** German: Kriminalsekretär. Every SS member had an SS rank and also a police/military rank. Kriminalsekretär is a police rank, equal to Detective Inspector or Detective Sergeant. https://bit.ly/41FXFhx. In this book, Viebahn

is in the role of Inspector Javert in *Les Misérables*. Or Ahab in *Moby Dick*.

679 **Hugo.** Resistance pseudonym of Teus van Vliet.

680 **New contacts.** Friedrich Viebahn, statement to postwar Special Court.

681 **Willy Lages** was leader of the Amsterdam SD local branch from 1941 until the liberation. Hanns Albin Rauter was the Higher Police Chief (in German: höhere Polizeiführer) in the Netherlands and Commissioner General of Public Security. Schaap, 2014, **Note 76,** 149.

682 **"German honor! German faithfulness!"** Deutsche Ehre, Deutsche Treue!

683 **Rühl.** Emil Rühl worked with Friedrich Viebahn at the SD. He tracked down Hannie Schaft, who was executed. Rühl's story is juxtaposed with hers in the Resistance Museum (Verzetsmuseum) exhibit in Amsterdam that opened on December 1, 2022. https://www.nytimes.com/2023/01/25/arts/design/resistance-museum-amsterdam.html.

684 **LO.** *Landelijke Organisatie,* Dutch for "National Organization." It helped *onderduikers,* "people hiding."

685 **Keep secret.** Presumably also this way Viebahn could obtain photos of the people going to the meeting, for future use.

686 **Van Vliet.** In the book *The Greatest Commandment* (Het Grote Gebod), Van Vliet is said to have been arrested in the Alexander Boerstraat, while he tapped on a window of the place where three members of the Resistance were in consultation at the time. However, he tapped on the wrong window, so no one noticed his arrival. While Van Vliet was waiting to enter, he was arrested. Schaap, 2014, **Note 77,** 151.

687 **Teus van Vliet** stated in May 1949 before the Special Court in Amsterdam that his diary had the note "Land. W. 12.30 Lg." Gijs van Hall mentions the same words in his autobiography. Schaap, 2014, **Note 78,** 151.

688 **Friedrich Viebahn** and Emil Rühl said to the Special Court on May 10, 1949: "There was no address, only "12.30 Land. W." The suspect explained it, but not spontaneously. We had to pull it out of him." In a report dated November

17, 1945, Rühl further said: ' Hugo (Van Vliet) informed me that they had given the WC (Werkcommissie) the name of "Landwacht." This established the meaning of "Land. W." Schaap, 2014, **Note 79,** 151.

689 **Domestic Forces. BS.** The armed units of the Resistance, combined under Prince Bernhard ion the closing months of the Occupation.

690 **Herengracht.** The Men's Canal, one of the three main residential and commercial canals in the historic Grachtengordel starting southwest of Central Station in Amsterdam.

691 **Brinkie.** Nickname for Weeda's pseudonym, Van den Brink.

692 **Morning meeting.** Eikema said Friday, but it was on Saturday. Schaap, 2014, **Note 80,** 153.

693 **Five men.** Hanneke Eikema is mistaken here. Not five, but four men were held at gunpoint. Schaap, 2014, **Note 81,** 153.

694 **Groan from his father.** Frits Nieuwenhuijzen.

695 **NC.** Nationaal Comité. One of the smaller Resistance groups.

696 **The last time.** Hanneke Eikema.

697 **Natura.** This was a food pantry organization for the relief of the Dutch famine in the winter 1944-45.

698 **Inner voice.** Henk van Randwijk.

699 **Death Row candidates.** German: *Todescandidaten.* These were prisoners awaiting execution. They were treated like hostages and executed whenever the SD decided some act of the Resistance should be punished.

700 **The February 9 Execution.** On February 9, 1945, a total of ten prisoners, none from Zaandam, were executed. It was a retaliation for the recent liquidation of a Collaborator, Zaandam police inspector Franciscus D. Willemse. The ten were Jan Bakker, Stephanus JP Bakker, Catrinus Douma, Jacob I. de Haan, Jan D. Janssen, Johan de Jonge, Jan Overeem, Johannes Ruijter, Gerrit C. Stapel and Gerardus J. van Wetering. Schaap, 2014, **Note 82,** 155.

701 **The February 17 Execution.** The following men were also executed with Willem P. Speelman: Pierre H. de Booij, Hillebrandt Dirkzwager, Jan Dol, Gabriel Philipsen, Dirk A. van Rees, Anton Vermaat, Andries P. de Visser, Abraham B. van Waarden, and Louis J. M. van der Weyden. Wim Speelman was buried after the war at the Eerebegraafplaats in Bloemendaal. He is in section 35, near Walraven van Hall. Schaap, 2014, **Note 83**, 155.

702 **A note.** In Dutch, *Briefje* (a little letter). Presumably about news, messages.

703 **1940-1945 Foundation.** By February 1945, this foundation was taking over some functions that the NSF had been performing.

704 **National Assault Gang.** In Dutch, the Landelijk KnokPloeg, LKP. (Local groups were just called a *KP.*) As previously noted, the National group was one of the three major armed groups in the Dutch Resistance, and were under the umbrella of the the the Domestic Forces n(BS).

705 **He denied everything at first.** Van den Donk, *De affaire-Sanders.*

706 **Northern Cemetery.** Noorderbegraafplaats.

707 **I believe in him.** Non van Lom, *Notes.*

708 **South Holland.** Zuid-Holland. This densely populated province includes two of the three largest Dutch cities—the Hague (den Haag) and Rotterdam.

709 **I never understood.** Peter Plantenga.

710 **SD.** *S*icherheitsdienst, the Security Service, the investigative arm of the Nazi police.

711 **The SD did not know yet.** Gijs van Hall, *Testimony.*

712 **Walraven's ID.** See Schaap, 2014, 196.

713 **Nothing could avert Walraven's fate.** Remmert Aten, *Walraven van Hall, 10 februari 1906—12 februari 1945*, 65.

714 **Gijs van Hall.** His daughter Marleen told Het Parool in February 1998: "My father survived the war, but his brother Wally was shot. I think people have underestimated the guilt he carried about it." To the reporter's

suggestion that "he might have been able to save his brother if he'd called in the right high-placed people," she responded affirmatively, "That's how he felt." Schaap, 2014, **Note 84.**

715 **Source:** Jaap Buijs.

716 **Source:** Jan Smallenbroek.

717 **Scheveningen.** The high-security "Orange Hotel" prison. It is now a museum and I have visited it with my wife Alice and some Dutch relatives.

718 **Two inches by four inches.** Original reads "ten centimeters by five centimeters."

719 **Hidden between pieces of clothing.** Aad van Hall, interview with Erik Schaap.

720 **The greatest of these is love.** St. Paul, Letter to the Corinthians, 13.

721 **RVV.** One of the three armed Resistance groups then under the command of Prince Bernhard as the Domestic Forces (*BS*).

722 **German military police.** In German, the Feldgendarmerie (Field Police).

723 *SiPo. SicherheitsPolizei.* Secret Police.

724 **Local branch.** Aussenstelle in German.

725 **Viermann.** Not to confuse with Viebahn. Both have the first name Friedrich.

726 **He asked.** The name of the officer is not known.

727 **The Canal.** *Jan Gijzenvaart* is the name of the canal. On either side of the canal are the Jan Gijzen quays or paths. The canal was dug into the sand around 1537, between the Spaarne River and Santpoort-Zuid, which was then referred to as the hamlet of Jan Gijzenvaart.

728 **The Bridge.** The Jan Gijzenburg bridge, where the monument has been placed to the victims. It is where the Rijksstraatweg crosses the canal, halfway between the Spaarne river and the canal's termination at Santpoort-Zuid.

729 **Train guard unit.** *Wachzug*, a German unit that ordinarily guarded trains. But few trains were running, so they did other things. The patrol unit leader was Hans Stöver, who does not merit even this small End Note.

730 **Rijkstraatweg.** This means a state highway. It is a major intersection in that part of Haarlem.

731 **Zeeweg.** The Zeeweg (road to the sea) connects Overveen with the North Sea, ending just north of Zandvoort.

732 **Bastards.** Dutch Ploerten "plodders, cads, scoundrels," English words not much used in the mid-20th century. In Michael C. Van Hall, *Three Centuries*, 112-113, he translates the word as "Rats."

733 **I cried like a child.** Laurens Weeda ("Brinkie").

734 **As a retaliatory measure. (**See copy of notice in German: *Als Vergeltungs-massnahme für den feigen Mordanschlag . .*

735 **Work Assignment:** *Arbeidsinzet* (Dutch), *Arbeitseinsatz* (German). The Nazi euphemism means "work mission," but the real meaning was: forced, slave labor.

736 **Sloping upwards.** Handwriting analysts consider this to be a sign of optimism.

737 **Strong Walraven!** Cited as well in Michael C. Van Hall, *Three Centuries*, 113.

738 **Overveen Artillery Street.** Overveense Artillerieweg.

739 **Seaway.** Zeeweg.

740 **"Murder!"** Toon Lavertu.

741 **Burst into tears.** Attie van Hall.

742 **German Honor.** Deutsche Ehre. Honor in the sense of keeping his word.

743 *Landelijk Werkcomité.* The National Work Committee.

744 **Second offense only.** Van Vliet argued on the first count that he had expected the meeting to be called off. That apparently was persuasive.

745 **The Emperor's Crown.** De Keizerskroon. This is an early-blooming and hardy variety of tulip flower with intense red edged with "gold" (yellow). https://www.brecks.com/ product/keizerskroon-tulip. Deventer in 2023 has a restaurant advertised online named De Keizerskroon but not a hotel.

746 **Landlubber.** Landrotten.

747 **83.8 million guilders.** 83,765,787 guilders, to be exact.

748 **2024 dollars.** In 1938, a Dutch guilder was worth about 56 U.S. cents. https://iisg. amsterdam/en/research/projects/hpw/calculate. php. The Nazis declared the guilder worthless but the Queen in exile said guilders would be good money after the war. A 1945 dollar was worth seventeen 2024 dollars. (BLS.gov inflation calculator.)

749 **Resistance Cross.** A lesser honor, similarly named, was given more widely.

750 **Worked voluntarily for the intelligence service.** Ministry of War.

751 **Six houses.** Woningen. Means "Houses," i.e., Big House. The address includes Westside 40 as well as the 42 that was the home of Walraven and Tilly van Hall.

752 **Zaanlandse Schoenhandel.** This was in 2023, when I visited for the second time, the Ankara Marrakesh furniture store.

753 **One of the most central and inspiring figures.** Prime Minister Willem Drees Sr. (in office 1948-1958), speaking about Walraven van Hall.

754 **Completely central and leading figure.** Prime Minister Willem (Wim) Schermerhorn (in office 1945-1946), speaking about Walraven.

755 **Zaan Region.** De Zaanstreek.

756 **Great inspirer.** De Zaanstreek (newspaper).

757 **No one contributed more.** Loe de Jong, Erasmus Lectures (Cambridge, Massachusetts: Harvard University Press, 1988), speaking of Walraven van Hall.

758 **Geert Mak.** Een Kleine Geschiedenis van Amsterdam ("A small history of Amsterdam"), Amsterdam: Atlas, 1994, 1997, Chapter X, 287-297 and 354-355. In fairness to the Van Hall family, Maurits Cornelis van Hall wrote *Drie Eeuwen* "Three Centuries") in 1961, but it did not get such wide circulation as Geert Mak's book.

Milton Keynes UK
Ingram Content Group UK Ltd.
UKHW021934110424
440788UK00005B/97